Florida
Place Names

Florida
Place Names

BY ALLEN MORRIS

UNIVERSITY OF MIAMI PRESS
Coral Gables, Florida

Designed by Bernard Lipsky
Manufactured in the United States of America

Library of Congress Cataloging in Publication Data

Morris, Allen Covington, 1909-
    Florida place names.

    Bibliography: p.
    1. Names, Geographical—Florida. 2. Florida—
History.   I. Title.
F309.M67   917.59   74-13949
ISBN 0-87024-256-3

For Joan,
in lieu of Chicago

PREFACE

"Let's go down to St. Marks for a seafood dinner tonight," or "I'm going to run over to Five Points—anything you want me to get?" These expressions and variations of them are heard in virtually all households. What they have in common is the use of a place name.

Everyday communication demands that places be consistently identified by a given name. So it is easy to believe the rule of thumb of place name specialists: a place name for every square mile. Florida then would have 54,136 place names.

This compilation obviously does not attempt to list all Florida place names. The foundation for this book is the highway map of the State Department of Transportation. The sectional map of the State Department of Agriculture also has been used. To the names of communities have been added the names of counties, present and past, and place names of special historial interest, such as names of forts. The choice has been selective, for no useful purpose seemed served by including sawmill towns and other small settlements long gone. I must confess, too, to being partial to those places having something of human interest about them.

I have included ghost towns, even though Florida has very few towns that remain after the people are gone. There are lost cities, however; St. Joseph is an example. My personal view is that no community ever passes totally out of existence as long as we remember that people once lived there. In Magnolia, for example, history still lives even if all that remains is a cemetery.

This compilation began in 1946 when I drew together information on the origin of county names for the first edition of *The Florida Handbook*. Subsequently, for the fifth biennial edition, an effort was made to account for the names of all incorporated cities. This updating has been followed with each *Handbook* edition. Incidentally, some idea of how fast Florida has produced cities may be gained from these figures: in 1930 Florida had one hundred and ten cities whereas in 1973 there were three hundred and ninety-one. At the time of the 1970 federal census, there were one hundred sixty-eight unincorporated communities of one thousand or more inhabitants.

The collection of county histories and other Florida materials in the Florida State Library has been a basic source for information. An unpublished survey of Florida place names, compiled in the 1930s by the Works Progress Administration, was an extremely helpful beginning, particularly for the smaller communities. Another source of information was the responses to a 1953 questionnaire I prepared and the Florida State Advertising Commission mailed to postmasters and other officials.

Compiling this book has been fascinating and frustrating. It has been interesting to see the vignettes of community life revealed from my research. The author of a county history commented that one central Florida town had a nineteen-piece brass band. What more need be said of that town's spirit! What an image that sentence creates of families gathered around a bandstand on a Saturday or Sunday afternoon.

My research has been informative in disclosing anew that those making a choice between Flagler and Miami as the name for the new Dade County community thought Miami meant "sweet water." Of what real importance, then, is all the hair-splitting over what *miami* may have meant to this or that Indian tribe?

And, there have been frustrations, too. I invested much time in trying to determine the origin of Bunker Hill, a name that appears with some prominence on maps of Collier County. For no special reason except curiosity, I wanted to know if those who named Florida's Bunker Hill had in mind the American Revolution's misnamed Battle of Bunker Hill. The search went unrewarded although I talked with seven authorities on the area and read several regional histories. Incidentally, there had been an earlier Bunker Hill in Jefferson County, the source of its name also lost to history, at least for this moment. Thus, neither of the Bunker Hills appear in this book.

Finally, it should be remembered that this book gathers together the knowledge and beliefs of many people. Sources disagree. The most often cited source in the Works Progress Administration's unpublished "Florida Place Names" is "local tradition." What is a compiler to do when there is a conflict of traditions? Here it has been resolved usually by relating all versions or picking the one which seems, on the basis of other evidence, to be more logical. Readers who either disagree or possess other facts are invited to write me at 2015 East Randolph Circle, Tallahassee, Fla. 32303.

I hope readers will find this book as entertaining and informative to read as I have found it to compile.

Allen Morris

ACKNOWLEDGMENTS

I am indebted to many persons for their help. First, as always, is Dr. Dorothy Dodd, state librarian-emeritus. Next, Miss Mary O. McRory, head of the reference section, and Miss Patty Paul, documents librarian, both of the Florida State Library.

Miss Dena Snodgrass shared her vast store of Florida facts, and Mrs. Lucy DeCosmo helped in organizing the raw materials as well as making other contributions to this book.

Others I would like to thank, in alphabetical order, are: Judge Charles C. Anderson of Monticello; Mrs. Carol Jo Beaty of Perry; Miss Jeanne Bellamy (Mrs. John T. Bills) of Miami; Mrs. Ada Bilbrey of Duette; Representative R. Ed Blackburn, Jr., of Tampa; Mrs. James D. Bruton, Jr., of Plant City; Daniel B. Cameron, Jr., of Palm Bay; Mr. and Mrs. Harold Chapman of Tallahassee; C. L. Clark of Tallahassee; James A. Clendinen, the *Tampa Tribune*; Representative Vince Fechtel of Leesburg; Dr. C. A. Gauld, Miami-Dade Community College; Representative William L. Gibson of Orlando; J. Ralph Hamlin, Sergeant's Office, Florida House of Representatives; T. E. Holcom of Lakeland; Homer Hooks of Lakeland; Mrs. Nell Hutchins of Fort Walton Beach; Representative and Mrs. C. Fred Jones of Auburndale; Mrs. A. J. Knecht of Palm Bay; Holmes Melton of Mayo; Representative Jerry G. Melvin of Fort Walton Beach; Representative Tom McPherson of Fort Lauderdale; Emmett B. Peter, Jr., of the *Orlando Sentinel*; Senator Curtis Peterson of Eaton Park; Representative Ted Randell of Fort Myers; W. D. Roberts of Collier County; Representative Jane Robinson of Cocoa; Mrs. M. G. Shuman of Duette; Nixon Smiley, columnist and author of Miami; Mrs. Elizabeth F. Smith of the *Magnolia Monthly*, Crawfordville; Wm. R. Spear of the *Fort Myers News-Press*; Mrs. Bonita Swann of Wauchula; Representative Pat Thomas of Quincy; George L. Thurston of Tallahassee; Representative Fred N. Tittle, Jr., of Tavernier; Mrs. Juanita S. Tucker, postmistress of Christmas; Mrs. Peg Twichell of Tamarac; Dr. Robert O. Vernon of the State Department of Natural Resources; and Marvin Witt, Sergeant's Office, Florida House of Representatives.

The many persons who helped in the early years of my research are acknowledged in *The Florida Handbook*, 1955 edition, pages 39-41.

County Map of Florida

INTRODUCTION

Perhaps nothing reflects the history of a state, and the personalities of the people who settled it, as much or as well as its place names. Florida's colorful history under the flags of Spain, Great Britain, France, the Confederate States, and the United States is matched by the great variety of names for its cities and communities.

From the day in 1513 when Ponce de León named the peninsula he had discovered Florida to the present-day nickname of the "Sunshine State," place names here have indicated the influences of the Indians, of the early settlers and railroad men, and now of the developers.

The Indian names in Florida, as elsewhere in this country, described places in terms useful to the Indians, for example, "cow ford," bloody creek," "rabbit creek," "sunning turtles," and "fallen tree." So, beware of Indian names that have been translated, as was Itchepackesassa, in such idyllic terms as "where the moon put the colors of the rainbow into the earth and the sun draws them out in the flowers." In Creek, Itchepackesassa, pronounced Itch-e-puck-ah-saś-sa, simply meant "tobacco field."

Indian names were signposts distinguishing places within a relatively small area from one another (Stewart, 1945). A big river seldom had the same name throughout its course because, as Stewart wrote, a tribe often had no idea from where its rivers came or where they went.

There was no universal Indian language. "To say that a name is Indian is even less than to say that it is European, for among the tribes the languages differed much more than English from French, Dutch, or Russian," said Stewart. The native Florida tribes that were numerous and powerful for a century and a half after the discovery of America contributed little to the catalog of Florida names. These early tribes disappeared long ago, and with the exception of the Timucua, little or nothing is known of their languages.

According to the standard work for this state, *Florida Place-Names of Indian Derivation* by J. Clarence Simpson, published by the Florida Geological Survey in 1956,

> We are immediately impressed by the observation that most of the surviving Indian place-names are derived from the language of those

immigrant bands from the North who moved into Florida after the decline and disappearance of the native Floridians. The newcomers were principally speakers of Hitchiti and Creek, or of other tribes whose language indicated affiliation with the basic Muskogean linguistic stock.

Simpson cautions us to remember that none of the old Indian languages had a written form with either an original alphabet of any description or an established orthography. The various Europeans who heard the Indian words spoken and attempted to express them in writing followed the usages of their own European languages.

Other authoritative books in the field of Indian names are Professor William A. Read's *Florida Place-Names of Indian Origin and Seminole Personal Names* and Minnie Moore-Willson's *The Seminoles of Florida*.

In the early days of settlement after Florida passed into American possession, names were chosen to honor postmasters and early landowners or to honor railroad officials. For example, Jacksonville gained its name from the first American governor of Florida, Andrew Jackson, and Bradenton from a pioneer sugar grower, Dr. Joseph Braden. Plant City was named for Henry B. Plant of the Atlantic Coast Line Railroad, and the name of Flagler County came from Henry M. Flagler of the Florida East Coast Railway. In later years Floridians sought names for cities that were intended to create the image of a good place to live. Interestingly, when settlers named the 7,712 lakes in Florida, however, they broke away from these patterns of name-choosing and usually said what they thought.

Cockroach Creek in Hillsborough County is an example of some now-forgotten incident that resulted in a place name. It is easy to guess what precipitated the naming of the two Baptizing Ponds in Washington County and the Baptizing Hole in Sumter County.

Sunday picnics come to mind with the names of the six lakes or ponds called Dinner. Booze Lake in Madison County well could commemorate a pioneer family of that name rather than something alcoholic. There is Beer Can Pond in Leon County, Polecat Lake in Polk County, Starvation Lake in Hillsborough County, Yankee Lake in Seminole County, Stealing Lake in Walton County, Up and Down Lake in Putnam County, Squaw Pond in Marion County, Lake Confusion in Polk County, and River Styx Lake in Alachua County. Other interesting names are the five lakes called Hiawatha, Kitchen Cow House Pond in Levy County, Camel Pond in Liberty County, Lake Hellen Blazes in Brevard, and, wonder of wonder, Lake Morality in Franklin County.

Repetitive names include: thirty-seven variations of Sand Lake, including Sand Mountain Pond in Washington County; fifty-nine names prefaced by Little, including Little Hell Lake in Suwannee County; twenty-nine Long Lakes or Ponds; twenty-seven versions of Mud Lake or Pond; twenty Silver Lakes; seventeen Black Lakes; fourteen Buck Lakes; fifteen Crystal Lakes; twelve Duck Ponds; twelve Horseshoe Lakes; five Rattlesnake Lakes or Ponds; and three Red Bug Lakes.

Sentiment likely dictated the frequent use of the names of women to identify lakes. The roll call of these include: Ada, Adelaide, Alice, Alma, Amelia, Ann, Anna Maria, Annette, Annie, Bess, Bessie, Blanche, Caroline, Carrie, Catharine or Catherine, Cathy, Charlotte, Cindy, Clara, Claire, Cloe, Cora Lee, Daisy, Dora, Effie, Elizabeth, Ella, Ellen, Erin, Fanny, Florence, Frances, Gertrude, Grace, Helen, Hettie, Hilda, Ida, Idamere, Irene, Ivanhoe, Jane, Jennie, Jessie, Jewel, Josephine, Katherine, Kathryn, Kitty, Lou, Lena, Lenore, Lillian, Lily, Lizzie, Louisa, Louise, Lucie, Lucy, Lulu, Mable, Margaret, Maria, Marie, Martha, Mary, Mary Ann, Mary Jane, Miranda, Minnie, Molly, Myrtle, Nan, Nellie, Nona, Ola, Opal, Sara, Sarah, Stella, Susan, Susannah, Sylvia, Victoria, Virginia, Violet, Violetta, Wilma, and Yvonne.

Anyone not yet honored has plenty of opportunity for this to be done. The census taken in 1969 by the State Department of Conservation, now the Department of Natural Resources, showed literally hundreds of unnamed lakes in Florida.

Another historical influence on Florida place names has been the unusually large number of forts built here. Florida often has been called the nation's most fortified state. Even many of those who use the term do not realize just how true it is. Counting the Spanish, French, and British forts for which we have recorded history, more than three hundred forts, batteries, redoubts, and named camps existed in Florida from earliest settlement to 1903, according to the meticulous research of Francis B. Heitman, compiler of the *Historical Register and Dictionary of the United States Army.*

The great forts—Clinch at Fernandina Beach, Castillo de San Marcos at St. Augustine, Jefferson in the Dry Tortugas, and Pickens and Barrancas at Pensacola—are the exceptions among the hundreds of Florida forts. Virtually all American forts of the Seminole wars were simple defensive works, usually a combination of ditches and embankments of earth and trees to protect relatively small military units for short periods of time. Their temporary nature means that traces of them have disappeared.

Although Spanish, French, and British forts usually were named for saints or members of royal families, American forts generally were named after officers of the local command. Of the surviving forts, therefore, Fort Lauderdale was named for Maj. William Lauderdale, Fort Meade for Lt. George Gordon Meade (later General Meade of Gettysburg), Fort

Myers for Lt. Abraham Charles Myers (afterward General Myers), and
Fort Pierce for Lt. Col. Benjamin Kendrick Pierce. But there were the
usual exceptions, that is, Fort Pleasant and Camp Lang Syne.

Seven incorporated cities retain today the names of forts: Fort Lauderdale, Fort Meade, Fort Myers, Fort Pierce, Fort Walton, and Fort
White.

A number of forts survive in communities that have dropped Fort
from their name: Maitland once was Fort Maitland, Jupiter once was
Fort Jupiter, and Dade City once was Fort Dade. Still others are known
now by different names: Miami was Fort Dallas, Jacksonville was
founded across the river from the old site of Fort San Nicholas, and
Tampa grew up on the fringe of Fort Brooke.

Finally, I would like to mention that no place names are more important to the typical man or woman than those of the streets on which he
lives and works. Unfortunately, this book does not have room for the
inclusion of all the names of interest. By mentioning a few in these final
paragraphs, however, I would like to encourage each of my readers to
appreciate the sense of history that surrounds us if we will but notice it.

I reside on land within the Lafayette grant (*which see*), and my office
window overlooks the columned face of Florida's Capitol. I have no
problem identifying with Florida's history because I am so near to it.
You may not be as fortunate, but history has touched everywhere in our
state. The names of streets of many communities recall significant events
in Florida's life. Miami's Flagler Street, Pensacola's Palafox Street, Jacksonville's Bay Street, and Tampa's Lafayette Street are among those
streets of memories. As Malcolm Johnson, editor of the *Tallahassee
Democrat,* once wrote: "The street names of an old city . . . provide an
index to its history." Let us take the capital for example: Tallahassee's
main street, Monroe, was named for President James Monroe, who was in
office when Florida was acquired from Spain. Paralleling Monroe is
Adams Street, named for John Quincy Adams, who was Monroe's
secretary of state and who succeeded him in the presidency. Duval Street
was named for William P. DuVal, who was the first territorial governor.
Other Tallahassee street names recall persons whose identification with
Florida may be found elsewhere in this book: Gadsden, Lafayette,
Gaines, and Call.

There is a street name in Tallahassee that evidences the love of liberty
that existed when the nation was young and also how place names are
corrupted through the passage of time. Boulevard started out as Bolívar,
named for the South American liberator Simón Bolívar, who was a hero
of the hemisphere when Tallahassee was established. Eventually some
French people settled on Boulevard. "Bolivar sounds very much like
Boulevard, as the French pronounce it, so gradually that's the way it
came to be spelled," explained Johnson.

ACTON. *Polk County.* In 1884 a group of Englishmen established Acton, named for the British author Lord Acton. The community lasted until 1894, when its residents scattered after a severe freeze. During its decade of existence, Acton had about 200 inhabitants, a hotel, a sawmill, some stores, and a church. Its atmosphere, dress, and customs were typically English, with polo, fox hunting, and cricket being a part of life. Lakeland has now absorbed the site of Acton.

ADAM, EVE, and **PARADISE.** *Alachua* and *Levy counties.* Adam, in Alachua County, and Eve, in Levy County, were separated by a few miles, but linked by a railroad. At the turn of the century, sawmills, turpentine stills, and phosphate mines were served by the railroad, whose officials named Adam and, likely, Eve. Adam remains on the sectional map of the Florida Department of Agriculture, but Eve has disappeared from maps. Unlike Adam, Eve had a post office, between 1899 and 1909. Paradise, in Alachua County, remains on the sectional map about 18 miles from Adam as the crow flies. Jess Davis of Gainesville, Alachua County historian, says Paradise was a bustling community with a post office between 1885 and 1908. The town was named when the landowner, negotiating with a railroad for right-of-way, remarked that the track "would go right through Paradise."

ALACHUA. *Alachua County.* The town can be traced back to the first half of the eighteenth century. Name derives from Seminole-Creek Indian word *luchuwa,* meaning "jug," and was apparently given when the place was first settled by Creeks who came down from Oconee in Georgia. The "jug" was a large chasm in the earth about two and one-half miles southeast of the present site of Gainesville. The name, with slight variations in spelling, indicates a Creek settlement on maps of 1715, 1720, and 1733. When the town became a center of white population following the British acquisition of Florida in 1763, the name was left unchanged and later applied to the county formed here, whose seat is at Gainesville.

ALACHUA County. The ninth county, established December 29, 1824.

ALADDIN CITY. *Dade County.* Developed during the boom of 1925, it was built so rapidly in the rich farmland of south Dade County that it was named for the lad in *Arabian Nights* who acquired the magic lamp. Later, the land reverted to its agricultural use in the Redlands and may remain agricultural. It is west of Goulds and south of Richmond on the Seaboard Railway Railroad.

ALDERMANS FORD. *Hillsborough County.* For years the traditional place for beginning political campaigns in Hillsborough County by state and county candidates.

ALFORD. *Jackson County.* Named for S. A. and Chauncey Alford, who were pioneer naval stores operators in the vicinity in the early part of this century.

ALLANDALE. *Volusia County.* Once known as Halifax City, the place later was known for two brothers, Thomas and William Allen, who settled here in the 1880s. At that time there already was an Allendale, in Osceola County; hence, Allandale.

ALTAMONTE SPRINGS. *Seminole County. Altamonte* is Spanish for "high hill." The town was established in 1887.

ALTHA. *Calhoun County.* The post office was established in 1901, and the postmistress, Lula M. Richards, chose the name. Mrs. Richards studied a postal guide containing 5,000 names and chose Altha because there was only one other office with that name and it was far away. Old maps show an Indian village called Hyhappo or Savannah nearby.

ALTOONA. *Lake County.* Either Thomas J. Hinson, a pioneer lumberer, or Augustus Gottschee, an early merchant, named this town in the 1880s for their former homes in Altoona, Pa.

ALVA. *Lee County.* The founder of the community in the 1880s was Capt. Peter Nelson, a Dane, who conferred the name because of a small white flower that he found growing here. Alva derives from the Latin *alba,* signifying "white."

AMERICAN BEACH. *Nassau County.* Before integration of Florida's improved beaches, blacks had few places on the ocean or gulf to swim. Employees of the Afro-American Life Insurance Company of Jacksonville established American Beach in the 1930s to meet this need. A seaside tract of 20 acres, American Beach offered summer cottages and year-round homes.

ANDALUSIA. *Flagler County.* For a region in southern Spain, bordering on the Atlantic Ocean and the Mediterranean Sea.

ANDYTOWN. *Broward County.* Andy Poulus, then a linen service operator in Philadelphia, Pa., stopped in 1947 at a small cafe at the junction of U.S. 27 and S.R. 84 for a cup of coffee. He returned the next day and bought 10 acres at the junction for $50,000. Poulus retired to south Florida, and the junction developed into a sizeable community. Poulus died in 1972 during a visit to his native Greece, a place he left at the age of 10.

ANNA MARIA ISLAND. *Manatee County.* Ponce de León is said to have visited this island in 1513 and to have named it for the queen of his sponsor, King Charles II. Indians of the Timucua tribe lived here, and their burial mounds have been the source of artifacts for archeologists studying the Timucua. Pronunciation of the island's name is disputed: Anna Mar-EYE-a has been the favorite of many old-timers, but islanders nowadays are said to prefer Anna Mar-EE-a.

ANTHONY. *Marion County.* First called Anoty Place, the town was named for Col. E. C. Anthony, who, in 1882, was one of a group that established the community as a center for citrus, cattle, lumbering, and sheep raising.

APALACHICOLA. *Franklin County.* One of the most musical names on the map of Florida and associated in the minds of most people with excellent and delicious oysters. According to some authorities, *apalachicola* is a Hitchiti Indian word meaning "the people on the other side." Simpson, however, says *apalachi* is a Choctaw word signifying "allies." The settlement of the present site of the town dates back to the times of the Creek Indians, and since it is located at the tip of a considerable peninsula, just west of the mouth of a river, the first version explains how the word might have become the designation of those who lived there. It later was applied to the river and the bay into which it empties. Apalachicola is the county seat of Franklin County.

APOLLO BEACH. *Hillsborough County.* Named by its developers in the 1950s for the Greek and Roman god of light because of the pleasing suggestion of a sunlit beach.

APOPKA. *Orange County.* Authorities seem to agree that the Indian word from which this town derives its name has something to do with eating, but just what was eaten is uncertain. One source gives two Creek words, *aha,* "potato," and *papka,* "eating place," and asserts that the original spelling was Ahapopka. Another ascribes the name to the word *tsalopopkohatchee,* "catfish-eating creek"; still another gives *tsala apopka,* "trout-eating place."

ARCADIA. *DeSoto County.* First called Waldron's Homestead, then Tater Hill Landing, and finally Arcadia. Local tradition denies that the name has anything to do with Arcadia in Greece or Arcadia in Louisiana or the French-Canadian Acadia, also in Louisiana. Instead, say the old-timers, the town was named by Rev. James (Boss) Hendry, who began a sawmill here on July 23, 1884, his forty-fifth birthday. The name honors Arcadia Albritton, daughter of pioneer settlers at Lilly on Horse Creek, who had baked him a birthday cake. Arcadia is the county seat of DeSoto County.

ARCHER. *Alachua County.* Established in 1852 by the Florida Land Company of Fernandina, and first called Deer Hammock. Later the town was renamed in honor of Brig. Gen. James J. Archer of the Army of the Confederacy. Early settlers were drawn to this section for planting orange groves. A company of Quaker settlers from Indiana and Ohio planted oaks throughout the vicinity to act as windbreakers.

ARGYLE. *Walton County.* Established in 1883 and thought to be named after Argyll, a county in West Scotland, perhaps at the suggestion of one of the many Scots who settled in the Euchee Valley beginning in 1823.

ARIEL. *Volusia County.* Named for Lake Ariel in Pennsylvania by settlers in the early 1900s.

ARIPEKA. *Pasco County.* Named after Sam Jones, a famous Miccosukee chief, who was called Aripeka or Arpeika. The name is possibly corrupted from Creek *abihka,* "pile at the base," "heap at the root." An ancient Creek town near the upper Coosa River was so named because "in the contest for supremacy its warriors heaped up a pile of scalps, covering the base of the war-pole."

ARRAN. *Wakulla County.* Established in the 1890s and believed to have been named for the Scotch island in the Firth of Clyde.

ARREDONDO. *Alachua County.* Named for Don Fernando de la Maza Arredondo, who received a grant of 290,000 acres of land in this vicinity from the Spanish government in 1817 just prior to the ceding of Florida to the United States.

ASHTON. *Osceola County.* Formerly called Ashton Station on what was in the 1880s the Sugar Belt Railroad. Named for an English family who were the first settlers.

ASTATULA. *Lake County.* Although local legend says Astatula means either "Lake of Sunbeams" or "Lake of Sparkling Moonbeams," Read suggests another meaning from Seminole-Creek *isti,* "people," and *italwa,* "tribes,"—"people of different tribes." Still another authority points out that *atula* is the Timucuan word for arrow. The name dates from 1880.

ASTOR. *Lake County.* First named Fort Butler for Lt. P. M. Butler, the officer in charge of erecting the fort. The fort was occupied by Union troops during the Civil War and was captured in 1864 by Confederate Capt. J. J. Dickison, whose calvary exploits caused north central Florida to be known as "Dixie's Land." The name was changed to Astor for the New York financier, William Astor. In the 1870s Astor purchased the grant that Moses Levy, a Portuguese Jew, had obtained in hopes of establishing a colony for oppressed European Jews. Astor bought a railroad and built hotels and a telegraph line. When steamboat traffic on the St. Johns River declined, however, the resort almost disappeared.

ATLANTIC BEACH. *Duval County.* Three seaside communities, now called (north to south) Atlantic Beach, Neptune Beach, and Jacksonville Beach, lie contiguous to one another about 18 miles southeast of the metropolis of Jacksonville. Formerly the territory of all three was included in what was called Pablo Beach, after the Spanish form of Paul. First named Ruby Beach, the Pablo was derived from names of Pablo Creek and Pablo Point, both of which date from Spanish days. A post office was established here in October 1884. Pablo Beach was incorporated May 22, 1907, and a paved highway leading from Jacksonville was built in 1910. In 1925, when the present town of Jacksonville Beach was incorporated, Atlantic Beach and Neptune Beach broke away and established themselves separately. The name, of course, comes from the name of the Atlantic Ocean.

AUBURNDALE. *Polk County.* When Oliver Goldsmith disguised his native village, Lishoy, under the name of Auburn in *The Deserted Village* and began with the lines:

> *Sweet Auburn! loveliest village of the*
>   *plain,*
> *Where health and plenty cheer'd the*
>   *laboring swain,*

he did not anticipate that today there would be Auburns in ten states and Auburndales in Massachusetts and Florida. Established in 1882, first under the name of Sanatoria, from a hotel erected there by the early settlers, the site was shifted when the railroad came through, and some citizens from Auburndale, Mass., suggested that it be rechristened after that town. The most influential of these seems to have been Mrs. Ralph Pulsifer, wife of the publisher of the *Boston Herald.*

AUCILLA. *Jefferson County.* An ancient community of many names: Aucilla, Ocello, Ocilla, Ocillo, Williamsburg, and Station Four. The first post office appears to have been established under the name Ocello in 1834, and in 1884 the name finally became Aucilla for the nearby Aucilla River. Eight Walker brothers were among the early inhabitants, and their progeny still live here. In the mid-1800s Aucilla was an overnight stop on the Salt Road, the trail followed by wagons carrying salt from Florida's Gulf coast to Georgia and beyond. Later, when the railroad went through, the stop was known as Station Four, because it was the fourth station east from Tallahassee. Aucilla is a Timucuan Indian word of unknown meaning.

AVON PARK. *Highlands County.* Site of this town was selected around 1885 by O. M. Crosby, of Danbury, Conn., who was president of the Florida Development Company. Shortly thereafter Crosby visited England, where he recruited many settlers for his new town and brought them back with him. Among these were Mr. and Mrs. William King, who came from Stratford-on-Avon, and it was they who named the town.

BABSON PARK. *Polk County.* Formerly known as Crooked Lake because it is situated on the northeast end of the lake by that name. In 1923 Roger W. Babson, an economic forecaster of national reputation, purchased 400 acres of land that included the town site; the name was changed to Babson Park in 1925.

BAGDAD. *Santa Rosa County.* For the port of the Bagdad Land and Lumber Company on the Blackwater River from which, beginning in 1850, millions of feet of pine and cypress were shipped. There is a belief that the company took its name from the Bagdad of the *Arabian Nights.* Like Bagdad, the queen city of Mesopotamia, Florida's Bagdad lies between two rivers—in Florida the Escambia and Blackwater rivers—on a grassy pine-covered peninsula. The area once was known as Simpson's Mill, for an earlier timberman.

BAHIA HONDA KEY. *Monroe County.* From the Spanish "deep bay." Bahia Honda Key marks the geologic transition from the upper to the lower keys. Since about 1870, botanists from all over the world have been visiting Bahia Honda Key to study the plants brought here by birds, hurricane winds, and ocean waves from islands of the West Indies and the Caribbean Sea. Very rare plants growing as native plants on Bahia Honda Key are the West Indies satinwood, or yellowwood tree (*Zanthoxylum flavum*), the Catesbaea, Jamaica morning glory (*Jaquemontia jamaicensis*), and the wild dilly (*Minusops*).

BAKER County. The thirty-eighth county, established February 8, 1861. Named for James McNair Baker (1822-92), Confederate States senator and judge of the Fourth Judicial District in Florida.

BALDWIN. *Duval County.* First called Thigpen, but in 1860 renamed to honor Dr. A. S. Baldwin, who had played a leading role in securing the building of the first railroad into Jacksonville. The town had sprung up at the point where the road from the west branches to Jacksonville and to Fernandina. Doctor Baldwin had served in the

Florida legislature in 1852, and during the Civil War was a prominent surgeon in the Army of the Confederacy.

BARBERVILLE. *Volusia County.* Named for J. D. Barber when the post office was opened in 1884. Barber had settled here two years earlier. This was not pioneer land, however, for Rev. J. J. Baker, a physician and Methodist minister, had homesteaded in the area prior to the Civil War.

BARTOW. *Polk County.* Seems to have had two previous names; the first was Peas Creek. Later, when Redding Blount came with Jacob Summerlin to pioneer the raising of cattle in Florida, the town was renamed Fort Blount. In 1867 its name was changed again, this time to honor Confederate Gen. Francis F. Bartow, who had been the first general officer of either side to fall in the Civil War. Nowadays Bartow, the county seat of Polk County, likes to be spoken of as "The City of Oaks."

BASCOM. *Jackson County.* Established in 1890 by the Bevis family, and named for a member of that family.

BAY County. The forty-ninth county, established April 24, 1913. Named for St. Andrews Bay, on which the county borders.

BAY HARBOR ISLANDS. *Dade County.* As might be guessed, this community derives its name and fame from Biscayne Bay. Stepping down in 1973 after 26 years as the community's first mayor, Shepard Broad said he had been "elected unanimously by 750 empty lots" in 1946, a year after the developer acquired two low-lying, sand-covered islands in Biscayne Bay.

BAY LAKE. *Orange County.* One of the twin cities—Lake Buena Vista being the other—whose legislatively conferred municipal powers are used to administer a fairyland, Disney World.

BEE RIDGE. *Sarasota County.* A Baptist preacher named Isaac Redd came this way and settled here around 1900. The story goes that most every hollow tree had a bee hive. Because of the bees and the ridge terrain, Rev. Redd named it Bee Ridge.

BELL. *Gilchrist County.* Incorporated in 1903 shortly after a branch of the Seaboard Air Line Railroad had been built through. The name was selected by means of a beauty contest in which the winner's name was to be given to the new station and post office. Bell Fletcher, the daughter of Daniel E. Fletcher, a native of Florida and a successful farmer of Alachua County, was elected queen. She later married G. W. Everett and lived in the Bell community until her death in 1919.

BELLAMY ROAD, THE. The 1824 Congress authorized a public road between St. Augustine and Pensacola, the capitals of the territories of East and West Florida. The road between St. Augustine and the present area of Tallahassee was to follow as nearly as practical the old

Spanish Mission Trail. Congress appropriated $20,000 for construc-
tion and authorized the use of troops stationed in Florida. Contracts
were awarded to John Bellamy, a South Carolinian who had moved to
Jefferson County, for sections extending from the St. Johns River (St.
Augustine) to the Ochlockonee River (Tallahassee). The western half of
the project finally was undertaken and completed by troops. Although the act of Congress authorizing the St. Augustine-Pensacola
road stated a width of 25 feet, the specifications given in the adver-
tisements by the territorial government for the eastern half required
only 16 feet. Bellamy regarded his task as completed by May 19,
1826. Critics complained that the road was too narrow, that stumps
had been left standing to a height that impeded the passage of
wheeled vehicles, that the bridges were flimsy, and that the causeways
over swampy areas were inadequate and unstable. Bellamy's defenders
argued that the stumps did not bar the passage of carriages and wagons and declared that it was impractical to cut a wide roadway, as the
admission of too much sunlight and air would promote the growth of
underbrush and scrub oak. The Bellamy Road was used until the
beginning of the Civil War. Traces can be seen today. *See also* El
Camino Real and Kings Road.

BELLEAIR. *Pinellas County.* Named to indicate the excellence of the
air in these parts by Henry B. Plant in 1896, when he purchased most
of the land now included in the town and built his Belleview Hotel.
The town was incorporated in 1925. The soothing name of the older
community has been appropriated for three nearby Pinellas County
cities: Belleair Beach, Belleair Bluffs, and Belleair Shore.

BELLE GLADE. *Palm Beach County.* Located on the south shore of
Lake Okeechobee and until 1921 known as the Hillsborough Canal
Settlement. In that year a post office was sought, and a prerequisite
was a more euphonious name. F. M. Myer, proprietor of the Pioneer
Hotel, placed a blackboard in his lobby and solicited suggestions. One
day a group of tourists came down the canal from West Palm Beach
and stayed at the hotel after making a trip through the Everglades.
One of them remarked that the Hillsborough Canal Settlement was
the belle of the 'Glades. Mrs. Elsie Myer, wife of the hotel proprietor,
quickly added Belle Glade to the list of names on the blackboard, and
when an informal poll was later taken it was voted the favorite. The
town was incorporated in 1928. Bellglade Camp, nearby, takes its
name from the larger community.

BELL SHOALS. *Hillsborough County.* First known as Bell's Ford
for Louis Bell, who settled here on the Alafia River in 1846 and
operated a cattle ferry much in use during the annual transporting of
cattle to Gulf ports. Bell was harassed by Indians and often took

refuge in a small log fort he had built. Once his six-year-old son was captured and returned only after Bell gave up all the family's blankets. Bell Shoals gained worldwide fame as the locale of Jules Verne's fantastic novel, *From the Earth to the Moon* (1865). Here the 900-foot cannon was supposed to have been cast and erected. In the first edition of the novel the man-bearing projectile was not properly aimed and so remained whirling in a vast orbit around the moon. Readers objected so strenuously to this tragic ending that in later editions Verne brought the adventurers back to earth unharmed. For 60 years a semiburied piece of machinery on the banks of the river was believed by some to be a fragment of the gigantic cannon. On being unearthed, it was found to be a 10-foot steel shaft with vanes attached at the ends. Although the origin and use of the shaft is unknown, it probably was a part of an old water-driven grist mill that served pioneers in this region.

BENTON. *A former county.* Displaced Hernando as the name of the twenty-second county from March 6, 1844, until December 24, 1850, when the former name was restored. Named for Thomas Hart Benton (1782-1853), U.S. senator from Missouri for 30 years (1821-51). His vociferous opposition to paper money and a national bank earned Benton the nickname "Old Bullion." Florida's recognition of Benton was, however, the result of his sponsorship of the Armed Occupation Act of 1842, which opened central Florida to settlers.

BEVERLY BEACH. *Flagler County.* Claude Varn; a St. Augustine attorney, named the area for his granddaughter Beverly when the land was subdivided.

BIG CYPRESS. The name of (1) a Seminole Indian reservation in Hendry County, (2) stands of cypress trees, mainly in Collier and Hendry counties, and (3) the Big Cypress National Freshwater Reserve, together with contiguous land and water areas ecologically linked with the Everglades National Park, estaurine fisheries, and the freshwater aquifer of south Florida in Collier, Hendry, Dade, and Monroe counties. The name Big Cypress seems to refer to the size of the original trees concentrated in the area. These grew as tall as 100 feet. Many of the trees remaining are as old as any cut, but their stunted nature saved them from timbering. The Big Cypress known to hunters has spawned its own place names, among them: Devil's Garden, Dark Strand, Lost Dog Prairie, Airplane Prairie, Lard Can Slough, and Thompson's Pine Island.

BISCAYNE (Bay, Key, Park). *Dade County.* Juan Ponce de León, sailing south in 1513 from his landing near St. Augustine, found "the bright nameless great bay that John Cabot [1499] had seen, and like him found fresh springs in the limestone rocks" (Douglas, 1967). There are several stories about how the bay got its name. Most assume this name is merely a variant on the Bay of Biscay, in the Atlantic Ocean north of Spain and west of France. Fontaneda (1854) says Biscayne Bay was named because of the wreck there in the mid-1500s of a ship belonging to a man called El Biscaino (the Biscayan, from the Spanish province of Biscaya). Douglas accepts this, but Muir, in *Miami, U.S.A.,* says that on one of the islands in the bay lived Don Pedro el Biscaino, who had been Keeper of the Swans at the Spanish court. The name *Vizcaino* appears on a Spanish map of 1765. Vizcaino is said to have been the name of a prosperous Spanish merchant in Manila, who set out from Mexico to colonize lower California. Interestingly, the bay was called Sandwich Gulf on John Lee Williams' map of 1837. *See also* Cape Florida.

BITHLO. *Orange County.* Derives from the Seminole-Creek word *pilo* for "canoe." In the transliteration of this Indian language the voiceless "l" was often written "thl." The town was established in 1822.

BLACK CAESAR'S ROCK. *Dade County.* A tiny island between Old Rhodes and Elliott keys in the island chain separating the Atlantic Ocean and Biscayne Bay, once the headquarters of the legendary pirate, Black Caesar. Many different and conflicting tales are told of Black Caesar, but it is agreed generally that he was a black who escaped from a wrecked slave ship. After a successful career as a single-handed wrecker, Black Caesar became a lieutenant of the notorious Teach, better known as Blackbeard. *Florida: A Guide to the Southernmost State* reports: "Flying the skull and crossbones, their ship, the *Queen Ann's Revenge,* was captured by Lieutenant Robert Maynard in 1718. Teach was killed during the battle, sustaining 25 wounds before he fell dead. Caesar attempted to blow up the ship and all on board by dropping a match into the powder magazine, but one of the men prevented him. Taken to Virginia, Black Caesar was hanged."

BLITCHTON. *Marion County.* Named for a pioneer family, among whose distinctions was that of having two brothers serving simultaneously in the State Senate of 1895-97. The community achieved post office status in 1888.

BLOUNTSTOWN. *Calhoun County.* Named for John Blount, a Seminole Indian and the distinguished chief of the Indian tribe who occupied the reservation that once lay just east of here. Blount had been given this Anglo-American name because it was said that he had many traits in common with William Blount of North Carolina, whom President Washington appointed superintendent of Indian affairs in 1790. When the Florida reservation was ceded to the United States by a treaty made at Tallahassee, October 11, 1832, John Blount led a delegation of Seminoles in exploring the new reservation west of the Mississippi, and later he led the Seminole band to take up the new territory. The first white settlers named the town after the great Seminole. Blountstown is the county seat of Calhoun County.

BLOXHAM. *Almost a county.* Named for William Dunningham Bloxham, a leader of Florida Democratic party activities during the last 40 years of the nineteenth century. A planter-lawyer, he served in the 1861 House of Representatives from Leon County, he organized and commanded an infantry company during the Civil War, he was defeated for lieutenant governor in 1870 by a questionable count of the ballots, he was defeated for governor in 1872, he was appointed secretary of state in 1877, and he was elected governor in 1880. He declined appointment in 1885 as American minister to Bolivia but served as U.S. surveyor for Florida. He was appointed comptroller in 1890 and was elected comptroller and reelected. He then was reelected governor in 1896. He died in 1911. In 1915 the legislature voted to establish Bloxham County, with Williston as the temporary seat, subject to ratification by voters in the affected areas of Levy and Marion counties. The voters rejected the new county. Bloxham thus is remembered on the map only by a Leon County community best known for having given its name to a stretch of road called the Bloxham Cutoff.

BLUE SPRINGS. *Marion, Taylor,* and *Hamilton counties.* Named for the color of the springs here. The Indians called the Marion spring Wikaiwa and the Spaniards Las Aguas Azules, or "blue water."

BLUFF SPRINGS. *Escambia County.* Established in 1819, and first known as the Old Pringle Mill after Abraham Pringle. The formal name, which came later, suggested the bluffs and springs in the locality.

BOCA CIEGA. *Pinellas County.* Named for Boca Ciega Bay, southwest of St. Petersburg. Literally, the Spanish word *boca* means "mouth," and *ciega* means "blind." In this use, however, the words mean "obstructed or closed passage"—a reference, probably, to what looked like the entrance to a river but proved impassable, either because there was no river or because of dense vegetation.

BOCA GRANDE. *Lee County.* On Gasparilla Island. A Spanish name that means big mouth or large entrance and refers to a passage from the Gulf. *See also* Captiva Island, Gasparilla Island.

BOCA RATON. *Palm Beach County.* Established in 1924 and named for Boca Raton Sound. The Spanish words *Boca de Ratones* mean "rat's mouth," a term used by seamen to describe a hidden rock that gnaws or frets a ship's cables.

BONE VALLEY. *Hillsborough, Polk, Hardee,* and *Manatee counties.* A roughly circular area in Hillsborough, Polk, Hardee, and Manatee counties and the source of huge land-pebble phosphate deposits. In this subsurface area, once perhaps a large delta or estuary before the sea receded, fossils can be found of much of the rich and bizarre animal life that roved what now is Florida.

BONIFAY. *Holmes County*. Established in 1882 and named for a prominent old family of that vicinity. This is the county seat of Holmes County.

BONITA SPRINGS. *Lee County*. Derived from the Spanish "pretty." The community dates from 1912.

BOULOGNE. *Nassau County*. Probably named for the city in France. Established in 1880 by Andrew Price.

BOWLING GREEN. *Hardee County*. Known as Utica until the late 1880s, when a number of farmers from Bowling Green, Ky., purchased large holdings in the district and renamed the town after their former home.

BOYNTON BEACH. *Palm Beach County*. Founded in 1896 and first called simply Boynton, after Maj. N. S. Boynton of Port Huron, Mich., who erected a hotel on the beach. In 1925 the name was changed to Boynton Beach.

BRADENTON. *Manatee County*. In 1854 Dr. Joseph Braden, a pioneer sugar planter in this section, built his home here, close to the point where some say Hernando De Soto first landed on the Florida peninsula in 1539. When a post office was established in 1878, the spelling was erroneously given as Braidentown. The "i" was later dropped, and in 1924 the "w" was eliminated to make the present spelling. Bradenton is the county seat of Manatee County.

BRADFORD County. The thirty-sixth county, established December 21, 1858, as New River County. Named for Capt. Richard Bradford, the first Florida officer killed in the Civil War. He died in the Battle of Santa Rosa Island, October 9, 1861, and the county was given his name on December 6, 1861.

BRADLEY JUNCTION. *Marion County*. Established in 1910, but not incorporated until April 25, 1912, as Bradley. It is not clear when Junction was added.

BRANDON. *Hillsborough County*. Named by John Brandon, who with his family and possessions moved to Florida from Alabama in 1857. He lived several places in Florida before 1874 when he homesteaded 12 miles east of Tampa and named the place for his family.

BRANDY BRANCH. *Nassau County*. Known also as Brandy Creek, this community lost its alcoholic connotation in 1886 with a change of name to Bryceville. Brandy Branch was so-called because of the color of the water entering the St. Marys River. *See also* Bryceville.

BRANFORD. *Suwannee County.* Henry B. Plant, the great Florida developer who was president of the Savannah, Florida, and Western Railroad, now the Atlantic Coast Line, named this town in 1882 after Branford, Conn., where he had formerly lived. The Connecticut town, it is said, was named by variation after the town of Brentford in England. The Spanish mission of Ajoica stood a few miles northeast of the present site of Branford.

BREVARD County. The twenty-fifth county, established March 14, 1844. Named for Theodore Washington Brevard (1804-77), a North Carolinian who came to Florida in 1847 and later became state comptroller (1853-61). The county was originally named St. Lucie, but the name was changed to Brevard on January 6, 1855. Saint Lucie was restored to the map in 1905 when another county was created and given the name.

BREWSTER. *Polk County.* Named for a chemical company that had phosphate operations hereabouts in 1913.

BRIGHTON. *Highlands County.* Despite its English sound, the town was not named for the seaside resort but, rather, for James H. Bright, who had a cattle ranch here. Bright was a partner of Glenn H. Curtiss in the founding of Hialeah, a community that survived the collapse of the land boom in the 1920s to become one of the state's large cities.

BRISTOL. *Liberty County.* The first post office was established in 1852 at Ridleyville, with J. Clarke Ridley as the postmaster. Bristol followed in 1859. It has been assumed that Bristol also was a family name, but E. E. Callaway, repository of local lore, says the town was named for Bristol, England, although he does not know why. During the mid-1900s, the mayors of Bristol, England, and Bristol, Florida, exchanged greetings, so that if England's Bristol was not the original source of the Florida name, now it has been accepted as the adopted source. Bristol is the county seat of Liberty County.

BROADBRANCH. *Calhoun County.* Likely named for a nearby waterway. Broadbranch twice enjoyed recognition as a post office: between 1911 and 1915 and between 1919 and 1933.

BRONSON. *Levy County.* Established during the Civil War, and first called Chunky Pond, through a mistaken transliteration of an Indian word meaning dance. When the town was incorporated in 1884, it was given its present name to honor an early settler of great popularity. This town is the county seat of Levy County.

BROOKER. *Bradford County.* In 1892 Thomas R. Collins, a native of nearby Columbia County, bought a piece of property about a mile southwest of the present site of Brooker. His petition for a post office was granted in August of 1894, he was named postmaster, and he named the post office after the old Brooker Bridge across the Santa Fe River. The bridge had been named after Ed Brooker, a farmer in that area. A settlement had been established in this vicinity in 1838.

BROOKSVILLE. *Hernando County.* Said to have been named for Congressman Preston Brooks of South Carolina. On May 20, 1856, during the debate on the Kansas-Nebraska Bill, Sen. Charles Sumner of Massachusetts denounced Sen. A. P. Butler of South Carolina, who was then absent from the chamber and who was an uncle of Preston Brooks. The latter, having heard of the verbal attack on his relative, found Sumner in the Senate chamber after adjournment that day, broke a gutta-percha cane over his head, and left him insensible on the floor; he was said never to have recovered fully from the assault. A move to expel Brooks from the House of Representatives failed, but he resigned and was promptly reelected by his constituents. He was the recipient of a number of gold-headed canes and gold-handled whips. Congressman Anson Burlingame of Massachusetts, on the other hand, publicly denounced Brooks as a coward. Brooks challenged Burlingame to a duel; the latter accepted and named the Canadian side of Niagara Falls as the place. Brooks said he could not make his way with safety through the northern states to this site, and refused to go. He died about a year later. Brooksville is the county seat of Hernando County.

BROWARD County. The fifty-first county, established April 30, 1915. Named for Napoleon B. Broward, who, as governor of Florida from 1905 to 1909, played a leading part in the draining of the Everglades. Earlier, he was the owner of a steam tug, *The Three Friends,* which he commanded in eluding both U.S. and Spanish authorities to supply war materials to Cuban revolutionists. He had a stormy political career.

BROWARD'S NECK. *Duval County.* The paternal grandfather of Gov. Napoleon B. Broward settled near where Cedar Creek, now Broward River, enters the St. Johns River and forms a neck (an isthmus or cape. Broward's Neck entered history in its own right when the "Ladies of Broward's Neck" petitioned the state government on November 6, 1860, to withdraw Florida from the Union. On December 28, 1860, two weeks before Florida's secession, Miss Helen Broward presented Gov. Madison Starke Perry with a new state flag, the handiwork of the Ladies of Broward's Neck. Governor Perry, in acknowledging the gift, described the flag thus: "a bright and effulgent star . . . on a field of azure. . . ."

BROWNSVILLE. *Escambia County.* Named for L. S. Brown, who was known as "Clean-Sweep Brown" after he and all his chosen candidates were elected to the first city council when the municipal government was formed.

BRYCEVILLE. *Nassau County.* Founded and named in 1886 by George W. Bryce, at one time the largest landowner in the county. *See also* Brandy Branch.

BUCKINGHAM. *Lee County.* Formerly called Twelve Mile Creek. Edward M. Williams, formerly of Bucks County, Pa., served as first postmaster, and he suggested the name in 1889 when the government objected to the former name. The name may honor Buckingham Smith, nineteenth-century federal reclamation commissioner for Florida and historian, or Mr. Williams' former home, or both.

BUMPNOSE. *Jackson County.* Who's nose was bumped? History does not say. Bumpnose was a post office from November 11, 1896, until March 2, 1899, when its postal functions were absorbed by Marianna.

BUNNELL. *Flagler County.* Founded in 1880 by Alva A. Bunnell. At first it was only a sawmill site, but as the soil in the area proved to be especially fertile it became a great farming center, of which the principal product is now potatoes. Bunnell is the county seat of Flagler County.

BUSHNELL. *Sumter County.* First settled in the 1870s but not named until 1884. Name honors the young chief engineer of the surveying crew that laid out the railroad right-of-way. It is now the county seat of Sumter County.

CALHOUN County. The twentieth county, established January 26, 1838. Named for John C. Calhoun, the South Carolina senator who was the foremost proponent of the doctrine of states' rights.

CALL. *Not quite a county.* The Territorial Council passed an act on November 23, 1828, providing for the creation of a county to be known as Call, but Gov. William P. DuVal vetoed the act and so Call County never was established. Call County apparently was to have been situated where parts of Leon, Gadsden, and Jefferson counties now exist because a description in the laws bounded Leon County, in part, "on the north and east by the County of Call." The county obviously was to honor Richard Keith Call, who first came to Florida with Andrew Jackson in 1814 as a soldier and personal aide and returned with him to Pensacola in 1821 to set up the American gov-

ernment for the new territory. DuVal likely vetoed the act creating
Call County because of political differences. Call, however, had the
satisfaction of twice serving as territorial governor. His stately mansion, "The Grove," stands today in Tallahassee, overlooking the home
across the street of Florida's present governors. Call stood on the steps
of "The Grove" in January 1861 and was taunted by Secessionists
when Florida left the Union. A slaveholder but a Unionist, Call
responded: "Well, gentlemen, all I wish to say to you is that you have
just opened the gates of hell." In 1974 a descendant lives in "The
Grove,"—Mrs. Mary Call Collins, wife of LeRoy Collins, twice governor.

CALLAHAN. *Nassau County.* Settled in 1860, this community was
named for one of the contractors engaged in the construction of the
cross-Florida railroad between Fernandina and Cedar Key.

CALLAWAY. *Bay County.* Named for a sawmill operator; the town
gained a post office of its own in 1903.

CAMPBELLTON. *Jackson County.* Established in 1840 or earlier and
named for Judge R. L. Campbell.

CANAL POINT. *Palm Beach County.* Named for its location at the
point where the Palm Beach Canal enters Lake Okeechobee.

CANTONMENT. *Escambia County.* So named because this place was
the cantonment, or site of encampment, for Gen. Andrew Jackson's
troops in 1814 while conducting a punitive expedition against the
Spanish in Florida, and again in 1821 while awaiting transfer of Florida from Spain. Later this was Cantonment Clinch for Gen. Duncan L.
Clinch, who was ordered in March 1836 to enforce President Andrew
Jackson's proclamation that the Seminoles must leave Florida. General Clinch represented the United States at the confrontation when a
fiery young warrior named Osceola, after eight chiefs had signed an
agreement to leave, stabbed a dagger through the paper and said in
effect, "This is the way I sign! "

CAPE CANAVERAL. *Brevard County.* Canaveral is the Spanish word
for "a place of reeds or cane." The Spaniards named the cape Canaveral because they found cane or reeds growing here. Ponce de León
called the point the Cape of Currents, but the name Canaveral
appeared on the earliest Spanish maps of Florida. A community,
established in 1961, and the space center were also named Cape Canaveral. Following the assassination of President John F. Kennedy in
1963, the names of the geographical area and the space center were
changed in memory of the late president. Cape Kennedy became Cape
Canaveral again in 1973; the space center remains the John F. Kennedy Space Center. *See also* Cape Kennedy.

CAPE CORAL. *Lee County.* Advertised as the "New City," and it is indeed that. Not listed in the 1960 Federal Census, Cape Coral had grown to 10,193 by 1970 and to an estimated 20,000 by 1974. On the Caloosahatchee River, four miles from the Gulf of Mexico, Cape Coral suggests by its name cool, casual, waterfront living—the image that its developers intended.

CAPE FLORIDA. *Dade County.* John Cabot is said to have rounded this point, the southern tip of Key Biscayne, in 1499 and to have named it the Cape of the End of April. Later mapmakers (as early as Le Moyne, ca. 1565) changed the name to Promentorium Floridae or Cape Florida, probably because it was the first landfall on the Atlantic mainland. Soon after the United States acquired Florida from Spain, planning commenced for a lighthouse on the cape. The tower was completed in 1825 and is one of the oldest structures remaining in south Florida. Indians attacked the lighthouse in July 1836, driving the keeper and a black helper to the metal platform surrounding the light. The helper was killed. Faced with the dilemma of being roasted by a fire the Indians had started inside the tower or being killed by other means, Keeper John W. B. Thompson dropped some gunpowder into the fire. The explosion extinguished the flames and left Thompson still clinging to the platform, from which he was rescued the next day by the crew of a passing ship. A temporary army post, Fort Bankhead, was established on the cape in 1838 by Indian fighters commanded by Col. William S. Harney. The lighthouse was raised to its present height of 95 feet in 1855. The light was wrecked during the Civil War, restored in 1867, and extinguished finally in 1878 when the Fowey Rock light took its place as a guardian of the coast.

CAPE KENNEDY. *Brevard County.* Cape Kennedy became the name of Cape Canaveral by order of President Lyndon B. Johnson on November 29, 1963, following the assassination of President John F. Kennedy. At the same time, Station No. 1 of the Atlantic Missile Range was renamed the John F. Kennedy Space Center by President Johnson. Because Cape Canaveral had been recognized as the oldest continuously used place name on the American Atlantic coast, efforts were made to have the federal government restore the ancient name to the land mass, while retaining Cape Kennedy for the Space Center. When these efforts remained unsuccessful, the 1973 Florida legislature decreed that "all public maps and documents in Florida designate the geographical area as Cape Canaveral." Shortly afterward the U.S. Department of Interior, upon the recommendation of the interagency Committee on Domestic Geographic Names, acquiesed in the state's action, restoring the ancient name to the geographical area. *See also* Cape Canaveral.

CAPTIVA ISLAND. *Lee County.* According to legend, the island where the pirate, Gaspar or Gasparilla, handed over to his crew the eleven beautiful Mexican girls who, in 1801, were traveling to Spain for education when their ship was captured. Gaspar kept for himself, so the story goes, a Spanish princess, Maria Louise, who also had been captured. A skeptic, however, has pointed out that the island bore its name before Gaspar roved the seas. The community on the island is also named Captiva and has had a post office since 1902. *See also* Gasparilla.

CAROL CITY. *Dade County.* Named as a convenience for sign painters and printers. The developer, Julius Gaines, had originally planned to call it Coral City and draw "some of the magic of Coral Gables." All the name drew, he said wryly, was a law suit from Coral Gables. Signs and stationery were ready to go, so Gaines merely changed "a" to "o" and "o" to "a" and made the name Carol City. The city capitalized on its name—a carolling party on the banks of the waterways was a Christmas custom.

CARRABELLE. *Franklin County.* Established here, near Dog Island Harbor, in 1877 by O. M. Kelly, who served as postmaster. A certain Miss Carrie Hall reigned as the belle of the town, and it was named Rio Carrabelle in her honor. The Rio was later dropped. The name appears in an 1886 gazetteer as Carrabella.

CARYVILLE. *Washington County.* First settled in 1845 and later named Half Moon Bluff. In 1884, upon the advent of the Pensacola and Apalachicola Railroad, it was renamed Caryville in honor of a Pensacola businessman, R. M. Cary.

CASSELBERRY. *Seminole County.* Formerly known as Fern Park because of the numerous extensive ferneries here, and still thus referred to by many of its residents. The town was renamed during the 1940s by Hibbard Casselberry, a local horticulturist who had undertaken the development of the area.

CASTILLO DE SAN MARCOS. *St. Johns County.* A defensive stone fort built by Spain after the sacking of St. Augustine by the English in 1586 and in 1668. The Castillo was named for Mark, an early disciple if not an apostle of Christ. Construction began in 1672 and continued with interruptions until 1763. The English twice besieged the Castillo, in 1702 and 1740. The British garrisoned and held the Castillo during the American Revolution after having ceded Florida to Spain for British-occupied Havana. The fort was returned to Spain in 1783, and it was ceded to the United States in 1821. The Castillo was known to the Americans as Fort Marion, in honor of Gen. Francis Marion, the Revolutionary patriot of South Carolina popularly called the Swamp Fox. Fort Marion housed Indian prisoners. Confederate forces occupied the fort briefly during the Civil War, and it was used during the Spanish-American War as a military prison. Fort Marion was declared a national monument in 1924, and the ancient name was restored afterward.

CEDAR GROVE. *Bay County.* Named for the large cedar trees in the community. In 1900, Jefferson Davis bought a homestead with a number of large cedar trees. A settlement grew up, and when it was incorporated 50 years later the trees were still a feature of the place. The residents voted to name it Cedar Grove.

CEDAR KEY. *Levy County.* Located on a Gulf island that is part of a cluster known collectively as Cedar Keys. The town was established in the 1840s and named for the abundant growth of cedar trees that formerly covered all the islands here. Three pencil-manufacturing plants located in Cedar Key closed down when the cedar was depleted.

CENTER HILL. *Sumter County.* Established in 1883 by Thomas W. Spicer, who became postmaster and gave the town its name. He liked to think of the hill on which it is located as the center of things.

CENTURY. *Escambia County.* First called Teaspoon, but renamed when construction of a lumber mill began in the first month of the twentieth century.

CHARLIE APOPKA CREEK. *Hardee County.* Name signifies "trout (or bass) eating place," inasmuch as charlie is a corruption of *chalo,* "trout or bass," and *apopka,* "place for eating." (Simpson, 1956).

CHARLOTTE County. The fifty-seventh county, established April 23, 1921. Named from the body of water, Charlotte Harbor. Some authorities say Charlotte is a corruption of Carlos or Calos, in turn a corruption of Calusa, the name of the Indian tribe. Calos appears on Le Moyne's map of 1565 (T. De Bry, 1591), with the name applied to the southern part of the Florida peninsula. In the free-handed way of mapmakers, the English surveyors who followed the Spanish appropriated and anglicized the name as a tribute to their queen, Charlotte Sophia, wife of King George III. The Jeffreys Map of 1775 shows Charlotte Harbour, formerly Carlos Bay.

CHATTAHOOCHEE. *Gadsden County.* First established about 1828, and its name taken from the Chattahoochee River. The word is Seminole-Creek for "marked rock," derived from the peculiarly colored and patterned stones that are found in the bed of the river. For part of its history this town was known as River Junction because the Flint and Chattahoochee rivers join nearby to form the Apalachicola River. In 1681 the Spanish located their mission of Santa Cruz de Sabacola here.

CHERRY LAKE. *Madison County.* Established by Lucius Church in 1827 and named by him for the large number of wild cherry trees near the water. A flourishing Indian village known as Ochoawilla was situated on a hill near the lake in 1827. The Indian word seems to be derived from two words meaning slimy water.

CHIEFLAND. *Levy County.* When hostilities in the Seminole War ceased in 1842, a Creek chief chose this site for his farm home and went extensively into the raising of corn, wheat, potatoes, and other crops. A number of other Indians did small farming nearby and helped operate the chief's farm.

CHIPLEY. *Washington County.* Originally known as Orange, but renamed in honor of Col. William D. Chipley, a railroad official.

CHOKOLOSKEEE. *Collier County.* Name of an island, a creek, a community, and a bay. The island is one of the Ten Thousand Islands. Tebeau (1955) says the name of the first modern-day settler is difficult if not impossible to determine. "That he came in the 1870's is fairly certain," Tebeau opines, adding, "people now living at Chokoloskee recall that it was sometimes called Big Island. But the name Cokoliska appears in the Seminole War literature for the island and for what is now Turner River." This name is formed from two Indian words—Seminole-Creek *chuka,* "house," and *liski,* "old." Through the energies of C. G. McKinney, the "Sage of Chokoloskee" who came to the island in 1880, a post office was established on November 27, 1891. The new post office bore the name Comfort, which was changed on June 30, 1892, to Chokoloskee.

CHOSEN. *Palm Beach County.* According to Will (1964), the name was promoted by J. R. Leatherman, a Church of the Brethren preacher from Virginia. The community wanted a post office in 1921 and for that a name was necessary. "Leatherman's bailiwick decided on the name of Chosen, a good Bible name, because theirs was the Chosen Place . . . ."

CHRISTMAS. *Orange County.* Named in 1835 when a detachment of the U.S. Army, engaged in the war against the Seminoles, established a fort about halfway down the east coast of Florida on Christmas Day. This settlement has become a center of busy annual holiday activity. Shortly after the Seminole War began, a report that a large number of braves were gathering in the upper St. Johns valley caused Brig. Gen. Abraham Eustis to leave Fort Mellon (Sanford) on December 17, 1835, with more than a thousand men. The column took seven days to travel 25 miles, arriving at a point opposite Lake Cone on the St. Johns River on December 25. General Eustis ordered a fort built. Writing in the *Miami Herald,* Nixon Smiley reports, "Fort Christmas was built eighty feet square, of pine pickets with two substantial block houses twenty feet square." No battle ever occurred there, and Fort Christmas disappeared long ago, the log-constructed pickets and block houses becoming victims of decay or forest fire. No one knows now exactly where the fort stood. But as recently as 1950 the old military road between Christmas and Chulota—the road created by the troop movement in 1835—was still in use. Today the town of Christmas purveys a volume of Yuletide spirit disproportionate to its size. People from all parts of the United States send their holiday cards and letters to be posted here with the official postmark "Christmas, Florida." Mrs. Juanita Tucker, commissioned postmistress in 1932, designed and added an extra imprint of her own—a Christmas tree, the words "Glory to God in the Highest, Christmas, Orange County, Florida," and the year. The town's fame originated in 1935 when Christmas celebrated its one hundredth anniversary and received considerable publicity. Since then the early part of November each year brings a steady flow of mail, more than 300,000 pieces each season.

CHULUOTA. *Seminole County.* Combines the Creek *chule,* "pine," and *ote,* "island," for this was an open area of pine surrounded by hardwoods. Another version says the name is Seminole for fox den. Just why the town received its musical Indian name has been forgotten, but Nixon Smiley reported in the *Miami Herald,* that Robert A. Mills, who developed a community on nearby Lake Mills in the 1880s, is said to have named the place. But Mrs. Josie Jacobs Prevatt, who was born at Chuluota in 1883, told Smiley in 1968 that the area may have been known by the name when her grandparents arrived from North Carolina in 1866. Residents smile when they tell still another story about the origin of the name—a very corny one: A Seminole brave courting a maiden named Luota brought her some sassafras roots. "What am I to do with these?" asked Luota. "Chew, Luota," replied the brave. Chuluota was one of the stations on Henry M. Flagler's abandoned railway division that swung away from the east coast at New Smyrna and ran past Geneva, Bithlo, Holopaw, and Yeehaw to wind up at Okeechobee.

CHUMUCKLA. *Santa Rosa County.* Formerly called Chumuckla Springs. The year of origin is as confused as the meaning of the name. The Federal Writers Project (1939) said Chumuckla was settled about 1813 by the McDavid family, the the Florida State Gazetteer (1886) gives 1883 as the beginning date. Perhaps there were two starts as an organized community. Read (1934) is uncertain about the derivation of the name, saying the Creek *chumuklita,* "to bow the head to the ground," closely resembles Chumuckla in form, but the reason why a place name of this peculiar meaning should have been selected is not apparent. The first syllable of Chumuckla may possibly be connected with Hitchiti *ichi,* "deer," and the last two syllables with *imokli,* "its den,"—hence, "deer den," or "deer retreat."

CINCO BAYOU. *Okaloosa County.* Originally the Cocke family homestead but named Cinco Bayou when subdivided because it bordered Five Mile Bayou. In turn, Five Mile Bayou gave way to the more stylish Spanish name; the waterway now also is called Cinco Bayou. The community was incorporated in 1951.

CITRA. *Marion County.* Named about 1881 by a group of men: among them were Messrs. Harris, Wartmann, White, Hoyt, and Rev. P. P. Bishop. Inasmuch as citrus production was the principal industry, Rev. Bishop suggested the name Citra, which was unanimously accepted.

CITRUS County. The forty-fourth county, established June 2, 1887. Named as a tribute to Florida's main agricultural product.

CLARCONA. *Orange County.* Origin of the name obscure. The long-settled town became a press service dateline in 1972 when Bill Herman bought the building that housed the post office. Wanting to call attention to the area's horse-breeding industry, Herman put up a sign picturing a rider on horseback and the words "Pony Express Station, Clarcona, Florida." A postal official said the sign did not conform to post office regulations and asked Herman to take it down.

CLAY County. The thirty-seventh county, established December 31, 1858. Named for Kentucky's Henry Clay, secretary of state under John Quincy Adams and author of the saying, "I would rather be right than be President."

CLEARWATER. *Pinellas County.* Panfilo de Narvaez landed here in 1528 on what is now the Pinellas Peninsula. Early in the nineteenth century some fishermen attempted citrus culture here, but were unsuccessful because of trouble with the Seminoles. After the establishment of Fort Harrison near here in 1841, a group of settlers under the leadership of James Stevens built homes and farms under the Armed Occupation Act. The town was first called Clear Water Harbor, because of a spring of sulphated water that bubbles up in the Gulf near the shore, making the water usually clear and sparkling. Later Harbor was dropped, and the other two words merged into one. The city is the county seat of Pinellas County.

CLERMONT. *Lake County.* Established about 1884 by the Clermont Improvement Company, whose manager, A. F. Wrotniski, had been born in Clermont, France. Today, in addition to the French name with its ancient associations, Clermont uses the designation "The Gem of the Hills," since it is situated amid seventeen lakes and a group of rugged green-gold hills, at an altitude of 105 feet above sea level.

CLEVELAND. *Charlotte County.* Named in 1886 for Grover Cleveland, who had been inaugurated as president for the first time in the previous year. Dr. A. T. Holleymon of Georgia was responsible for the name. He had bought extensive property on the Peace River and developed it.

CLEWISTON. *Hendry County.* In 1922, when the Atlantic Coast Line Railroad was extended from Moore Haven to Sand Point, a settlement here was named in honor of A. C. Clewis, a Tampa banker who had provided the capital for the extension of the railroad. The town was platted and developed in 1925 and incorporated in 1932.

CLOUD LAKE. *Palm Beach County.* Named for Yaholoochee or "Cloud," one of the famous war chiefs of the Seminoles during the Second Seminole War of the 1840s. When Kenyon Riddle developed a subdivision here in the 1940s, he excavated about five acres and named the resultant lake Cloud Lake after the warrior. Several years later the people of the platted area decided to incorporate, and the name was used for the new town.

COCOA. *Brevard County.* Two widely varying accounts explain this unique name. One says that it came from the coco plum (*Chrysobalanus icaco* L.) that grows along the whole Florida east coast and is particularly profuse in this area. The other explanation says that while a group of citizens were seeking a name for the town an old Negress, standing near a landing at the foot of Willard Street, was inspired by the label on a box of Baker's Cocoa; her suggestion was adopted. Either route would have involved a little misspelling ("cocoa" is a corruption of "cacao"), but in any event Cocoa-ites claim there is no other town in the world that bears the same name. The community was founded by fishermen very early in Florida's history, and in 1871 a post office was established at Magnolia Point, some two miles north of here, but the town of Cocoa was not incorporated until 1895. Cocoa Beach is on the beach peninsula across the Indian and Banana rivers from Cocoa.

COCONUT CREEK. *Broward County.* Incorporated in 1967 and named for the dense coconut palms and the canals and small lakes present here.

COCONUT GROVE. *Dade County.* Once known as Jack's Bight, for John Thomas (Jolly Jack) Peacock, an Englishman who in 1863 homesteaded 160 acres by the side of Biscayne Bay. Jack's Bight (bight: the land beside a bend in a shore) came to be known more formally as Cocoanut Grove because of the grove of coconut trees here. When the area was incorporated in 1922 the "a" was dropped, largely through the energies of Kirk Munroe, a local resident and nationally known writer of juvenile stories and other fiction who argued that the coconut palm had nothing to do with cocoa, the roasted, husked, and ground seeds of cacao. Coconut Grove, although a part of Miami since 1925, still retains its distinctive village charm.

COLEMAN. *Sumter County.* Settled in 1882 and named for an early settler, B. F. Coleman, who was a physician, orange grove and farm owner, and the first postmaster.

COLLIER County. The sixty-second county, established May 8, 1923. Named for Barron G. Collier, one of the leading developers of the southern part of the state and the owner of extensive land holdings in this area. Born in Memphis, Tenn., March 23, 1873, he was graduated from Oglethorpe University. He entered the advertising business in 1890 and became one of the first great advertising tycoons, particularly in "car cards" on New York streetcars, subways, and elevated trains. East Naples is the county seat.

COLLIER CITY. *Collier County.* By an interesting coincidence, this community had the same name as its county but derived the name from a different source. William R. Spear, editor of the *Fort Myers News-Press,* explained in personal communication: "The first settler at Marco Island was W. T. Collier from Tennessee, no relation of Barron [Collier], who settled there in 1870 after an earlier stay at Fort Myers. He had eight children, the most prominent of whom was Capt. William D. Collier. In 1927 when a New York syndicate . . . promoted a big boomtime development there they got the Legislature to incorporate all Marco Island as a city and named it Collier City. Whether it was named for W. T. or William D. is uncertain. . . . There is no such place today as Collier City. Captain William D. Collier became postmaster of Marco in 1888. In 1908 he invented a clam-dredging machine which gave rise to the big Doxsee clam industry there."

COLUMBIA County. The sixteenth county, established February 4, 1832. Named for the poetical name of the United States, the name that was formed from Columbus, the discoverer of America.

COMPASS LAKE. *Jackson County.* Established in 1885. Named for the lake, which is round like a compass.

CONANT. *Lake County.* A post office was established in 1884. The town was named in tribute to Maj. Sherman Conant, one of the principals of the Florida Southern Railway. Kennedy (1929) relates that "Conant would have been a good city of today with its promising start, but its promoters went in for snobbery and 'cut' all who did their own work or who sent their children to public school instead of a private school that was opened in Conant." Kennedy concluded by saying that "it is, within any recollection, the only town that made this practice of snobbery, for the usual spirit of the communities in Lake County was comradeship, helpfulness, and hospitality. All that marks [in 1929] the site of the once flourishing town of Conant is the railroad sign at the siding."

COOPER CITY. *Broward County.* Morris Cooper, founder and landowner, gave his name to this community in the 1950s.

CORAL GABLES. *Dade County.* This city, home of the University of Miami, took its name from the house built in 1906 by the Reverend Solomon Greasley Merrick, a Congregational minister in Duxbury, Mass., who in 1898 purchased sight unseen for $1,100 a Dade County 160-acre homestead. Under the guidance of his son, George, this land became the nucleus in the 1920s of the subdivision and city known as Coral Gables. Reverend Merrick had built his home of a local stone that he thought was coral. He was an admirer of U.S. President Grover Cleveland, whose Princeton, N.J., home was known as Gray Gables. Reverend Merrick put together his name for the stone and part of the name of the Cleveland house for "Coral Gables."

CORAL SPRINGS. *Broward County.* An officer of Coral Ridge Properties, developers of the 21-square mile community west of Pompano Beach, in 1972 explained the choice of name: "This area has been known since Indian times for the purity of the natural spring water. In order to give it our own continuity, we merely added the 'Coral' to 'Springs.' "

COREYTOWN. *Pinellas County.* Once incorporated and later "decorporated" community named for the Corey Causeway to St. Petersburg. The town is located at the eastern end of the causeway, which was named for one of the Pinellas County commissioners in office at the time it was built.

CORK. *Hillsborough County.* See Plant City.

COTTONDALE. *Jackson County.* Established by railway hands in 1882 and named because of the surrounding cotton farms.

CRACKERTOWN. *Levy County.* A riposte to nearby Yankeetown. There once was also a Crackertown in Duval County. Floridians are known as "crackers," but Morris and Waldron (1965) suggest the nickname should be used with care. Its acceptance by Floridians depends upon the person and, in some measure, upon the section of the state. A number of origins for the nickname have been suggested. Goulding (1869) thought the name was derived from Scotch settlers in whose dialect a "cracker" was a person who talked boastingly. Lambert (1810) wrote: "The wagoners are familiarly called *crackers* (from the smacking of their whip, I suppose)." Burke (1850) said some Georgians were called crackers "from the circumstance that they formerly pounded all their corn, which is their principle article of diet." Two modern historians, A. J. and Kathryn Abbey Hanna (1948), said: "The name 'cracker' frequently applied to countrymen of Georgia and Florida is supposed to have originated as a cattle term." Florida cowboys popped whips of braided buckskin, 12 to 18 feet long. The "crack" sounded like a rifle shot and at times could be heard for several miles. As the writer of the syndicated Florida newspaper column "Cracker Politics," I suggest it might be prudent to accompany the nickname with a smile.

CRAWFORDVILLE. *Wakulla County.* Named for the Crawford family, two of whose members, Dr. Jno. L. and his son, H. Clay, served as Florida's secretary of state for 48 years, from 1881 until 1929. Crawfordville is the county seat of Wakulla County.

CRESCENT CITY. *Putnam County.* Named by Mrs. Charles R. Griffin of New York City, who came here with her husband soon after the close of the Civil War. There were two lakes in the vicinity, one of them shaped like a moon in crescent, Crescent Lake, and the other, Lake Stella, positioned like a star nearby. The town took its name from Crescent Lake, which was known as Dunn's Lake during the Civil War and before. Dunn's Creek, which flows out of the lake is still called Dunn's Creek; in this creek the famous original sailing yacht *America* was scuttled by the Confederates and raised by the Unionists.

CRESTVIEW. *Okaloosa County.* Named for its position on the top of a high hill, 223 feet above sea level, the highest point on the old Pensacola and Atlantic Railroad. It is the county seat of Okaloosa County.

CROSS CITY. *Dixie County.* Two public roads, one from Perry to old Archer, the other from Branford to Horseshoe, crossed at this point. W. H. Matthis, who conferred the name, seemingly wanted to make it clear that Cross City was something more than a mere crossroad. It is the county seat of Dixie County.

CROWS BLUFF. *Lake County.* E. H. Crow was among those who settled here on the St. Johns River in the 1850s. The name then was Ledworth Camp after a timbering operation for the U.S. Navy. Crow changed this name to Osceola, but confusion resulted, with freight shipments for Ocala arriving here and those for Osceola turning up in Ocala. The name again was changed in 1858 to Hawkinsville, and finally in 1888 to Crows Bluff. This was the site of an early free bridge across the St. Johns River to link Lake and Volusia counties.

CRYSTAL RIVER. *Citrus County.* On the Taylor war map of 1839 a stream appeared designated as Weewa-hiiaca. In Seminole-Creek the word *wiwa* means "water," and *haiyayaki* means "clear" or "shining." The name Crystal River is the English translation, and by the time the Davis Map of 1856 was published the Indian name had disappeared. The town takes its name from the river.

CUDJOE KEY. *Monroe County.* Stevenson (1970) relates a story worth retelling about how this key may have gotten its name. Aggravated by the bustle of Key West in the 1880s, writes Stevenson, a member of a family there left for the isolation of this key. "He selected a pleasant spot and his family used to visit him frequently, upon Cousin Joe's key." Whether Cudjoe took its name from Cousin Joe or from the fragrant little tree there known as joewood, or cudjoewood, no one knows.

CUTLER RIDGE. *Dade County.* Dr. C. F. Cutler of Chelsea, Mass., came here in 1884, started a settlement, and built a mill to grind coontie, an arrowroot starch used for bread. The Seminoles were the first to grind coontie. Before Dr. Cutler arrived, this area was known as Big Hunting Ground.

CYPRESS. *Jackson County.* Named for the large number of cypress ponds in this vicinity. Established in 1873.

DADE County. The nineteenth county, established February 4, 1836. Named for Maj. Francis Langhorne Dade, U.S. Army, the Virginian commanding a detachment of 110 men ambushed and slaughtered near the present site of Bushnell by Seminoles, December 28, 1835. The column from Fort Brooke (Tampa) was on its way to relieve Fort King (Ocala). Only three soldiers survived. When news reached Tallahassee of the Dade Massacre, the territory's Legislative Council inserted Dade's name in a bill that was pending to create a new county. (Otherwise, Dade would be known today as Pinkney County, for William Pinkney, lawyer, statesman, diplomat, soldier. As a U.S. senator from Maryland, Pinkney gained national recognition as a champion of the slave-holding states during the debates on the Missouri Compromise.) Today this county is the most populous in Florida, the site of Metropolitan Miami. A curiosity among Florida maps is one from 1838 which shows Dade County between Alachua and Hillsborough counties. Apparently a northern cartographer assumed that the lawmakers would recognize the area of the massacre in creating a new county.

DADE CITY. *Pasco County.* Named for Maj. Francis Langhorne Dade of King George County, Va., the U.S. Army officer killed by Seminoles December 28, 1835. The Dade Massacre marks the opening of the Second Seminole War—as tragic a war as the pages of history have to show. This is the county seat. *See also* Dade County.

DANIA. *Broward County.* Named by Danes for their own people. The community was founded by the Florida East Coast Railroad's Model Land Company, whose officials named it Modello. Later a group called the Danish Brotherhood came from Wisconsin, under the leadership of A. C. Frost, and provided the new name. The town was incorporated in 1927. It is the center of the county's tomato-growing district and the seat of the Seminole Indian Agency. Incidentally, the thrifty railwaymen again used the name Modello for another community in south Dade County.

DAVENPORT. *Polk County.* Some say this town, founded about 1883, was named after a colonel; others say it was named after a conductor. The military officer was Col. William Davenport, who commanded a military camp located about 12 miles northwest of the present site of the town during the Second Seminole War. The gentleman honored according to the other version was a conductor named Davenport on the old South Florida Railroad.

DAVIE. *Broward County.* Formerly called Zona, this community was named in 1914 for a developer, R. P. Davie, who bought 25,000 acres of black muck by the South New River Canal, north of Miami.

DAYTONA BEACH. *Volusia County.* Mathias Day, of Mansfield, Ohio, is the man whose name lives in the rather unusual name of this world-famous seaside town. He was its founder in 1870. Two years later a committee consisting of himself, Mrs. William Jackson, and Mrs. Riley Peck was commissioned by the settlers to select a name from among three suggested versions: Daytown, Daytonia, and Daytona. The city now encompasses a business and residential section on the mainland west of the Halifax River, as well as a residential and resort section on the beach and peninsula between the river and the ocean; but, until they were consolidated in 1926, these were three separate municipalities called Daytona, Daytona Beach, and Seabreeze. The broad, hard beach has been the scene of many automobile races and speed trials, including those of Sir Malcolm Campbell.

"DEADENING, THE." *Polk County.* Fort Meade was settled in a tract known as "The Deadening" about 20 miles square on the west side of Peace Creek. Hetherington (1928) says the tract was so named because "years before all the large timber in that area had died. Indians say that there was a very heavy hail at one time, and the stones were so large and fell with such force, that they bruised the trees, and worms got into the bruised places and killed the trees."

DeBARY. *Volusia County.* Named for Baron Frederick DeBary, German-born of Belgian ancestry, who came to the United States in 1840 as an agent for Mumm's champagne. The baron came here in 1868 and built the handsome residence known now as DeBary Hall. His Florida estate of some hundreds of acres, with its hunting and fishing, attracted many notables of the era, including presidents Grant and Cleveland. The baron's steamboats plying the nearby St. Johns River facilitated these visits. In the 1960s, DeBary gained occasional national attention as the winter home of U.S. Senator Everett K. Dirksen of Illinois, colorful Republican leader.

DEERFIELD BEACH. *Broward County.* Originally called Hillsborough, this town adopted the name Deerfield about 1907 when deer were plentiful in the hammocks west of town.

DeFUNIAK SPRINGS. *Walton County.* Colonel Fred DeFuniak of Louisville, Ky., an official of the Louisville and Nashville Railroad, gave his name to the town, which was called Lake DeFuniak in 1883, then DeFuniak Springs in 1885. Around the lake, which is a mile in circumference and was known in the early days as Open Pond, not only a business district developed but also a Chautauqua building that attracted widely known speakers and large audiences. When established in 1885, the institution was called the "Chautauqua that began under a tree" because its organizers met under a large oak to plan for the building beside the spring-fed lake. Chautauquas were assemblies in a nationwide system of lectures, concerts, and dramatic performances that flourished in the late nineteenth and early twentieth centuries. The assemblies originated at Lake Chautauqua, N.Y. DeFuniak Springs is the county seat of Walton County.

DeLAND. *Volusia County.* Henry A. DeLand, a New York baking powder manufacturer, came to Florida on a visit in 1876 and purchased a homestead at the site of this town. A group of the people in the vicinity visiting at a home where DeLand was being entertained resolved to obtain a post office and decided to name it after him. John B. Stetson, the world-famous Philadelphia hat manufacturer, also had a part in the founding of the town. In 1883 DeLand established an academy here and gave it his own name. Stetson became a great financial benefactor of the institution, and when the university was finally incorporated DeLand suggested that its name be changed to honor Stetson. Because of the university the city calls itself "The Athens of Florida." Great branching oaks planted long ago beautify its streets; these trees have caused some aviators to call DeLand "the city of the forest." The Spanish mission of Antonico stood near here. DeLand is the county seat of Volusia County.

DeLEON SPRINGS. *Volusia County.* Once known as Garden Springs and earlier as Spring Garden, but named in 1885 for Ponce de León. A plantation here was visited in 1831 by the naturalist John James Audubon. There were two springs but one ceased to flow. Gold (1927) states this place was named De Sota (sic) in 1882, but the Post Office Department refused to recognize the name because of a De Soto elsewhere, so Ponce de León was honored. Near here stood the Spanish mission of San Salvador de Maiaca.

DELLWOOD. *Jackson County.* Settled in 1840 or earlier. The beauty of the wooded land on a ridge overlooking lakes and streams prompted the name.

DELRAY BEACH. *Palm Beach County.* This name may be simply a corruption of the Spanish words *del rey,* meaning "of the king." It was originally named Linton after Congressman Linton of Michigan, who platted the town about 1892. In 1895 the town was reorganized as Delray. One story has it that the settlers named the town for a neighborhood in Detroit called Delray. Beach was added to the name in the 1930s when the area along the beach was consolidated with the city on the mainland.

DELTONA. *Volusia County.* Started virtually from scratch in the 1960s and approximately midway between DeLand (Del-) and Daytona Beach (-tona).

De SOTO County. The forty-second county, established May 19, 1887. This is one of two counties in Florida bearing parts of the name of the Spanish explorer Hernando De Soto—with Hernando being the other, an interesting circumstance.

De SOTO City. *Highlands County.* Named for Hernando De Soto, the great Spanish conquistador. It was founded in 1916.

DESTIN. *Okaloosa County.* A city proud of its New England atmosphere, an inheritance from Capt. Leonard Destin of New London, Conn., who used this area as a base in pioneering the snapper fishing industry more than a century ago.

DEVILFISH KEY. *Lee County.* President Theodore Roosevelt was one of the many presidents of the United States who relaxed in Florida. Fishing off Captiva Island in the early 1900s, President Roosevelt hooked a giant devilfish, or manta, which he landed after an all-day battle. The creature, measuring 30 feet across and weighing more than two tons, was beached on a small island in Blind Pass. The island was thereafter known as Devilfish Key. Nearby Roosevelt Beach also commemorates the president's visit.

DEVIL'S MILL HOPPER. *Alachua County.* Located 17 miles from Gainesville, this sink is a funnel-shaped depression with a surface area of 5 acres, sloping to a depth of approximately 100 feet. The sink was caused when the surface collapsed as a result of the eroding action of an underground waterway on the limestone. Robert O. Vernon, state geologist, says seepage from underground water fills a pool and drains through an underground outlet. Violets, ferns, dogwood, and magnolia grow in profusion here, and the rim of the sink is surrounded by dense stands of hardwood. The name appears to stem from the international custom of using the concept of a devil to indicate something unusually bad in terrain or formation, plus mill hopper from the inverted cone of a container through which grain of anything else to be ground feeds into a grist mill. Davis (1969) says the natural wonder formerly was known as the Devil's Hopper and earlier as the Washpot.

DEVIL'S PUNCH BOWL. *Hernando County.* A dry sink an acre wide and from 60 to 80 feet deep. About three and one-half miles west of Brooksville, this sink resembles a mammoth punch bowl with steep sides.

DISSTON CITY. *Pinellas County.* Florida's almost forgotten developer, Hamilton Disston, lacks the distinction of the two Henrys—Henry M. Flagler and Henry B. Plant—of having a city or county named for him. Two lakes, in Flagler and Pinellas counties, bear his name. Disston City now is Gulfport. Disston City was not a part of Hamilton Disston's hugh Florida undertaking but appears to have been an effort in 1884 by other, small-scale developers to interest him. The first bid for his attention was frustrated because there already was a town called Diston in Pasco County, so the townsite was called Bonafacio, probably after the middle name of William B. Miranda, one of the original promoters. By the time the name Disston became available (through Diston changing its name to Drexel) and was adopted in 1889, Hamilton Disston was too busy dredging canals that would drain and open a vast area of south-central Florida to waterway transportation. Then a new generation of developers sought to woo former military men (Straub, 1929), so the town's name was changed to Veteran City in 1905. Gulfport emerged in 1910 and that name clicked.

DIXIE County. The fifty-ninth county, established April 25, 1921. Named from the lyric name for the South.

DOG ISLAND. *Franklin County.* At the entrance to St. Georges Sound in the Gulf of Mexico off Carrabelle, Dog Island first appeared on maps as the *Isles aux Chiens*. It is speculated variously that there were wild dogs on the island when the French explored or that the island to a shipboard observer resembled a crouched dog. Dog Island, of approximately 2,000 acres, is seven miles long. Once there was a federal government reservation here, including a lighthouse and quarantine station as a port of entry for the vessels serving Carrabelle, then an important port for the worldwide shipment of lumber. Dog Island today serves primarily as an escape for those desiring to exchange the mainland's problems for white sand dunes and surf.

DOGTOWN. *Gadsden County*. Pat Thomas, state representative, reported in 1973 that Dogtown gained its name many years ago as a place where dogs were pitted to fight.

DOVER. *Hillsborough County*. Named Sydney in 1882, then Cork in 1884 (the second Hillsborough community of that name), and believed to have received its third name in 1890 from settlers who came from Dover, the capital of Delaware.

DOWLING PARK. *Suwannee County*. Called Charles Ferry on J. L. Williams' map of 1837. At one time it was a turpentine camp owned by Thomas and Robert L. Dowling. Thomas Dowling, uncle of Robert L. Dowling, gave a large acreage to the Advent Church for an orphanage. Near here stood the Spanish mission of San Francisco de Chuayain. The Spanish explorer Panfilo de Narvaez may have crossed the Suwannee River near here.

DRY TORTUGAS. On his exploratory voyage along the Florida coast in 1513, Juan Ponce de León landed on some rocky islets that he called Las Tortugas because the crew took one hundred and sixty tortoises here. As Bickel (1942) said: "Here they restored their larder with turtles, manatee—which they called seal—pelicans and terns. Not dainty fare, but filling. The Spaniard of the early sixteenth century in the Indies enjoyed strange food and grew fat on it." Now, the great ruins of Fort Jefferson stand on an island of the Dry Tortugas: a fortress never to fire its cannon in anger but to earn infamy as the prison of Dr. Samuel A. Mudd, an innocent victim of John Wilkes Booth, the assassin of President Lincoln.

DUETTE. *Manatee County*. Two versions explain the origin of this name, but the one commonly accepted is this: Prior to 1930 the community had a church, the Dry Prairie Baptist, but no other name. The need for a name arose with school consolidation, and at a community meeting Mrs. Susie Wilkins, who had donated money for the new school, suggested "Duette." There was no disagreement. Another version is that the name was that of an early Canadian settler.

DUNDEE. *Polk County*. The first new town to be platted along the line when the railroad was built from Haines City down to Sebring, and the first depot was erected here. The name was obviously taken from that of the famous town in Scotland. Development of the town was begun about 1911 by William W. Shepard, who organized the Florida Highlands Company.

DUNEDIN. *Pinellas County*. The old Gaelic name for Edinburgh, Scotland, so this Florida town is named for a more important Old

World city than one might think. It vies with Clearwater for the distinction of being the second-oldest town on the Florida west coast between Cedar Key and Key West, Tampa being the oldest. It was established in the late 1860s, and at first was called Jonesboro, after the general store proprietor, George L. Jones. The new name change occurred in 1878 when J. O. Douglass and James Somerville, two Scotsmen, arrived on the scene. Dun is a form of "town" and edin derives from an Irish saint Edana, for whom many Scotch churches were named.

DUNNELLON. *Marion County.* Named for an early railroad promoter, J. F. Dunn. This point, near Rainbow Springs, is probably where the Spanish explorer Panfilo de Narvaez crossed the Withlacoochee River. Albertus Vogt discovered hard-rock phosphate here in 1889 and caused Dunnellon to become a boom town. The Tiger Rag, Early Bird, and Eagle mines were among the most valuable.

DuPONT. *Flagler County.* Takes its name from Abraham DuPont, who came to St. Augustine in 1825 and settled in 1829 on Spanish grant land adjacent to the Matanzas River. He was appointed justice of the peace for St. Johns County on February 17, 1833. He died at his Matanzas home in 1857.

DUVAL County. The fourth county, established August 12, 1822. Named for William Pope DuVal, first territorial governor of Florida. DuVal was born at Mount Comfort, near Richmond, Va., in 1784, the son of William and Ann (Pope) DuVal. DuVal was of French Huguenot forbears. His father was associated, as a lawyer, with Patrick Henry in the British debt cases and, as a major of riflemen, with the capture of a British vessel becalmed in the James River during the Revolution. Young DuVal left home at the age of fourteen for the Kentucky frontier, settling in Bardstown to study law. He was admitted to the bar at nineteen. He served as a captain in the mounted rangers in 1812 and as Kentucky representative in the Thirteenth Congress (1813-15). He came to Florida as a territorial judge, having been appointed by President Monroe upon the recommendation of DuVal's friend, John C. Calhoun, then secretary of war. He served about a month at St. Augustine. He was appointed governor of the Florida territory in 1822 by President Monroe; he was reappointed by presidents Adams and Jackson. His administration was notable for the confidence that he enjoyed with the Indians. The capital was established at Tallahassee during his tenure. He was a friend of Washington Irving, who wrote of him in "Ralph Ringwood." James K. Pauling also wrote of him as "Nimrod Wildlife." DuVal uniformly signed himself as DuVal, though the name usually appears in print as Duval. DuVal moved to Texas in 1848, and Texas was his home when he died on

March 18, 1854, in Washington, D.C. He was buried in the Congressional Cemetery.

EASTPOINT. *Franklin County.* The name apparently is derived from the community's location on the east point of a peninsula where the big Apalachicola River empties into Apalachicola Bay. At the turn of the century, East Point (spelled then as two words) was the site of an experiment in cooperative living. A promotional guide to Franklin County, published in 1901, had a page describing how "the Co-operative Association of America has secured a thousand acres of land with sea front and is establishing a co-operative colony there." The Reverend Harry C. Vrooman, manager for Florida, said the "Association means to organize industry in departments—like a huge department store, only on the co-operative plan—so that all the profits of industry go to the workers. Each member must deposit $300 before he is guaranteed employment. This $300 may be paid in installments. Retiring members are guaranteed their money." Members had a choice of employment at Lewiston, Me., or East Point. Persons not wishing to participate in cooperative living could become associate members at $2 a year and "enjoy all the commercial and social advantages." Associate members could "buy good land for farm, garden or fruit, fronting the sea if desired, near good fishing and oystering." Eastpoint today remains a center for fishing and oystering.

EATON PARK. *Polk County.* Once known as Pauway, Eaton Park near Lakeland was another of Polk County's phosphate centers. The name Eaton may have been derived from State Senator O. M. Eaton, who represented Polk in the 1920s about the time the name was changed.

EATONVILLE. *Orange County.* Incorporated August 18, 1888, as a black community; some say the first in the country. The *Eatonville Speaker* capsuled the purpose of the town in this advertisement on January 22, 1889: "Colored people of the United States—Solve the great race problem by securing a home in Eatonville, Florida, a Negro city governed by Negroes." This description remained true in 1974. A *Miami Herald* reporter (Hines, 1972) described Eatonville in February

1972 as "an all-black town, run by blacks and populated solely by blacks," and a *St. Petersburg Times* reporter (Ogleby, 1972) who visited Eatonville in April 1972 said the community of 2,024 inhabitants was "virtually" all black. Yet the town takes its name from a white man, "Capt." Joshua (or Josiah) C. Eaton of Maine, a retired Navy paymaster who settled with other Union veterans at nearby Maitland after the Civil War. Blacks joined with whites in an election at Maitland, and a black, J. E. (Tony) Clarke, became mayor. Clarke had the dream of an all-black town and enlisted the aid of Eaton and two other white Union veterans. They bought a 500-acre tract a mile west of Maitland for the townsite of Eatonville. Among those lured to Eatonville was John Hurston, a master carpenter and Baptist preacher who became the father of Zora Neale Hurston, who alone would give the town more distinction than many small towns ever receive. She wrote about Eatonville in her remarkable autobiography, *Dust Tracks on a Road,* and impressions of her life there may be found in other of her books, including *Mules and Men.* The late Theodore Pratt, the novelist, said that Zora Neale Hurston was the "only first class native-born Florida author."

EAU GALLIE. *Brevard County.* Authorities agree that *eau* is French for "water," but they differ as to the meaning of *gallie.* Some say it is French for "bitter" (like gall); others say that it is an Indian word for "rocky." The water referred to is that of the Indian River, which is salt water. Where Americans use the words salt and fresh, Europeans often use the equivalent of bitter and sweet. In any event, the town was established soon after the Civil War by William H. Gleason, who is said to have given it its name. He had been commissioned by the federal government to ascertain whether Florida was suitable for colonization by blacks; finding that capital was required for developing the natural resources of the country, he reported adversely on this matter, but settled in Florida himself. The name is pronounced "Oh, galley" and not "Oh, golly!"Eau Gallie merged with Melbourne in 1969, but letters sent to Eau Gallie still reach there.

EBRO. *Washington County.* This community is believed to have gained its name from Spain's Ebro River. Its post office opened in 1897.

EDEN. *Walton County.* A lovely estate and mansion built with elaborate Victorian trimmings in 1895 by lumberman William Henry Wesley. Bought in 1963 by Lois Genevieve Maxon, the mansion was restored in antebellum style with a formal garden and given to the state by Mrs. Maxon in memory of her parents. The restoration fulfills a local legend that claims the original design was inspired by an antebellum plantation house in which the builder was sheltered on his way from the Civil War.

EDGEWATER. *Volusia County.* Dr. John M. Hawks bought property here in 1865 and settled it about 1872, naming it Hawks' Park. The name, which refers to the town's location at the edge of Mosquito Lagoon, was changed in 1924.

EDGEWATER GULF BEACH. *Bay County.* Incorporated as Edgewater Gulf Beach Apartments in 1953. The town consists almost entirely of the resort facility of that name.

EGLIN AIR FORCE BASE. Named in honor of Lt. Col. Frederick I. Eglin, an Army Air Force aviator who was killed in the crash of his airplane near Anniston, Ala., on January 1, 1937. Eglin Field was a redesignation on August 4, 1937, of the Valparaiso Bombing and Gunnery Base, which had been activated on June 14, 1935, as a subpost of Maxwell Field, Ala., with a detachment of 15 enlisted men under the command of Capt. Arnold H. Rich.

EL CAMINO REAL. A Spanish name meaning "the royal road," which conjures up an image of a thoroughfare that certainly did not exist in early Spanish Florida. Overland travel was by trails or footpaths, and most Spanish trails could be called El Camino Real since the king paid for developing them. Freight moved on the backs of Indians. The use of pack mules instead of Indians still was under consideration in 1686, although the Spanish had been thrusting out from St. Augustine since 1565. Boyd (1951) cites two examples that evidence the nature of travel. Some idea of the primitive nature of the path may be inferred from the fact that a Capt. Enrique Rivera obtained a contract in 1688 for transporting supplies and foodstuffs along the Apalachee Trail to missions between St. Augustine and the country around present-day Tallahassee. He could not fulfill the contract inasmuch as his carts were unable to proceed more than 40 miles west of St. Augustine because of swamps and streams. The Apalachee Trail, when later developed, became one of the roads known as El Camino Real. A county road and city street in Tallahassee still known as the "Old St. Augustine Road" follows an early Spanish trail.

EL JOBEAN. *Charlotte County.* Once known as Southland, but in 1924 during the great land boom the Spanish-sounding name El Jobean was substituted. In actuality, Joel Bean, a developer, twisted his name around to produce El Jobean.

ELKTON. *St. Johns County.* Legend says B. Genovar bought property here simultaneously with being initiated into the Elks Lodge at St. Augustine. In commemoration he named the townsite Elk Town, which usage corrupted around 1905 to Elkton.

ELLAVILLE. *Madison County.* Little is left today to suggest that Ellaville once was a busy lumber port on the Suwannee River. Obviously named for a woman, Ellaville was the site of a large lumber mill owned by George F. Drew, governor of Florida from 1877 to 1881.

ELLENTON. *Manatee County.* The Gamble Mansion is here, a duplicate of "Waukeenah," the homestead near Tallahassee that Maj. Robert Gamble left after the crash of the Union Bank. Starting life anew, Major Gamble constructed a two-story mansion with thick walls, shuttered windows, and wide verandas out of "tabby," a combination of marl, burnt shell lime, oyster shell, and sand. This mansion is said to have sheltered Judah P. Benjamin, secretary of state in the Confederacy, as he escaped to England by way of Florida and the Bahamas. Who was Ellen? She remains a mystery.

ELLIOTT KEY. *Dade County.* This key became the city Islandia and then was taken under the protective wing of the federal government in the 1960s as a part of the natural preserve known as the Biscayne National Monument. Dr. Gilbert Voss of the University of Miami, a marine scientist who has familiarity with the key and its background, believes Elliott is a misspelling of the name of Andrew Ellicott, who best may be remembered as the American commissioner for the survey of the Georgia-Florida boundary in 1798-1800. Ellicott was in the vicinity of the key in November 1799 with a survey party. Elliott Key was not shown by that name on maps prior to his visit.

ELLZEY. *Levy County.* The name remembers Rev. R. M. Ellzey, who settled here in 1876.

EL PORTAL. *Dade County.* Spanish for "the gate," the name came from a subdivision developed during the boom of the 1920s at what was then the highway entrance to Miami from the north.

ENGLEWOOD. *Sarasota County.* Herbert, Howard, and Ira Nichols, three brothers from Englewood, Ill., laid out and promoted this community. An exhibit about the new community at the Columbian Exposition in Chicago in 1898 attracted new residents.

ENSLEY. *Escambia County.* Once called Fig City because of its fig production. Established about 1912, the town was renamed for Fred B. Ensley, a prominent resident.

ENTERPRISE. *Volusia County.* Once the southern terminus of shipping on the St. Johns River. This community on Lake Monroe was founded in 1841 by Maj. Cornelius Taylor, cousin of Zachary Taylor. Enterprise first was known as Fountain Place, then Enterprize, then Benson Springs in 1924, and then Enterprise (with the present spelling) in 1937. Until 1888 Enterprize was the seat of Volusia County. In the mid-1900s Daytona Beach tried to wrest from DeLand the honor of being the seat of Volusia County. Ironically, in 1888 Enterprize had lost the seat to DeLand by a vote of 1,003 for DeLand to 439 for Enterprize (seven other communities were in the running, with Daytona receiving only 3 votes).

ERIDU. *Taylor County.* On your way from Tallahassee to Perry on U.S. 19 and U.S. 27, just after crossing into Taylor County, you will come to a little place called Eridu. If you happen to be a classical scholar, you will recognize the name as the Latin name for the River Po—or, maybe I had better say, a derivative of that name, which in full was Eridanus. M. S. Rose, who retired to Vero Beach from Pittsburgh in 1969, wrote that Eridu was named in 1926 by J. E. Welloughby, the chief engineer of the Atlantic Coast Line railroad. "I was a young engineer on Mr. Welloughby's staff and believe that I probably produced the first map showing Eridu as a town," Mr. Rose said. Eridu was one of the three unusual names applied by Mr. Welloughby to points in Taylor County along the new track then being placed to connect existing Atlantic Coast Line lines at Thomasville, Ga., and Dunnellon, Fla. The other two names were Iddo and Secotan, both apparently from ancient lore. Secotan's meaning has not been found, but Iddo is from 2 Chron. 9 : 29—"Now the rest of the acts of Solomon, first and last, are they not written in the book of Nathan the prophet, and in the prophecy of Ahijah the Shilomite, and in the visions of Iddo the seer against Jeroboam the son of Nebat?" In 1863 many Confederate deserters and draft evaders hid out in the wilds near here. Although Confederate cavalrymen failed to round them up, the cavalrymen drove off the lifestock, burned the houses, and in some instances put the families of the deserters into a concentration camp at Tallahassee until an outraged community forced their releases.

ESCAMBIA County and River. Escambia shares with St. Johns the distinction of being one of the first two counties, each having been established July 21, 1821. The Escambia River divides Escambia and Santa Rosa counties. Simpson (1956) reports the river was shown on a 1693 map as the Río de Jovenazo, apparently honoring the Duke of Jovenazo. It also was referred to at the same time as the Pensacola River. Simpson goes on to say that while the word Escambia might be derived from the Spanish *cambiar* "to exchange or barter," "it more likely has an Indian origin, even though the derivation is unknown." Justification for this belief, he continues, "is afforded by the existence in Apalachee during the mission period of an Indian village called San Cosmo y San Damian de Escambé (or Scambé). It is possible that the prefixed 'E' represents the Spanish pronunciation of the letter 'S' when before a consonant."

ESTERO. *Lee County.* Spanish for "estuary." In 1892 Dr. Cyrus Read Teed, founder of the Koreshan Unity, established his "college of life" here as a cooperative community in the spirit of Christ's teachings. Koreshans believe "we live inside the World." The Guiding Star Printing House at Estero published *The Cellular Cosmogony* and other books, magazines, and newspapers. The Koreshan Nursery was world famous for its subtropical plant life. In 1961 the Koreshan Unity deeded 305 acres of their Florida landholdings to the state as "a gift to the people."

ESTO. *Holmes County.* Named for one of the earliest settlers; he was here before the railroad was built. Before "old man Esto"—as the federal writers (1939) characterized him—was honored, the place was known as Hutto.

EUSTIS. *Lake County.* There is some question as to which member of the Eustis family gave his name to this town. The town is situated on Lake Eustis, named for Brig. Gen. Abraham Eustis, who served in Florida during the Seminole War and was one of the officers who favored ending the war by allowing the Indians to remain within a small territory to be given them in the southern part of the state. The community itself was established in 1881 by James A. McDonald, a Scotch engineer, and was first called Highlands, to distinguish its homesteaders from others settling in the lowlands; then Pendryville, because it was on A. S. Pendry's homestead; then Lake Eustis; and finally Eustis. Another authority says that the Eustis honored was Gen. Henry Lawrence Eustis, the son of Abraham, who was a Civil War soldier, engineer, and professor, first at West Point and then at Harvard.

EVERGLADES. *Collier County.* Named for the great primeval "river of grass" on whose western edge it lies. An Indian trading post was established here, at the mouth of the Barron River, in 1873, and soon became the center of a farming community. Around 1880 farmers began calling it Everglades, when they needed a trade name for their produce. A post office was established in 1892. W. S. Allen built the first home on the south bank of the Barron River, then known as Allen's River, and used the spot as a shipping point for his produce. The principal agricultural product today is tomatoes. The community first was known as Everglade; the s was added locally in 1923 and by the post office department in 1925.

EVERGLADES. An area covering 2,500,000 acres and dubbed "the River of Grass" (Douglas, 1947). In 1847 the federal government sent Buckingham Smith of St. Augustine to gather facts about the Everglades, in particular about whether or not the land could be "reclaimed and made valuable." His report contained a lyrical description of the great marsh. At that time the Everglades extended, unbroken, 100 miles from Lake Okeechobee to Cape Sable. It has been described by author Jeanne Bellamy as "the widest, shallowest and strangest river in America—fifty miles wide in places, averaging around nine inches deep in fall, the wettest season, but parched for weeks in springtime, the driest time of year" (Morris, 1973). Buckingham

Smith found the Everglades in 1847 to be "a vast lake of fresh water . . . studded with thousands of islands . . . which are generally covered with dense thickets of shrubbery and vines." The Everglades cover all or parts of seven counties: Glades, Hendry, Martin, Palm Beach, Broward, Dade, and Monroe. Douglas traced the name from the Spanish *El Laguno del Espiritu Santo* to the first English mapmaker's "River Glades." On later maps this became "Ever Glades." Douglas said the word glade is of the oldest English origin, coming from the Anglo-Saxon glaed, with the ae dipthong shortened to glad. The word glaed or glyde or glade has meant an open, green, grassy place in the forest. And, in the America of the English colonies, the use was continued to mean stretches of natural pasture, naturally grassy. "But most dictionaries nowadays end the definition," observed Douglas, with the qualifying phrase, "as of the Florida Everglades," and thus this area has become unique.

EVINSTON. *Alachua County.* Evinston or Evanston? Here is a fascinating example of how an ancient argument lives in a place name. Joseph Judge, assistant editor of the *National Geographic,* wrote about Evinston in the magazine's issue of November 1973. Judge wrote that he had been driving a back road in Florida's countryside, past moss-covered hamlets of weathered houses with tin roofs sloping against a chill rain, when he came to a highway marker designating Evanston. Yet the ancient post office and general store bore an old sign proclaiming Evinston P.O. Inside, reported Judge, Mr. Fred Wood addressed himself to the question. "There were two brothers," he said, "who came from England. My forebears. Their name was Evans, with an 'a'. During the war they took opposite sides." "The Civil War?" assumed Judge out loud. "Lord, no, man, the Revolution," corrected Wood. "The colonist got so mad at the loyalist that he changed his name to Evins, with an 'i'. No highway department knows much about history, or cares."

FAIRYLAND. *Brevard County.* One of a string of old-time Florida settlements within sound of the takeoffs of spacecraft from Cape

Kennedy. On Merritt Island, Fairyland, Tropic, and Georgiana are among the communities on what now is known as the Scenic Drive but once was called the Tropical Trail. Nixon Smiley of the *Miami Herald* said "driving about the byways and backways one still can find a few scenes of a bygone era"; Scenic Drive on Merritt Island is one of those scenes.

FALMOUTH. *Suwannee County.* Once known as Peacock, but Colonel Duval, an influential resident, had a pointer dog named Falmouth that he prized highly. Local legend says that when Falmouth was killed while hunting the colonel gave the community his dog's name. For whatever reason, the change of name occurred in 1906.

FANLEW. *Jefferson County.* A railway distribution center serving the sawmills and turpentine stills once in this area, moving supplies in and timber and naval stores out. Fanlew likely was named for an Atlantic Coast Line railroad superintendent.

FAYETTE. *The lost county.* Established in 1832 and extinguished in 1834, the only Florida county ever to pass completely out of existence. Presumably named for the Marquis de Lafayette, who died in the same year as the county, Fayette filled the v of the converging Chipola and Apalachicola rivers, with Alabama's boundary as the crossbar. Fayette was reincorporated in Jackson County.

FELDA. *Hendry County.* About 1920, Felix Taylor, a mailman, changed the name of Eddy to Felda, combining syllables of his first name and that of his wife, Ida.

FELLSMERE. *Indian River County.* Founded by E. Nelson Fell, who in 1910 acquired title to about 144 square miles in the northwest corner of what is now Indian River County. Fell was one of the English settlers of Narcoosee, one of a group of British communities in neighboring Osceola County. He was "a distinguished mining engineer who served the Czar of Russia," according to Cantrell (1948). Mere is an Anglo-Saxon word meaning "a body of standing water" and probably refers to the St. Johns River, a few miles west. The present town of Fellsmere is located in the eastern end of the development, which is now under the direction of the Fellsmere Farms Company.

FERNANDINA BEACH. *Nassau County.* Everyone agrees about the great age of Fernandina; it claims to be the second oldest city in the United States, having been settled by Spaniards in 1567. Not everyone agrees, however, about the source of its name. Fernandina was the early name of Cuba, conferred upon it by Columbus in 1492 as a tribute to King Ferdinand of Spain, and it is presumed by some that the name was given to the Florida settlement for the same reason. A large tract of land, however, was granted to Don Domingo Fernandez in 1785, and other authorities say it was in his honor that the town was named. Still others say the name comes from Fort San Fernando, built by Spain in 1686. The county seat of Nassau County, it is located on Amelia Island. It calls itself "The Ocean City." Beach is a recent addition to the city's name.

FIDDLE LAKE. *Lake County.* A lake near Eustis named because of an accident. According to Kennedy (1929), "one day K. D. Smith was bringing a miscellaneous load of goods, containing nails, groceries, and fiddles among other things, from the St. Johns River to Fort Mason. As the day was hot, the haul a long and tiresome one, and the oxen very thirsty, they started on a run when they sighted a lake. The driver was so startled by their sudden stampede that he could not check them until they were almost completely submerged." The cargo, including the fiddles, was lost in the lake.

FISHEATING CREEK. *Glades County.* See Tasmania.

FLAGLER County. The fifty-third county, established April 28, 1917. Named for Henry Morrison Flagler, one of the two Henrys—the other being Henry B. Plant—who raced to open the east and west coasts of Florida by building railroads and hotels and operating steamships and land development companies. Flagler (1830-1913) lived two lives, the first as a Northern businessman and the associate of John D. Rockefeller in the Standard Oil Company, and the second as a promoter of Florida's east coast. The *Dictionary of American Biography* (1964) says that Flagler, "brought up in poverty and trained in the stern Rockefeller school," was a grim, shrewd, rather ruthless man until he was fifty-five. Thereafter, in Florida, he continued to work, but with a new attitude toward humanity. "He thoroughly enjoyed his role of builder of a state, and seemed to feel a sense of personal responsibility for every settler on his railroads and for every one of his many employees," reports the *Dictionary.* "They, in turn, repaid him with admiration and loyalty." Flagler first visited Florida in 1883. Good businessman that he was, even on a holiday, he believed full advantage was not being taken of Florida's natural assets. He thought the state needed better transportation and hotel facilities, and he set about providing these for the east coast. His first project was building the Ponce de León Hotel in St. Augustine, formally opened January 10, 1888. He bought the rickety, narrow-gauge Jacksonville, St. Augustine and Halifax River Railroad on December 31, 1885. Flagler's Florida East Coast Railroad paced the building of a chain of hotels down the coast until Key West was officially reached on January 22, 1912. The Overseas Highway still goes to Key West over bridges and viaducts constructed for Flagler's railroad. Building of the railroad brought Flagler more than a million and one-half acres of state land, and he vigorously sought settlers, making concessions including free seed and reduced freight rates to encourage colonizing, which in turn would produce revenue for the railroad. Flagler died May 20, 1913.

FLAGLER BEACH. *Flagler County.* Name honors Henry M. Flagler, who did so much for the development of the east coast of Florida through his building of the Florida East Coast Railroad. A settlement on the mainland side of the intracoastal waterway, earlier known as Ocean City, was granted a post office under that name in 1915. As more families built homes along the oceanfront, a post office was needed there. The name Ocean City Beach was first suggested, but the Post Office Department disapproved it because of its length and its similarity to others. Robert Tolan, real estate broker and promoter, who had been corresponding with the post office authorities, consulted George Moody, homesteader of the section. Moody said he would like it named Flagler Beach in honor of the later Henry Flagler, who had been a friend of his brother, I. I. Moody. Between Flagler Beach and Summer Haven stood the Spanish mission of San José.

FLAMINGO. *Everglades National Park.* Formerly the southernmost community on the mainland of the continental United States and now the southernmost headquarters for the Everglades National Park services and operations. Named in 1893 by the half-dozen families living here. According to Tebeau (1963) "they wanted it named for something characteristic of the area, and easily selected the flamingo as the most distinctive of the many birds that frequented the area." Tebeau says flamingoes are not native to south Florida, which lies on the outer fringe of their natural range. "But they once came in relatively large numbers from Cuba, the Bahama Islands and possibly other nearby places where they nested. Several hundred were sighted in 1902, but rarely any after that time." Tebeau comments later, when the presence of the long-legged birds in large numbers was largely forgotten, at least one writer surmised that Flamingo was so named "because the houses were 'long-legged', being built in many cases on stilts to raise them above the hurricane flood waters that sometimes swept over the low-lying land."

FLIRT, LAKE. *Glades County.* River traffic moved along the Caloosahatchee in the old steamboating days from Fort Thompson to Lake Okeechobee through open country with shallow lakes and drowned prairies. These lakes included Lake Flirt, some five miles by two. The lake is believed to have been named for the Army supply boat *Flirt*. Will (1965) quotes a state engineer, Fred Flanders, as having found "a most bodacious collection of old fossil bones of dinosaurs and all them old timey critters, with mammoth's teeth as big as a cow man's hat" after the lake dried up. He said Flanders opined this must have been a bog during prehistoric times.

FLOMATON. *Escambia County.* *See* South Flomaton.

FLORAL CITY. *Citrus County.* A search for orchids and other rare flowers led a Vermonter to what in the 1870s was known as Cove

Bend. His enthusiasm for flowers brought a change of the name to Floral Cove and subsequently to Floral City.

FLORIDA State. The first place name that Europeans brought to this mainland. On Easter Sunday 1513, Juan Ponce de León and those with him in three ships saw a small, unknown island. They sailed northwest for three days and then west-northwest for two days more. Again they saw land, but the coast was so long that they knew this was not an island like the one glimpsed five days before. The lawyers who served the king of Spain thought that possession could be cinched by naming places discovered by the explorers; thus, Ponce de León was faced with naming this land on which he had not yet stepped foot. Writing a hundred years later, the court historian Antonío de Herrera related that "Believing that land to be an island, they nam'd it *Florida,* because it appeared very delightful, having many pleasant groves, and it was all level; as also because they discovered it at Easter, which as has been said, the Spaniards called *Pasqua de Flores,* or *Florida*" [the Feast of Flowers at Easter time]. The Spanish pronounced it Flor-EE-da. The English, coming later, kept the name but changed the pronounciation to suit their tongues, so Flor-EE-da became FLOR-i-da.

FLORIDA CITY. *Dade County.* The southernmost mainland town in the United States. It was developed in 1905 by Miami realtors and incorporated in 1913. A group of settlers from Detroit, Mich., agreed to name the place after their home city, but the Post Office Department said this would be confusing. The name Florida City was then adopted by a vote of the residents.

FLORIDATOWN. *Santa Rosa County.* One of the oldest place names in this state. The town was a trading post in Spanish days. General Andrew Jackson first camped here in 1814. At the delta of Escambia River and Escambia Bay, the place served for the transshipment of goods and as a resting place for travelers. M. Luther King (1972) reports that Davy Crockett was here with Jackson; in Crockett's autobiography he tells how he "went 'bar' hunting up the 'Scamby'." Floridatown was the seat of Santa Rosa County in territorial days, losing this distinction when yellow fever ravaged the community in 1842.

FOLEY. *Taylor County.* Built in 1929 by the Brooks-Scanlon Lumber Company to house employees of a sawmill that the company located here. The town was named for J. S. Foley, the company's president for more than 30 years. Other milltowns named Foley for him still survive in Alabama, Louisiana, Minnesota, and Washington.

FORT BASINGER. *Highlands County.* Named for Lt. William E. Basinger of the 2nd Artillery, killed in the Dade Massacre. Colonel

Zachary Taylor, afterwards president of the United States, had a stockade built December 23, 1837, on a sandy hill on the west bank of the Kissimmee River. The fort consisted of pine logs standing upright, with sharp, pointed tops. Blockhouses and lookout towers were placed at the northwest and southeast corners. The stockade was intended to serve as a supply station for Taylor's expedition against the Indians in the Lake Okeechobee region. Visiting the area in 1972, George Lane, Jr., of the *St. Petersburg Times* could find no trace of the remains of Fort Basinger, only a historical marker at the intersection of U.S. 98 and S.R. 721. The name survives, however, in the twin communities of Fort Basinger in Highlands County and Basinger in Okeechobee County.

FORT BROOKE. *Hillsborough County.* Colonel George Mercer Brooke, directed to proceed from Pensacola with four infantry companies to establish a military post at Tampa Bay, arrived in January 1824 and moved into the plantation home of the absent Robert Hackley. Erecting a log fortification, Brooke called it Camp Hillsborough for its location on the northeast bank of the Hillsborough River. But the War Department assented to the desire of Brooke's fellow officers to name the fort for him, and thereafter it was known as Fort Brooke. Tampa grew up on the fringes of Fort Brooke. Colonel Brooke's son born here perhaps gained more lasting fame; he was Lt. J. M. Brooke, Confederate States Navy, who converted the captured Union ship *Merrimack* into the Confederate ironclad ram *Virginia*.

FORT CAROLINE. *Duval County.* Named for Charles IX. In 1564 France sent troops to the St. Johns River, where they built the sod-and-timber Fort Caroline as a toe step in the Florida wilderness that Spain claimed. Hunger, mutiny, and Indian troubles plagued the settlement, which the Spanish extinguished in 1565 by executing most of the garrison. The Spanish then garrisoned the place, which they called Fort San Mateo, only to have French vengeance strike them in 1568 with the hanging of those Spanish who survived the assault. The first record of a Protestant white child of the present United States was born at Fort Caroline some time just before 1565. The original site of Fort Caroline was washed away in the 1880s, but a replica has been erected nearby to help visitors visualize the scene. The Fort Caroline National Monument is 10 miles east of Jacksonville.

FORT CLINCH. *Nassau County.* Named for Gen. Duncan Lamont Clinch, who had served with distinction in the War of 1812, the Seminole wars in Florida, and the War with Mexico. Three forts and a camp in Florida were named for Clinch: Fort Clinch on Amelia Island, Fort Clinch on Lake Locha Apopka (now Lake Clinch) near Frostproof, Fort Clinch on the Withlacoochee, between today's Inglis and

Dunnellon, and Cantonment Clinch (now Cantonment) near Pensacola. The beautifully restored brick Fort Clinch in Nassau County was commenced in 1847 to guard the entrance to the broad Cumberland Sound, into which flow both the Amelia and St. Marys rivers. The fort was one of a chain of closed masonry forts on the Atlantic coast; Fort Jefferson in the Dry Tortugas was another. These forts were intended to withstand the penetration of smooth-bore artillery, but after the development of rifled bores they became obsolete. Construction of Fort Clinch was discontinued in 1867. The fort was far from complete at the outbreak of the Civil War, and the Confederates seized it in 1861, abandoning it a year later with the appearance of a combined Union Army and Navy force. Fort Clinch remained in Union possession for the remainder of the Civil War. It was strengthened and used during the Spanish-American War and had limited use as a communications and security post during World War II. In 1936, the state acquired Fort Clinch for development as a park. Fort Clinch is situated on Amelia Island, over which eight flags have flown since it was visited in 1562 by the French Admiral Jean Ribaut. The national flags were those of France, Spain, England, Mexico, the United States, and the Confederate States, and the local flags of the Patriots and Green Cross. *See* Fort Meade and Frostproof.

FORT DADE. *Hillsborough County.* Named for Major Dade (*see* Dade County) and erected in 1898 on Egmont Key at the mouth of Tampa Bay.

FORT DADE. *Pasco County.* Named for Maj. Francis Langhorne Dade (of the Dade Massacre—*see also* Dade County). Seven miles north of today's Dade City, the fort was built in 1837 on the south bank of the Withlacoochee River at the crossing of the Fort King Road and served for many years as a depot and observation post in the heart of the Seminole Indian settlement. On March 6, 1837 the Seminole leaders Jumper and Alligator met Gen. Thomas S. Jesup here to sign the "Fort Dade Capitulation."

FORT DENAUD. *Hendry County.* Named for Pierre Denaud, a French Canadian who traded here with the Indians for skins and hides before the soldiers came during the Seminole wars. This stockade guarded a crossing on the Caloosahatchee River on the military highway between Fort Meade and Fort Myers.

FORT GADSDEN. *Franklin County.* This place, affording a control of commerce on the Apalachicola River, was the site of fortifications occupied by English, free black, American, and Confederate forces. The site is near today's Sumatra. Although it was built in 1814 by the British as a rallying point to encourage the Seminole Indians to ally themselves with England against the United States in the War of 1812, the fort then was abandoned. In 1816 it was occupied by a band of free blacks. Its location in Spanish Florida did not deter Gen. Andrew Jackson from ordering its elimination because it was a threat to American commerce on the Apalachicola River. On July 27, 1816, Lt. Col. Duncan L. Clinch (later General Clinch), with U.S. forces and 150 Creek Indians, fired on the fort. A "hot shot" cannon ball penetrated the fort's powder magazine, and the explosion killed all but thirty of the three hundred occupants. In 1818 General Jackson directed Lt. James Gadsden to build Fort Gadsden here in spite of Spanish protests. Confederate troops occupied the fort during the Civil War until July 1863, when malaria forced abandonment.

FORT GEORGE ISLAND. *Duval County.* Named for Fort St. George, erected in 1740 by Gen. James Edward Oglethorpe of Georgia and named for the patron saint of England. The St. was dropped eventually, and the island simply called Fort George. Miss Dena Snodgrass of Jacksonville, an eminent Florida historian, picks up the story in personal communication: "Fort George Island is the body upon which is the Kingsley plantation. This is a true island and is connected with an island at its southern tip by a man-made causeway. That connecting island is Batten Island. On it is Pilot Town. The ferry across the St. Johns River from Mayport ends at this island and town. Each is erroneously called Fort George. Mr. John F. Rollins bought the true Fort George Island in 1869. He was appointed postmaster and shortly afterward he moved the post office from his residence to Batten Island because it was easier for river people to pick up mail there. And look what a mess he made!" Fort George Island is "important because the state's history is capsuled here. From the Indian village-mission-fort period through the struggles with the British colonies and the Republic of East Florida, on through the great plantation days and the early magic of Florida as a tourist mecca. It's all here on the island where the state maintains the Kingsley plantation house, the oldest plantation house extant in Florida."

FORT LAUDERDALE. *Broward County.* Named for Maj. William Lauderdale, of Sumner County, Tenn., who, on March 5, 1838, with a company of volunteers in the Second Seminole War, reached New River. Weidling and Burghard (1966) report that Lauderdale's command selected a site for a fort on the north bank "by the windings" of the river. On March 16, Maj. Gen. Thomas S. Jesup, in command of troops in the Florida war, issued Order No. 74, from headquarters at Fort Jupiter: "The new post lately established on the New River by the Tennessee Battalion of Volunteers and Company 'D' 3rd Artillery will be called *Fort Lauderdale.*" Major Lauderdale died at Baton Rouge, La., on May 10. Weidling and Burghard report the first land platted for sale within the present city of Fort Lauderdale was "Palm City," the 1887 dream of Arthur T. Williams of Fernandina. Fort Lauderdale, incorporated as a city in 1911, is now the county seat.

FORT LONESOME. *Hillsborough County.* Never a fort, but it is lonesome—a *Miami Herald* article by Nixon Smiley in 1971 said even the cows "sounded lonely." How the name was applied to this crossroads where S.R. 39 and S.R. 674 intersect has two explanations passed along by Mrs. James D. Bruton, Jr., of Plant City. One version says Mrs. Dovie Stanaland, who had a store here, gave the town this name because there was a sense of loneliness with only flat land as far as the eye could see. The other version, which has a martial ring to it, holds that the name was applied by a detachment of the National Guard stationed at the crossroads during the yearlong blockade of central Florida that was instituted to prevent spread of the Mediterranean fruit fly after the infestation was discovered in Orange County on April 6, 1929.

FORT MARION. *St. Johns County. See* Castillo de San Marcos.

FORT MEADE. *Polk County.* This site on the Peace River was at first the location of Fort Clinch, established in 1849, but the fortification was not maintained. Three years later, during a topographical survey of the area, the commanding officer of the party assigned 2nd Lt. George G. Meade to find the site of old Fort Clinch. This task was not easy because the description he had been given was ambiguous, but before nightfall he had found it. General Twigg, the commanding officer, exclaimed, "Here shall be Fort Meade!" Meade later gained fame at the Battle of Gettysburg. The modern town was incorporated in 1909.

FORT MYERS. *Lee County.* Named for Gen. Abraham Charles Myers, a distinguished officer in the U.S. Army. The fort was named by David E. Twiggs, federal commander in the Seminole wars, who later became the father-in-law of Myers. The city was developed in the later years of the nineteenth century, chiefly through the initiative of Stafford C. Cleveland, a New York newspaperman. The Florida estates of Thomas A. Edison and Henry Ford are located here. For awhile in the 1890s Fort was dropped from the community's name; but the citizenry paid no attention, and Fort came back into official usage. In the Seminole War of 1835-42, a fort was established here and named for Lt. John Harvie. Situated on the south bank of the Caloosahatchee River, Fort Myers is the county seat and the largest city in Lee County.

FORT PIERCE. *St. Lucie County.* Erected between 1838 and 1842 and named for Lt. Col. Benjamin Kendrick Pierce, a brother of President Franklin Pierce. The fort was the headquarters of the Army of the

South under General Jesup. A settlement about the fort began soon after its establishment. Fort Pierce is the county seat of St. Lucie County.

FORT WALTON BEACH. *Okaloosa County.* Named after the fort established here during the Seminole wars. The fort and the county adjacent to Okaloosa were named for Col. George Walton, who was secretary of West Florida during the governorship of Andrew Jackson, 1821-22, and secretary of the East-West Florida Territory, 1822-26. Walton was the son of George Walton, signer of the Declaration of Independence and governor of Georgia.

FORT WHITE. *Columbia County.* Named for a fort that stood here during the Seminole wars. Name source unrecorded.

FRANKLIN County. The seventeenth county, established February 8, 1832. Named for Benjamin Franklin.

FROSTPROOF. *Polk County.* Cowboys from the cattle regions just north of here were wont to herd their cattle southward into this highland lake region during the winter months because of the absence of frost here in the coldest seasons. It is said that they gave the meteorological name to this town. Frostproof once was known as Fort Clinch. Hetherington (1928) reported there was a tradition that a sea serpent used to haunt adjacent Lake Clinch. "The Indians many years ago insisted there was an immense serpent in this lake. In 1907 residents of Frostproof declared they had seen the monster, and that it must be thirty feet long." When Nixon Smiley of the *Miami Herald* visited Frostproof in 1969, he commented that the unique fact was that the community did not have a chamber of commerce. "But perhaps a town with the name of Frostproof doesn't need one," said Smiley.

FRUITLAND PARK. *Lake County.* Founded in 1876 by Maj. O. P. Rooks of Cincinnati, Ohio, this town was named after the Fruitland Nurseries of Augusta, Ga. There was already a Fruitland in Florida at this time, so postal authorities refused to permit the name of Fruitland Park; hence the town was officially renamed Gardenia. But the railroad had already issued its timetables, et cetera, with the name Fruitland Park and persisted in their use, so that everything except the mail was addressed in that way. Four years later the postal officials were brought round. The town was incorporated in 1925.

FRUITVILLE. *Sarasota County.* Named by the first settler, Charles L. Reaves, who came in 1876 and hoped to raise fruit.

GADSDEN County. The fifth county, established June 24, 1823. Named for James Gadsden (1788-1858), a native of Charleston, S.C., and a diplomat who served as aide-de-camp to Gen. Andrew Jackson during the 1818 campaign in Florida. Why the Territorial Council named the county for Gadsden is not known. He had been an associate of Jackson, however, and he had been commissioned to negotiate with the Indians for their removal either to then-remote peninsular Florida or completely out of the territory. Gadsden distinguished himself nationally for what is known now as the Gadsden Purchase, which occurred long after the naming of the Florida county. As an emissary from President Franklin Pierce in 1853, Gadsden negotiated a boundary dispute with Mexico that resulted in American acquisition of 27,640 square miles, now parts of New Mexico and Arizona, for $10 million. For a short time, until the creation of Leon County, Gadsden was the seat of territorial government.

GAINESVILLE. *Alachua County.* Named for Gen. Edmund Pendleton Gaines, the captor of Aaron Burr, but the story of its naming is not as simple as that. When De Soto marched through here in 1539, this area was called Potano Province; it was renamed Alachua when the Creek Indians took possession upon the English acquisition of Florida in 1763. A white settlement known as Hog Town grew up around a trading post established in 1830. When the Florida Railroad Company (the Yulee line) from Fernandina to Cedar Keys was built through in 1853, a more dignified name was plainly needed. County Commissioner William I. Turner, an Indian-war veteran and prosperous cattle raiser, proposed Gainesville, but a wealthy and influential planter named William R. Lewis offered his own name. Also in dispute was the location of the county seat, which had hitherto been at Newnansville. A barbecue picnic was held at Boulware Springs where all citizens of the county were to settle the issues, but the peace was almost ruptured before dinner was served. After everyone had eaten, some more peaceable negotiation and vote-swapping took place, and the present town was given both the courthouse and the name of Gainesville. The advocates of Newnansville referred in derision to their successful rival as "Gains-ville." Gainesville is the county seat and the home of the University of Florida.

GALAXY. *Palm Beach County.* From 1889 to 1895 there were a number of communities in what then was Dade County but now is Palm Beach County known collectively as the galaxy because their names— Jupiter, Mars, Venus, and Juno—suggested a galaxy of heavenly bodies. And, of course, the short railroad linking these communities came to be known popularly as the Celestial Railroad. Its proper name was the Jupiter and Lake Worth Railway, and its seven and one-half miles of narrow gauge linked steamboat landings on the Atlantic Ocean and Lake Worth. Juno's newspaper, the *Tropical Sun,* disapproved of the nickname, originated by travelers, thinking that they were poking fun which could obscure the worth of the area. When cold nipped the area, the editor wryly called the celestial roll—Jupiter, Juno, Venus, Mars, and the Sun—and said even Mercury had fallen there.

GASPARILLA ISLAND. *Charlotte County.* Named for the renegade Spanish naval officer, real or legendary, José Gaspar, who established a base here for his band of pirates. *See also* Boca Grande and Captiva.

GEM MARY, LAKE. *Orange County.* When William Randolph, an attorney, came to Orange County in 1868, an unnamed lake was adjacent to the Randolph home. To honor his wife Mary, whom he regarded as a gem, he named the lake Gem Mary. In so doing, Randolph followed the example of a neighbor, Dr. O. P. Preston, a Texan who settled in Orange County two years earlier. He named his lake for his wife Jennie, whom he said was a jewel, hence, Lake Jennie Jewel. These gems are from Gore (1949).

GENEVA. *Seminole County.* Named in 1880 for Switzerland's Geneva, lake and city.

GIBSONTON. *Hillsborough County.* Named for its founder, James B. Gibson.

GIFFORD. *Indian River County.* The Florida East Coast Railroad is said to have given this town in the 1880s the name of F. Charles Gifford, who in turn has been credited with selecting the site for nearby Vero Beach.

GILCHRIST County. The sixty-seventh county, established December 4, 1925. Named for Albert Waller Gilchrist, the twentieth governor (January 5, 1909-January 7, 1913). The legislature was about to create a new county to be known as Mellon when news came that former Governor Gilchrist was dying in a New York hospital. By amendment in floor consideration, Gilchrist was substituted for Mellon. Gilchrist was a descendant of the grandfathers of both George Washington and James Madison. A civil engineer, land developer, and orange grower at Punta Gorda, he was a member of the House of Representatives from De Soto County for the sessions of 1893-95 and 1903-5 and the speaker in 1905. A bachelor, he provided money in his will to supply Halloween treats for the children of Punta Gorda. This thoughtfulness was but one of Gilchrist's beneficences; his entire estate of a half-million dollars went to charities.

GLADES County. The fifty-eighth county, established April 23, 1921. Named for the Everglades, of which the county forms a part.

GLEN RIDGE. *Palm Beach County.* The name suggested by Mrs. Max Mosler when the residents met to incorporate. Mrs. Mosler said that the town's location on the bank of the Palm Beach Canal gave her the idea of "Ridge." Mrs. Mosler's suggestion was accepted by majority vote.

GLEN ST. MARY. *Baker County.* Established by Miss T. M. Tilton in 1882. She owned the hotel and served as postmistress. The name was prompted by the nearby St. Marys River, which forms the northern boundary of Florida. (St. Marys is easier to pronounce than the Indian name for the river was—it was Thlathlathlakuphka.)

GLENWOOD. *Volusia County.* Situated in one of the earliest cleared areas under American ownership of Florida. Grants of land in this vicinity were confirmed by special acts of Congress in 1832. Major George Norris of Batavia, N.Y., purchased a large tract on a high pine ridge in 1872 and may have been instrumental in selecting the name for its pleasing sound.

GOLDEN BEACH. *Dade County.* As happened so often, the name originally chosen by subdivision developers in the 1920s has been adopted for the successor community. Golden Beach is on the Atlantic, an extension northward of Miami Beach.

GOLF. *Palm Beach County.* Founded in the 1950s by men who had previously established Golf, Ill. These men were very interested in the game of golf.

GOMEZ. *Martin County.* Gomez has been an independent community at least since 1891, but the name derives from Eusobie M. Gomez, who received a Spanish land grant of 12,000 acres in 1815.

GONZALEZ. *Escambia County.* On at least three occasions, in 1814, 1818, and 1821, Gen. Andrew Jackson visited Don Mañuel Gonzalez at the Don's estate, Gonzalia (known also as Fifteen Mile House because of its location from Pensacola). Don Mañuel came to Pensacola as a Spanish soldier in 1784 and later served as the crown's Indian agent and commissary officer. He received a Spanish land grant almost encircling Pensacola and developed a cattle ranch. After the American acquisition of Florida, he became a citizen of the United States. M. Luther King (1972) relates that when Jackson was first about to capture Pensacola in 1814, the general requested that Don Mañuel have his son guide the Americans into Pensacola. King wrote that Don Mañuel refused, saying "Shoot him or both of us if you must but do not expect us to betray our King and our County." Such "plain talk . . . General Jackson could understand and respect."

GOULDS. *Dade County.* Once called Gould's Siding, a sidetrack of the Florida East Coast Railroad during the development of south Dade County in the early 1900s.

GRACEVILLE. *Jackson County.* A man named Stapleton established a grist mill here in 1824 and named the resultant town for Capt. N. B. Grace, a prominent builder, surveyor, landowner, and officer in the Confererate Army.

GRAND ISLAND. *Lake County.* Named in the 1880s by Captain Dodd, who had moved here from Fort Mason because he wanted to live on higher, hilly ground. Grand Island then was almost surrounded by lakes.

GRAND RIDGE. *Jackson County.* Founded in 1889 by John Thomas Porter, a native of Pennsylvania, and named for his old home in Grand Ridge, Ill.

GRANT. *Brevard County.* Originally named Grant's Farm for a settler on an island in the Indian River. The community's name was given by Mrs. Edwin Nelson in 1890.

GREENACRES CITY. *Palm Beach County.* In 1925, the developer, L. C. Swain, asked his twenty-six associates to suggest names other than his own and then vote for the final choice. Greenacres won. The post office department suggested that City be added because of the similarity to the numerous other Florida communities with Green in their name.

GREEN COVE SPRINGS. *Clay County.* Here the St. Johns River forms a curve and is sheltered by trees that are perennially green. Here also are located some celebrated sulphur springs, which at times have been said to be those that Ponce de León and others were seeking. The town was established by live-oak cutters in 1830. It is the county seat of Clay County.

GREEN RIVER SWAMP. *Collier County.* Place names do not necessarily have any relation to natural features, even when the names appear to be derived from local terrain. For example, "Green River Swamp south of Corkscrew Marsh is so named," observed Tebeau (1966), "because of a pile of nearly a hundred Green River whiskey bottles accumulated at a nearby hunting camp visited regularly by a party with a liking for that brand."

GREENSBORO. *Gadsden County.* In 1895, J. W. Green bought 160 acres near his birthplace in the Alamo community of Gadsden County. He moved into the place and soon secured a post office called Green's. When the Apalachicola Northern Railway was built in 1907, a depot was platted and named in honor of Green.

GREEN SWAMP. Named for its prevailing color and situated in central

Florida between Orlando and Tampa. When people began talking about the Green Swamp in the 1970s as an area of "critical state concern," many Floridians gained their first awareness of an area skirted by Panfilo de Narvaez and Hernando De Soto in the 1500s. It contains 870 square miles, bordered by U.S. 27 on the east, S.R. 544 on the south, S.R. 28 and S.R. 301 on the west, and S.R. 50 on the north, and it is not the typical low, wet land usually associated with a swamp. It is a composite of many swamps distributed with fair uniformity within the area. The largest continuous expanse of swamp lies within the Withlacoochee River environs and is more than a mile in width. The Green Swamp occupies a flat plateau with elevations varying from 75 to 200 feet above mean sea level. Ridges border the swamp on the east and west, with the higher land to the east being the Lake Wales Ridge. The area contains orange groves, marshes, improved pasture, open flatwoods, pine flatwoods, hardwood hammocks, and cypress swamps. Fish found in the area include largemouth bass, bluegill, redbreast, sunfish, chain pickerel (or jackfish), and channel catfish. Wildlife include white-tailed deer, bobwhite quail, mourning dove, common snipe, woodcock, and Florida duck. Some species have shown indications of noncyclical decline, such as, the white ibis, red-shouldered hawk, marsh hawk, Cooper's hawk, limpkin, and eastern bluebird. Rare and endangered species include the American alligator, bald eagle, and Florida panther. The climate of the Green Swamp is classified as humid-subtropical. The normal average rainfall is 52.7 inches. The swamp is a water reservoir vital to central Florida.

GREENVILLE. *Madison County.* First established in 1850 and named Sandy Ford. During the Civil War, however, the place was named Station Five, because it was the fifth station from the capital. A women's sewing circle was organized here to sew for the soldiers in the Confederate Army, and the first box of supplies that the women sent to the commissary in Richmond was designated as coming from Station Five. But the quartermaster wrote the president of the society that packages would have to be given in the name of some town. The ladies met and agreed to call the town Greenville, as a tribute to Mrs. U. M. Roberts, president of the society, who came from Greenville, S.C. The Spanish missions of San Miguel de Asylo and San Mateo de Tolapato were both near here.

GREENWOOD. *Jackson County.* Established in 1824 and first named Panhandle. Greenwood was chosen by settlers from South Carolina in remembrance of their former home.

GRETNA. *Gadsden County.* Established in 1897 by the Humphrey Company, naval stores operators, but not a town in any real sense of the word, consisting largely of a few widely scattered black families around the point where the railroad stopped to pick up wood. The blacks called the place Gritney, because there was so much sand, but this spelling may have been a corruption of the name as now officially spelled. In time the Humphrey Company built a turpentine still, homes for officials and workmen, and a commissary; a post office was established in the commissary, and J. W. Mehaffey, a son-in-law of the head of the firm, was appointed first postmaster. He decided Gritney was not a very "prominent sounding" name, and changed it to Gretna, perhaps influenced by his Scottish ancestors.

GROVELAND. *Lake County.* First called Taylorville, apparently after one of the original backers of the Orange Belt Railway, on which construction was begun late in the 1880s. About 1911 the town was renamed Groveland, in reference to the large number of flourishing citrus groves that had been planted in the vicinity.

GROVE PARK. *Alachua County.* A grove of great oaks grew here in 1883 as the area developed into a shipping point for truck farmers.

GULF County. The sixty-sixth county, established June 6, 1925. Named for the Gulf of Mexico, which washes the southern shore of the county.

GULF BREEZE. *Santa Rosa County.* Across Pensacola Bay from Pensacola and separated from the Gulf of Mexico by Santa Rosa Island, Gulf Breeze offers the pleasures of resort living year-round, with breezes from either the Gulf or the Bay. Since Milton was, and is, the county seat, Gulf Breeze (called Town Point) was a two- or three-day roundtrip for the sheriff, either by land or by water, in the 1800s.

GULF HAMMOCK. *Levy County.* This part of Levy County had dense hardwood stands, much of which have been timbered. It borders the Gulf of Mexico. The name first was given its post office in 1883.

GULFPORT. *Pinellas County.* See Disston City.

GULFSTREAM. *Palm Beach County.* Named for its proximity to the Gulf Stream, which flows nearest the Florida mainland in this area.

HACIENDA VILLAGE. *Broward County.* Originally a subdivision called Hacienda Flores—using Spanish words to convey the idea of homes and flowers. The name was changed to Hacienda Village when it was incorporated in 1949.

HAGUE. *Alachua County.* When Hague grew to post office size in 1883, it seemed natural to honor A. Hague, the postmaster and county commissioner. In 1885, Hague, on the Savannah, Florida, and Western Railroad, had a grist mill, a steam sawmill, and a cotton gin.

HAINES CITY. *Polk County.* First known as Clay Cut when it originated in 1883 with the building of the South Florida Railroad. It was on the railroad line, but the residents could not get the company to put a station here. This situation was remedied four years later by changing the name of the town to Haines City, in honor of Col. Henry Haines, an official of the railroad. After that, the railroad put up a station and stopped the trains at it. The post office was known for several years as "Hains City," the e possibly having been inadvertently omitted in the rush of getting the colonel's name to Washington. It took a while to unravel the red tape that mistake caused. Haines City calls itself "The Gateway to the Scenic Highlands."

HALLANDALE. *Broward County.* Evidently the namers intended to call it Hollandale, since the majority of the early settlers were Hollanders, but the name has somehow been changed in its first vowel. The community was incorporated in 1927.

HAMILTON County. The fifteenth county, established December 26, 1827. Named for Alexander Hamilton, embattled conservative and first U.S. secretary of the treasury.

HAMPTON. *Bradford County.* Henry Saxon, Sr., had a farmhouse at approximately the center of the present town of Hampton. When he moved to another farm, a family by the name of Terry moved into the farmhouse. As a community formed about the tracks near the Terry farm, it was given the name of the Terrys' 10-year-old son, Hampton.

HAMPTON SPRINGS. *Taylor County.* The story goes that Joe Hampton, an early Taylor County settler whose wife suffered from rheumatism, was directed to these springs by an Indian. The water eased her pain and stiffness, so Hampton obtained a government grant to the spring area for $10. A descendant of his built a hotel here in 1904 to accommodate visitors to the springs.

HARDEE County. The fifty-fifth county, established April 23, 1921. One of four counties—Highlands, Charlotte, and Glades being the others—created in a massive division of De Soto County. Named for Cary Augustus Hardee, who was in his first year as governor when De Soto was divided. Plowden (1929) reports those supporting a new county first had proposed calling it Seminole, but this name went to another new county. Later, Cherokee was suggested, along with Goolsby and Wauchula. When the bill was introduced, however, it bore the name of Hardee. Perhaps the promoters of county division wanted to make the idea more palatable to a governor who possessed veto power. Born in Taylor County, Cary Hardee taught school and studied for admission to the bar. Upon becoming a lawyer, he began practice at Live Oak. He served as state attorney and then was elected to the House of Representatives. His political genius may be evidenced by his selection as speaker before he took the oath as a member of the House. He served two terms as speaker, another rare happening, in 1915 and 1917. He was better known in later years as a banker at Live Oak than as a lawyer. He was defeated for the Democratic nomination for governor in 1932. He died at Live Oak on November 21, 1957.

HARD SCRABBLE. *Santa Rosa County.* King (1972) recalls how the Spanish licensed a trading firm to control the export-import business of West Florida. Persons seeking to evade the king's levy used the area of present-day Milton, which came to be known as Hard Scrabble "since often these landings were made at the bluffs on the basins above town where it was a hard scrabble to get from the boat on the water to the top of the bluff." *See also* Milton.

HAROLD. *Santa Rosa County.* Local legend says the town was named in 1909 for a son of the postmaster. The community was known earlier as Oscar.

HASTINGS. *St. Johns County.* A famous potato section of Florida named for the H. G. Hastings Seed Company of Atlanta, Ga.

HAVANA. *Gadsden County.* Cultivation of Cuban tobacco in this county began as early as 1829; long afterward, however, this town was named for the Cuban capital as a means of honoring this remunerative crop. A frame schoolhouse and a boxlike depot were the only buildings here in 1903 when the Georgia, Florida & Alabama Railroad was completed from Cuthbert, Ga., to Tallahassee (Stanley, 1948). The railroad caused people to gravitate to the place, which was named Havana at the suggestion of Jim Mathison, a schoolteacher. The name Havana is of Indian origin, though its exact significance has been lost. The Spanish mission of Santa Cruz de Cupali stood near here.

HAWTHORNE. *Alachua County.* Once known as Waits Crossing for Calvin Waits, a landowner. Adjacent land to the north was owned by James M. Hawthorn (sic) and called Jamestown. In 1880 the two settlements merged, and the town was named Hawthorn. People persisted in spelling the name with a final e, however, and this was adopted in 1950.

HAYDEN. *Sarasota County.* Dr. George Hayden, a traveling dentist, came here from Palmetto and founded this town about 1895.

HELL'S HALF ACRE. *Jefferson County.* A swamp in southeast Jefferson County whose rugged terrain is unusual even among the many swamps of the counties of Florida's Big Bend. Rather than half an acre, the swamp covers approximately 1,000 acres.

HENDRY County. The sixty-third county, established May 11, 1923. Name honors Capt. Francis Asbury Hendry, whose fascinating history is recited in *Hendry County's Golden Anniversary Issue of the Clewiston News,* July 12, 1973. Hendry married at nineteen and settled near Fort Meade to raise cattle. With the outbreak of the Second Seminole War, he became a dispatch bearer; riding to Fort Harvie (afterward Fort Myers), he became enchanted with the lands along the Caloosahatchee River. During the Civil War, he served the Confederacy as captain of a calvary troop he recruited in Polk County. His admiration for Gen. Robert E. Lee caused him later to give Lee's name to a new county he was instrumental in creating in 1887. After the war he moved the family home to the Caloosahatchee Valley, where cattle easily could be moved to Punta Rassa for shipment to Cuba. He platted the townsite he called LaBelle after his daughters Laura and Belle. He was elected state senator from Monroe County, which then encompassed all of the present Lee, Hendry, and Collier counties. He promoted the incorporation of Fort Myers and served as one of its first city councilmen. Similarly, he promoted the creation of Lee County and served as a member of its first county commission and then six terms as state representative. He pioneered the upgrading of Florida cattle. He bought purebreds and imported grass to improve herds and pastures. With his herd containing as many as 50,000 head at one time, he was known as the "Cattle King of South Florida." He died February 12, 1917, his life having spanned a monumental epoch in Florida's history.

HERNANDO County. The twenty-second county, established February 24, 1843. Named for the Spanish explorer, Hernando De Soto. Why his first name was chosen for the county must be a historical curiosity inasmuch as his last name was selected for the county seat. De Soto's last name finally achieved county status in 1887, thus giving Florida two counties named for the same person. The name of the county seat was changed from De Soto to Brooksville. Even the name of the county was briefly lost; it was changed to Benton on March 6, 1844, to honor Thomas Hart Benton of Missouri, U.S. senator, whose sponsorship of the Armed Occupation Act of 1842 won favor among Floridians eager to evict the Indians. Benton's moderation during the Missouri Compromise caused extremists in the legislature to switch the name back on December 24, 1850. *See also* Benton.

HERNANDO. *Citrus County.* Named for Hernando De Soto and located on Lake Tsala Apopka near the place where De Soto is believed to have crossed the Withlacoochee River during his expedition north through Florida.

HESPERIDES. *Polk County.* The name of this village, located nine miles east of Lake Wales on S.R. 60 and entirely surrounded by orange groves, is another of Florida's choice classical allusions. In the Garden of the Hesperides, far in the western part of the Grecian kingdom, grew the golden apples of Hera. The Hesperides were the maidens charged with guarding this precious fruit; some say they were the daughters of the giant Atlas, others that their father was Hesperus, the Evening Star. To assist them in their guardianship they had a dragon who never slept named Ladon. The eleventh of Hercules' twelve labors was to procure these Grecian oranges. Some accounts say he killed the dragon himself and made off with the fruit; another story is that he sent Atlas to get the fruit, holding up the sky for him while he was gone.

HIALEAH. *Dade County.* Of Seminole-Creek origin: *haiyakpo,* "prairie" and *hili,* "pretty." A settlement was established here in 1910 by James H. Bright, a Missouri ranchman, who transformed 1,000 acres of a 14,000-acre tract into a grazing meadow for his herd of cows, with a year-round dairy industry in mind. In 1917 Glenn H. Curtiss, of Jamestown, N.Y., pioneer aviator, collaborated with Bright in building a town on the banks of the Miami Canal. The cattle were moved further north. The town was incorporated in 1925. Nowadays, the name Hialeah is associated with two vastly different images: Hialeah Park race track, one of the nation's loveliest horse tracks, and light industries, whose numerous plants make Hialeah the industrial center of Metropolitan Miami.

HIGHLAND CITY. *Polk County.* Originally a station named Haskell on the Pemberton Ferry Railroad. In 1925 the name was changed to Highland City.

HIGHLANDS County. The fifty-sixth county, established April 23, 1921. The name suggests the pleasant hilliness of the area.

HIGHLANDS. *Lake County. See* Eustis.

HIGH SPRINGS. *Alachua County.* First founded in 1884 as Sanafee—a corruption of the name of the Santa Fe River, near which it was located. In 1886 the name was changed to Orion, after the hunter who was transformed into a constellation. In 1889 the name was changed to its present form, because of a spring located atop a hill within the townsite. The spring has since disappeared.

HILLCREST HEIGHTS. *Polk County.* So named because it lies on a hillside south of Crooked Lake. Irwin Yarnell, co-owner with F. E. Fairchild in the Southern Land Co., built a home on the crest in 1916.

HILLIARD. *Nassau County.* A trading post was established here in the early 1800s, but the present town was not founded until 1881. It was named for one of the members of the lumber company, Hilliard and Bailey, which operated a mill here.

HILLSBORO BEACH. *Broward County.* Named for an inlet and lighthouse here. They derived their names from a contraction of the Earl of Hillsborough. *See also* Hillsborough.

HILLSBORO RIVER. *Hillsborough County.* The name appears in two forms of present-day maps. The sectional map of the State Department of Agriculture spells it Hillsboro, both for river and bay, whereas the highway map of the State Department of Transportation uses Hillsborough for the river and merges the waterways on both sides of Tampa as Tampa Bay. The U.S. Board on Geographic Names decreed the usage should be Hillsboro River and Hillsborough County. The Indians knew the river as *locksa apopka,* or "place for eating acorns." *See also* Hillsborough.

HILLSBOROUGH County. The eighteenth county, established January 25, 1834. Named for Wills Hills, the Earl of Hillsborough (1718-93), an Irish peer who in 1768 became secretary of state for the colonies. Lord Hillsborough's office was responsible for amassing knowledge about England's possessions overseas. Those agents dispatched in Lord Hillsborough's name in turn affixed that name to places in Florida and elsewhere. Hillsborough was especially curious about Florida since he had received a large grant of land here, so he sent Bernard Romans, a surveyor and naturalist, to examine the east and west coasts of Florida. Romans regarded the Bay of Tampa exceptionally well suited to harbor a large fleet of heavy ships, with the surrounding countryside capable of furnishing timber and water. James Grant Forbes, who navigated the waters of the west coast in 1803, confirmed Romans' opinion, writing (Forbes, 1821; reprint 1964) that "Espiritu Santo, Tampa or Hillsborough Bay is the most spacious bay on the west coast of the peninsula . . . it may be justly considered the key to navigation of the British and Spanish islands to the leeward. . . ." Hillsborough appeared on some maps of the period, and later, as Hillsboro, and the shortened version may be regarded as a contraction. Lord Hillsborough, by then the first Marquis of Downshire, never saw his Florida domain. In 1956, however, a direct descendant, Arthur Wills Percy Wellington Blundell Trumbull Sandys Hills, Marquis of Downshire and Earl of Hillsborough, and his Marchioness, Maureen, were Tampa's distinguished guests during the Gasparilla festival.

HOBE SOUND. *Martin County.* The name is derived from the Indian pronunciation *Hoe-bay* of the Spanish *Jove.* During the excitement of the land boom of the 1920s, Hobe Sound was changed to Olympia, which suggested the dwelling of the gods of classical Greece, but when the boom collapsed the old name was restored. *See also* Jupiter.

HOLDER. *Citrus County.* A family named Holder owned a hard-rock phosphate mine here at the turn of the century. The community first was known (in 1895) as Hartshorn, then Cordeal (in 1897), and finally Holder (in 1901).

HOLLEY. *Santa Rosa County.* Settled in 1893 and said to have been named for a Baptist minister, Rev. W. D. Holley.

HOLLY HILL. *Volusia County.* Established about 1882 and probably named for the prevalence of holly trees along the ridge. The Federal Writers Florida Place Names Project (1939) said there also was a belief that "one Mr. Fleming named the place in honor of his old home in Delaware."

HOLLYWOOD. *Broward County.* Established in 1921, and christened Hollywood-by-the-Sea by its founder, Joseph W. Young of California, whose visions for establishing a great new city and port seemed limitless. Collapse of the boom of the 1920s retarded the unfolding of these plans but ultimately, as with so many other developments in Florida, most of his dreams came true. Today Young probably would be delighted if he could see what he initiated.

HOLMES County. The twenty-seventh county, established January 8, 1848. Named for Holmes Creek, the eastern boundary of the county (Utley, 1908). The creek was named for Holmes Valley, which received its name "either from an Indian chieftain who had been given the English name of Holmes or else from one Thomas J. Holmes, who settled in that vicinity from North Carolina about 1830 or 1834." Simpson (1956) says the belief the name derived from that of an early white settler cannot be substantiated. After Andrew Jackson occupied Spanish Pensacola in 1818, he sent a raiding party on a sweep along the Choctawhatchee River. During this raid, the troops came upon and killed the half-breed Indian known as Holmes. Holmes was one of the so-called "Red Sticks," the disaffected Muskogee or Creeks who fled to Florida from Alabama after the Creek War of 1813-14 (American State Papers, Military Affairs, Vol. 1, 1832-59). The first seat of Holmes County was at Hewett's Bluff, known later as Bear Pen. Cerro Gordon and Westville also served as the courthouse site before Bonifay finally was selected in 1905.

HOLMES BEACH. *Manatee County.* Situated on Anna Maria Island, this community derived its name in the 1950s from Jack E. Holmes, builder and developer.

HOLOPAW. *Osceola County.* This station on the abandoned Okeechobee extension of the Florida East Coast Railroad (FEC) bears a name apparently of recent Seminole origin. Minnie Moore-Willson (1920) translates *holopaw* as "walk" or "pavement." The naming has been credited to J. E. Ingraham, vice president of the FEC. A number of stations along the Okeechobee extension bore Indianlike names, among them Yeehaw, Pocataw, Nittaw, and Osowaw. Perhaps these names were chosen for their sounds rather than for their meanings.

HOMELAND. *Polk County.* One of the older communities in Polk County, having been known by that name since 1885. The settlement previously was known as Bethel for a Methodist church of the same name situated here. Hetherington (1928) reports "Jack McCormick, an Irish peddler, suggested the community's present name, noting that 'it' impresses one who views it as the 'home land' of contented people."

HOMESTEAD. *Dade County.* Known as "the Homestead Country" around the turn of the century because the pineland was U.S. government-owned and subject to homestead entry. When the Florida East Coast Railroad stretched its rails down from Miami in 1904, the abbreviated designation Homestead was tacked to the freight car first used as a station.

HOMOSASSA. *Citrus County.* The name of two communities— Homosassa and Homosassa Springs—and of springs, a river, a bay, a point, and a group of islands. A Seminole settlement is also named Homosassa; in 1836 it was at or near the site of the present town. Homosassa Springs has a flow of 70,000 gallons a minute. Read (1934) defines Homosassa as Seminole-Creek *homo,* "pepper," and *sasi,* "is there," or "a place where wild pepper grows." There are others who like to think the name means "smoking creek" from the dense vapor that on cool days envelops the warm springs and river.

HONGRY LAND. *Palm Beach County.* An area between Lake Okeechobee and the Jupiter Lighthouse "which has been known to cowmen and hunters for generations past as the Hongry Lane" (Will, 1964). During the Seminole wars, a starving band of Indians, their wives and children dying from the hardships of being fugitives so long, surrendered in the Everglades, asking only that they might be permitted to remain in Florida. An Army surgeon, James Rhett Motte, described the scene as the Army and the Indians waited for a reply from Washington. He said the Indians were a pitiful sight, especially the women. They wandered about the camp, picking up grains of corn dropped where the Army horses had been fed; the women "were poor as snakes, with hardly enough clothes to cover their nakedness, being dressed in corn sacks which the soldiers had thrown away." Then the word came from Washington: the war must continue until every Indian was dead or deported. So they were shipped to Arkansas, leaving the Hongry Land.

HOWEY-IN-THE-HILLS. *Lake County.* First known as Howey, for its founder W. J. Howey; the in-the-Hills was adopted during the boom of the 1920s when the town was incorporated. A leader in the Florida Republican Party, Howey was twice the GOP nominee for governor and received 39 percent of the vote against Democrat Doyle E. Carlton in 1928 and 33 percent of the vote against Democrat Dave Sholtz in 1932.

HYPOLUXO. *Palm Beach County.* Perhaps an Indian name, but Read (1934) suggests some skepticism by writing "if this is a genuine Indian name," it may be connected with Seminole *hapo,* "mound, heap, or pile," and *poloski,* "round, circular." Hypoluxo therefore could refer to one of the numerous shell mounds along the coasts of Florida. Pierce (1970), writing of pioneer life in southeast Florida, however, says an Indian woman told an early arrival that Lake Worth was called Hypoluxo and that this meant "water all around, no get out"; in other words, the lake was landlocked. In a subsequent discussion of the spelling of the name of an island in the lake on which a group of early settlers proposed to settle, the group agreed upon "hypo" instead of "hipo" for the first syllables; they did not want everyone to call it "Hippoluxo."

IMMOKALEE. *Collier County.* As early as 1869, trappers called this place Gopher Ridge. The first settlement came in 1884 when a sawmill was established to prepare lumber for the Episcopal mission to the Indians. The present name is Indian; authorities differ about whether the name is Miccosukee-Seminole for "his home" or "his people," or whether it is from the Cherokee *ama,* "water," and *kolola,* "tumbling." Tebeau (1966) says William "Billy" Allen, a Confederate veteran from Arcadia, settled here in 1872, building a log house. For 25 years it was known as Allen's Place. But, when the time came for a post office in 1897, Episcopal Bishop William Crane Gray suggested the name should be a Seminole word with pleasant associations; hence, reports Tebeau, "The 'Allen Place' now became Immokalee, meaning 'my home'," although strictly interpreted the word is "his home."

INDIALANTIC. *Brevard County.* Born in the boom of 1925. Mrs. G. F. Duren won a contest to name the town. Her name indicates its site—between the Indian River and the Atlantic Ocean.

INDIAN CREEK VILLAGE. *Dade County.* Incorporated in 1939, this municipality is an island in Indian Creek, from which it draws its name.

INDIAN HARBOUR BEACH. *Brevard County.* So named in 1955 because traces of an Indian village were found here on the shore of a sheltered cove on the Banana River.

INDIAN LAKE ESTATES. *Polk County.* Founded in the 1950s as one of the first big-scale land developments in Florida after the renewal of interest in the state following the collapse of the boom of the 1920s.

INDIAN RIVER County. The sixty-fifth county, established May 30, 1925. Named for the Indian River, which flows through it.

INDIAN RIVER SHORES. *Indian River County.* Named for its location on the shores of the Indian River.

INDIAN ROCKS BEACH. *Pinellas County.* The surrounding country has been settled since 1840; on early maps it is known as St. Clements Point. A number of large red rocks along the shore give the community its present name.

INDIANTOWN. *Martin County.* Once a trading center for the Seminole Indians.

INGLIS. *Levy County.* Named for Capt. John Inglis, whose family came from Glasgow, Scotland. He skippered a ship from Spain to the mouth of the Withlacoochee River during the 1800s and traded with the few inhabitants of this area. A community known as Port Inglis sprang up at the river's mouth, at that time the intersection of the "highways" of the Withlacoochee and the Gulf. Sometime later, a new community named simply Inglis grew up around a chemical plant eight miles upriver from the port. Its original name was Blind Horse. As roads developed and the inland population grew, ship trading declined and with it Port Inglis. Inglis, however, continued to grow.

INTERLACHEN. *Putnam County.* Settled in 1872 and first known as Wilcox. The present name is Scotch, meaning "between the lakes."

INVERNESS. *Citrus County.* Named by a Scotch settler for the ancient capital of the Scottish Highlands. On the shores of 18-mile-long Lake Tsala Apopka, Inverness is the county seat of Citrus County. *See also* Mannsfield.

ISLAMORADA. *Monroe County.* Viewed from the sea, Upper Matecumbe Key, which this community straddles, often appears mauve or lilac-tinted, hence, Islamorada, Spanish for "purple island." Here the Labor Day hurricane of 1935 overturned cars of a train dispatched to evacuate veterans of World War I, remnants of the popularly called Bonus Expeditionary Force, or "Bonus Army," which had assembled at Washington, D.C., seeking help during the depression of the 1930s. The veterans in the keys had been enlisted by the Florida Emergency

Relief Administration to close gaps in the Overseas Highway from the mainland to Key West. After the wind and water of the Labor Day hurricane swept Windley Key and Lower Matecumbe Key, 282 of the 684 veterans encamped were dead or missing. Civilian dead were officially placed at 164, although there were higher estimates. The storm destroyed sections of the Florida East Coast Railroad tracks, but the great bridges emerged undamaged and later were used to support a highway.

ISLAND GROVE. *Alachua County.* A high hammock among flatlands, settled in the 1880s. Here, unusually tall cabbage palms tower over citrus groves. Island Grove is famous as the *Cross Creek* of Marjorie Kinnan Rawlings, who also wrote *South Moon Under* and *The Yearling,* novels of the adjacent scrubland.

JACKSON County. The third county, established August 12, 1822. Named for Andrew Jackson, who had been U.S. commissioner and governor of the territories of East and West Florida and who later became the seventh president of the United States and the symbol of an emergent democracy.

JACKSONVILLE. *Duval County.* The St. Johns River has been crossed at this point as far back as the history of this area can be traced. The Timucuan Indians called it *wacca pilatka,* meaning "place where cows cross," though, of course, the Indians had never seen cattle until the Spaniards brought them (*wacca* is a variant of the Spanish *vaca,* "cow"). Two of the Spanish names for the area can be translated "Pass of San Nicolas" (Fort San Nicolas was nearby) and "the place where the cows cross." When the British gained possession of Florida in 1763, the name became Cow Ford. This name was revived by American settlers of Spanish Florida in the early 1800s. In 1822, under the urging of Isaiah D. Hart, a settler from south Georgia, a townsite was surveyed. Newnan, Market, Liberty, and Washington streets were laid out and named. Crossing these, Bay, Forsyth, Adams, Monroe, and Duval formed a 20-block area. Snodgrass (1969) reports John Warren, a settler who had served under Andrew Jackson as a soldier, suggested Jacksonville as the name, and this name was agreed upon without dissent. With so much known, the tantalizing fact is that so far no record has been found of the exact date in June 1822 when the city officially came into being. Probably the events were spread over a number of days. Every city must have a birthday, however, so Jacksonville has selected June 15, the date when the settlers petitioned Congress for recognition as a port of entry. Jacksonville is the county seat of Duval County.

JACKSONVILLE BEACH. *Duval County.* A seaside town about 18 miles southeast of Jacksonville and taking its name now from that city. This town was at first called Ruby and later Pablo Beach. *See also* Atlantic Beach.

JASPER. *Hamilton County.* Some fragmentary reports record a trading post here as early as 1830, established by families from Georgia and South Carolina. It was somewhat informally designated as Micco Town, the word thought to have been a reference to a tribe of Miccosukee Indians who lived nearby. In 1850 the town was incorporated as Jasper, in memory of the revolutionary war hero, Sgt. William Jasper, who rescued the American flag during the British assault on Fort Sullivan, now Fort Moultrie, in 1776, and who was later killed at age 29 in the siege of Savannah. Jasper is the county seat of Hamilton County.

JAY. *Santa Rosa County.* First named Pine Level. When a post office was established, the town is thought to have been named from the first initial of J. T. Nowling, who owned a store here in 1900 and was appointed postmaster in 1902.

JEFFERSON County. The thirteenth county, established January 20, 1827. Named for Thomas Jefferson, president of the United States, who had died on July 4th of the preceding year.

JENNINGS. *Hamilton County.* Two men by the name of Jennings may have contributed the name of this town. Robert Jennings settled here in 1860, operating a farm and general store. George Jennings came to this vicinity in 1884 on a raft on the Alapaha River. This community was an important shipping point for Sea Island cotton in the days before World War I and the boll weevil.

JENSEN BEACH. *Martin County.* Peter Jensen settled a fishing village here about 1868. After the promotional fashion of Florida coastal communities, the community added Beach to its name in 1943.

JULIETTE. *Marion County. See* Romeo.

JUNE PARK. *Brevard County.* Communities follow transportation. In Florida's first days the settlements were at ports; next, cities sprung up as railroads spread. Now interstate highway interchanges are spawning communities. June Park, on Interstate 95, appears to be one of those.

JUNO BEACH. *Palm Beach County.* The county seat of Dade County before Palm Beach County was organized. Named for the consort of Jupiter. A tiny, narrow-gauge railroad used to run the eight miles from Jupiter to Juno. Mars and Venus were other stations on this "celestial railroad." Trains ran from Jupiter to Juno, then they had to back up all the way to Jupiter. *See also* Galaxy.

JUPITER. *Palm Beach County.* A fascinating story explains how this community came to be named after a Roman god. The Indians called the place Jobe or Jove from the Indian names, Xega, Jega, and Jeaga.

Pronounced Hoe-bay, the name stuck to nearby Hobe Sound. English mapmakers, however, saw Jobe and Jove and wrote Jupiter. The name at any rate inspired the names of Juno, Mars, and Venus for nearby towns. Jupiter Inlet Beach Colony and Jupiter Island in Martin County are recent communities that have adopted part of the old name. There also is a Jupiter Inlet connecting the Jupiter River to the Atlantic Ocean. DuBois (1968) says the incoming tide through Jupiter Inlet brings clear, blue-green water far up the Loxahatchee River to a fork where General Thomas S. Jesup's soldiers raised the palmetto log stockade of Fort Jupiter after the Battle of the Loxahatchee on January 20, 1838, in the Second Seminole War. *See also* Galaxy, Juno Beach.

KATHLEEN. *Polk County.* Said to have been named for Mrs. Catherine Prine, who moved here from Hillsborough County when a small child and died here in August 1916 at the age of 76 (Hetherington, 1928). "The first reference to the place we find in print gives the spelling as Cathleen," wrote Mr. Hetherington. "That was in 1887." The postal register says the community first was entered as Polish in April 1886 and changed to Kathleen in July of the same year.

KENANSVILLE. *Osceola County.* Formerly a station on the Okeechobee extension of the Florida East Coast Railroad, and in 1914 given the family name of the third Mrs. Henry M. Flagler, the former Miss Mary Lily Kenan of Chapel Hill, N.C. Flagler built the Florida East Coast Railroad and its affiliated hotel, steamship, and land companies.

KENDALL. *Dade County.* A post office established here in 1914 and named for Major Kendall, resident vice-president of the British Land Company, which owned groves and other agricultural land.

KENNETH CITY. *Pinellas County.* Developed by Sidney Colen and named for his only son, Kenneth Colen. The community was incorporated in 1957; Kenneth was then six years old.

KEY BISCAYNE. *Dade County.* Known as the site of the Cape Florida lighthouse and as a protective barrier between the Atlantic Ocean and Biscayne Bay. The lighthouse here was completed in 1825 and remains as one of the oldest structures in south Florida. A temporary Army post, Fort Bankhead, was established here during the Seminole War of 1838. For residents of metropolitan Miami, Key Biscayne became accessible by motor vehicle during the 1940s through the building of the Rickenbacker Causeway and development of an outstanding recreation area, Crandon Park. Rickenbacker Causeway was named for the World War I flying ace, E. V. "Eddie" Rickenbacker, and Crandon Park for a Dade County commissioner, Charles H. Crandon, who was the spark plug in public acquisition and development of the oceanside park. Key Biscayne became a nationally recognized place name through the establishment here of a satellite White House during the administration of President Richard M. Nixon. *See also* Biscayne, Cape Florida.

KEY COLONY BEACH. *Monroe County.* As the name suggests, this resort and development is situated in the Keys, about midway between the mainland and Key West.

KEY LARGO. *Monroe County.* A motion picture titled "Key Largo," starring Humphrey Bogart and Lauren Bacall, was filmed here and named for this lovely island. A town on the key was once known as Rock Harbor, but developers sought to cash in on the movie's publicity by having the name of the post office changed to Key Largo in 1952. Some seventeenth-century maps described the key as *Caio de dose leguas,* "the key of twelve leagues" (Hathway, 1967). Twelve times the Spanish league of the seventeenth century would be 29 miles, roughly the length of the island. Key Largo is never more than 3 miles wide, and Hathway says its Spanish name has been translated variously as "large island," "long island," and "small big island."

KEYSTONE. *Hillsborough County.* During the days of the 1880s when many Florida communities maintained a shotgun quarantine to warn off travelers from areas affected by yellow fever, Keystone was the place where mail was left for summer campers along the Gulf coast in the vicinity of Clearwater. The postman would ride over (Straub, 1829) "selecting his own mail, stained with disinfectant to protect the receiver from yellow fever!'"

KEYSTONE HEIGHTS. *Clay County.* Originally called Brooklyn, but in 1922 J. J. Lawrence of Pittsburgh, Pa., settled here and was responsible for the adoption of the present name in honor of his home state, which is called the Keystone State.

KEY VACA. *Monroe County.* Possibly the name antedates St. Augustine inasmuch as the chief of the Map Division of the Library of Congress reported (Brigham, 1957) the key (as "C. d bacas") appeared on a map that evidentally was made between 1519 and 1565 since Havana is shown but St. Augustine is not. The antiquity of the place name is beyond dispute, but the meaning never has been settled. Perhaps there was a person named Vacas (or a name of that sound). Local legend attributed the English translation of *vaca* "cow" to cattle there, but nothing to substantiate this theory has been found. Charles M. Brookfield, field representative of the National Audubon Society, once questioned the cow theory on the basis of the limited grazing area and the swarms of mosquitoes and other insects in the early days. Brookfield believes a more likely source would have been the sea cows or manatees once so prevalent in the area. Key Vaca long was the southernmost key on which freshwater could be obtained by drilling. During the construction of the Overseas Extension of the Florida East Coast Railroad from the mainland to Key West, two unusual types of boats visited here—liquor boats enjoying a brisk trade among some of the workers and a "gospel boat" dispatched by Key West churches to serve the spiritual needs of the workers.

KEY WEST. *Monroe County.* One of the strangest and most amusing examples of moving names from one language to another not by meaning but by sound—what professors call folk etymology. Early Spanish explorers are said to have found quantities of human bones on this island, presumably the result of a battle between Indian tribes. The Spaniards called the island Cayo Hueso (pronounced Wesso), "Bone Island." It just happens that this is the westernmost of the string of islands that extends from the tip of the Florida peninsula, so it was no trouble at all to transliterate *hueso* into "west." Later U.S. settlers tried on several occasions to give it more dignified names: for example, Thompson's Island, Port Rogers, Allentown. These names recognized officials and heroes of the U.S. Navy; the last honored Lt. W. H. Allen, who, in November 1822, in command of the schooner *U.S.S. Alligator,* pursued a fleet of eight pirate vessels. He had 40 men against 125 in the pirate party. His men had muskets, swords, and pistols; the pirates had 14 cannon. The Navy vessel took five of the pirate ships, but Allen was wounded twice and died before final victory; his name became a Navy war cry. Neither his name nor the others, however, stuck to the town on the island, which has remained Key West. It was first settled in 1822 by John Simonton, who purchased it from a Spaniard, Juan P. Salas, to whom it had been granted by the Spanish monarchy. Key Westers know their island as "The Rock" (Proby, 1974). A person born off "The Rock," wrote Mrs. Proby, "although he has lived a long life there, is called a stranger, and a large percentage of the population claims to have never left the island." Key West, rising from a shimmering sea on a coral island approximately 4 miles long and 2 miles wide, 100 miles from the Florida mainland, is the county seat of Monroe County.

KINGSLEY. *Clay County.* A town and lake named for Zephaniah Kingsley, perhaps Florida's most prominent plantation owner and slave trader during 1803 to 1839. The area here was among his land holdings. Kingsley imported slaves from Africa and put them through a period of acclimation and schooling before their sale. "His slaves were so well trained and were put in such good physical and mental condition by his shrewd and humanitarian handling that he was able to ask and receive a price of fifty percent above the average market price for the slaves he brought in and smuggled over the border" (Williams, 1949). Kingsley's home on Fort George Island overlooking the St. Johns River in Duval County is a tourist attraction today. Among the structures is the two-story Ma'am Anna's House, so designated in recollection of the name given Anna Madegigine Jai, Kingsley's wife and the daughter of a chief of Senegal. Kingsley Lake once was known informally to aviators as Dollar Lake because its roundness resembled a silver dollar.

KINGS ROAD. A street and highway in Jacksonville built in the 1770s by the British, then the owners of Florida, and named for the king of England. This road was graded and the first in Florida wide enough to accommodate wheeled vehicles; other overland passageways were trails. Today the Kings Road is the principal reminder of British days in northeast Florida. The route of the old road approximates U.S. 1. It was originally planned to connect Florida, especially St. Augustine and Cow Ford (now Jacksonville), with the British colonies to the north and encourage settlers to come into the province.

KISMET. *Lake County.* Kismet means "fate or destiny." What happened to Kismet in Florida may be regarded as an example of how fate intervenes in man's plans. The community was founded in 1884 by the Kismet Land and Improvement Company, near Lake Dorr in what is now the Ocala National Forest. There was a fifty-room hotel for winter visitors amid flourishing groves and crops. The great freeze of 1889 wiped out Kismet, however, except for its hotel, which was carefully taken apart and hauled to Eustis. "Each piece was carefully preserved and the building set up on the corner of Grove Street and Magnolia Avenue exactly as it had stood at Kismet, and was named the Grand View Hotel of Eustis" (Kennedy, 1929).

KISSIMMEE. *Osceola County.* An Indian name for which no authority has been able to find a definitive source. This difficulty was encountered by some of the Indians too. Even Seminoles in modern times do not seem to know the name's origin, although they say that Indians named the city. Indians referred to where presumably the Ais Caloosas, a tribe antedating the Seminoles, was slaughtered by De Soto's cavalcade about 1540. Ethnologists at the Smithsonian Institution ascribe the origin of Kissimmee to these Indians. Simpson (1946) used Kissimmee as an example of the pitfalls of trying to translate Indian words into English or any other language simply by the sound of syllables or words. He said examples of this error could be found in the popular interpretations advanced for the names Micanopy and Kissimmee. "Whereas these names do sound like 'Me-can-no-pay' and 'Kiss-him-me,' the first has no connection with ability to pay and the second has no connection with amorous activities of some early Indian maiden." Cantrell (1948) says the Kissimmee *Gazette* of February 21, 1941, told of a map dated 1752 that used the name Cacema for the area. This could have been an English pronunciation of Kissimmee, a name first applied to a lake and a river here. Cantrell also quotes the Kissimmee *Leader* (undated) as saying: "Kissimmee is an Indian word meaning 'long water'. By the combined efforts of railroad employees and brakemen, the pronunciation is gradually being corrupted into Kis-*sim*-my, with the accent on the second syllable; but the correct pronunciation, and the one which citizens of the city hope will prevail, is Kiss-im-mee, with the accent on all syllables the same and a lingering on the last." The modern town was founded before the Civil War by the Bass, Johnson, and Overstreet families and has long been a center of the cattle industry. In 1881 Hamilton Disston gave impetus to the town through his drainage activities and sugar-growing empire. The town is located on Lake Tohopekaliga meaning "fort site." Kissimmee is the county seat of Osceola County.

KNIGHTS. *Hillsborough County.* Settled in the 1880s and named for William Knight.

KORONA. *Flagler County.* Polish settlers in 1918 adopted the Latin *corona,* "crown," but with K instead of C.

LA BELLE. *Hendry County.* The county seat of Hendry County named by Capt. Francis Asbury Hendry for two of his daughters, Laura and Belle. *See also* Hendry.

LACOOCHEE. *Pasco County.* A shortened form of Withlacoochee, from the Withlacoochee River.

LA CROSSE. *Alachua County.* Settled sometime prior to 1885 by people who came from La Crosse, Wis. That town had derived its name from the Indian ball game, to which the French had given the name *la crosse,* and which was regularly played at that spot.

LADY LAKE. *Lake County.* A village near here had been named Slighville. When the railroad came through in 1884, the residents moved to this site in order to be on the railroad line. Railroad authorities wanted to call the place Cooper, but the settlers preferred a more picturesque name. The Indians had already named the lake here Lady Lake, because of an unknown white woman they had found drowned in it, and the town took its name from that.

LAFAYETTE County. The thirty-third county, established December 23, 1856. Named for the Marquis de Lafayette 1757-1834. Lafayette pleaded the cause of American independence in France, lent both his prestige and military knowledge to the American Revolutionary Army by serving as a major general, and spent about $200,000 of his private fortune on behalf of the colonies. After his imprisonment and the confiscation of his estates during the French Reign of Terror, Lafayette looked to the United States to save his family from poverty. After other gifts of money and land, Congress in December 1824 appropriated $200,000 and a grant of a township of land anywhere in the unsold public domain. President Monroe was hopeful that Lafayette, then in the United States, would become a resident of Florida. "The General himself was keenly interested in the proposition, for while in Washington, he had come under the magnetic spell of Richard Keith Call, Florida's representative and her most ardent champion. A strong friendship grew up between the two men and before they separated, Lafayette half-way promised to visit Florida" (Hanna, 1932). Although Lafayette did choose a township in Florida at Tallahassee, the visit never was to be. Only once was a Lafayette in Florida; in 1850 Edmond de Lafayette and Ferdinand de Lasteyrie, grandsons of the marquis, visited the United States and conferred with their American land agent. The last of the Lafayette land was sold in 1855, although this sale could have been accomplished years earlier if the marquis had not wished to experiment with cultivating (by free labor) vineyards, olive groves, mulberry trees, and silkworms. Some fifty to sixty Normans unsuccessfully tried to reproduce the agriculture of the Old World on a bluff overlooking Lake Lafayette. The Lafayette Grant, as the township is known, is formally Township 1 North, Range 1 East, bounded in today's Tallahassee by Meridian Road on the west, approximately Gaines Street on the south, and extends six miles to the east and six miles to the north. The popularity of Lafayette in the United States was such that forty places were named for him. *See also* Fayette.

LAKE County. The forty-third county, established May 27, 1887, being taken from Orange and Sumter counties. Named for the large number of lakes within its boundaries. When lakes were counted in 1969 by the state, Lake County had 505 lakes either named or unnamed and of 10 acres or more.

LAKES. Listed according to their names; e.g., Lake Okeechobee appears as Okeechobee, Lake.

LAKE ALFRED. *Polk County.* A number of less poetic names were used for this community before the present one was selected in 1913.

The first of these was Fargo, after Fargo, N.Dak., from where a number of persons came who were interested in the Fruitlands Company, which developed this area. This name was discarded because of postal confusion with Largo, Fla. Next came Chubb (derivation unknown), which was discarded because it was not pleasant-sounding. Bartow Junction was tried out, but Bartow was 15 miles away and folks here did not want to be considered suburbanites. Finally the present name was chosen, being taken from the nearest large lake, which had been named for Alfred Parslow, who came to Florida in 1877 with $10,000 he received from injuries in a railroad wreck at Ashtabula, Ohio. With this nest egg, Parslow and a friend, William Van Fleet, procured a charter to build the first railroad through north central Polk County, the ambitiously named Jacksonville, Tampa, and Key West Railroad, which ran between Kissimmee and Tampa. President Cleveland is said to have fished in the lake here when he came to Florida for recreation.

LAKE BUENA VISTA. *Orange County.* With Bay Lake, this is one of the twin cities that serve the municipal needs of Disney World. For a while Lake Buena Vista was called the City of Reedy Creek. There also is a Buena Vista community in Osceola County and a Reedy Creek in Polk County.

LAKE BUTLER. *Union County.* Named for Col. Robert Butler, who received the surrender of East Florida from the Spaniards on July 10, 1821. A 420-acre lake named Lake Butler is here, and the community possibly took its name from the lake when the first settlement occurred in the 1840s. Continuous religious services have been held since 1844 on the site of the Mount Zion Primitive Baptist Church. This community became the county seat of Union County in 1921.

LAKE CITY. *Columbia County.* Named in 1858 by an act of the legislature. The name, selected by Mrs. James M. Baker, wife of an early Lake City attorney, refers to the myriad lakes that surround the city. Earlier, the town had been named Alligator, after an Indian chief, Halpatter Tustenugee, "alligator warrior." Alligator Lake, near the city, was named for the same chief. It may have been the site of the Indian town Uriutina. When the legislature was asked to change the name from Alligator to Lake City, a puckish House member moved to amend by substituting Crocodile for Lake. Fortunately for the Lake City boosters, the amendment failed. This is the county seat of Columbia County.

LAKE CLARKE SHORES. *Palm Beach County.* Named by the developer for the lake on which it fronts. The lake took its name from the Clarke family of Pittsburgh, Pa., which once had a fishing lodge on the lake.

LAKE COMO. *Putnam County.* The settlement was begun in 1871 by

E. C. Post and others and named Woodland. The change of name to
Lake Como occurred in 1877, perhaps because someone was reminded
of the Italian lake.

LAKE FERN. *Hillsborough County.* A luxuriant growth of wild ferns
by the lake probably suggested the name for both the lake and the
settlement, the latter of which is said to date from 1914.

LAKE HAMILTON. *Polk County.* Origin of the name of the lake on
which the town is situated, and from which it takes its own name, is
obscure; it seems formerly to have been spelled "Hambleton," ruling
out the obvious Alexander. The town was established in 1913. The
lake itself has a shoreline of 35 miles; there are seven smaller lakes
within the townsite. The town is called "The Top of Florida."

LAKE HARBOR. *Palm Beach County.* Named for its location on Lake
Okeechobee where the Miami drainage canal leaves the lake. Originally
named Ritta in 1912, an example of how man proposes but Washington sometimes disposes. When the Okeechobee Fruitlands Company
began to build a hotel to accommodate prospective land buyers that
the company was bringing into the area, a post office was needed. The
community settled on the name Rita, which was understood to mean
"small" and "lovely." However, "when the community sent in an
application for the establishment of a post office, a careless clerk in
Washington, D.C., put an extra 't' in the name and made it Ritta"
(Newhouse, 1932). The misspelled name lasted until 1931 when the
community was renamed Lake Harbor because of its location on Lake
Okeechobee.

LAKE HELEN. *Volusia County.* Both the town and the lake were
named by Henry DeLand for his daughter. The town was incorporated
in 1891. *See also* DeLand.

LAKELAND. *Polk County.* So named because of the nineteen lakes
within the city limits. The name was adopted at a mass meeting of
citizens on December 15, 1883, having been selected by a committee
consisting of P. R. McCrary, E. R. Trammell, and Dr. J. L. Derieux.
Abraham G. Munn, a wealthy manufacturer from Louisville, Ky.,
moved here in 1881 and is credited with founding the town; with S.
A. Hartwell he formed the Lakeland Improvement Company. The
town was incorporated on January 1, 1885.

LAKE MAITLAND. *Orange County. See* Maitland.

LAKE MARY. *Seminole County.* Founded in the 1880s and named for
the adjacent lake, which, in turn, was named for the wife of Maj.
William Randolph, father-in-law of Will Wallace Harney, an Orlando
poet.

LAKE MONROE. *Seminole County.* Named for the lake, whose name
honor James Monroe, fifth president of the United States. During
President Monroe's administration the United States acquired Florida.

The community originally was named Ahern, but the name likely was changed to take advantage of the geographic location.

LAKE PARK. *Palm Beach County.* A town here was laid out in the 1920s by Harry S. Kelsey, who called it Kelsey City. After his death, residents decided to rename the town, and since it lay along the shores of Lake Worth it was called Lake Park.

LAKE PLACID. *Highlands County.* A name transplanted intact from upper New York State, when the Lake Placid Club, famous site of winter sports, chose this site for its semitropical branch. The club had been founded by Melvil Dewey, inventor of the widely adopted system of library classification and the widely neglected system of simplified spelling (hence the missing le from his first name). The Florida site was chosen for its beauty and climate. Earlier, the community had been called Lake Stearns; it was founded in 1924 through a citrus development enterprise begun by A. H. DeVane, E. E. Stewart, and Ernest Morrow.

LAKE WALES. *Polk County.* *Century in the Sun,* the centennial history of Polk County, gives a new but logical version for the selection of the name of this city and its adjacent lake. The land around the present city was surveyed in 1879 by Sidney Irving Wailes, who changed the name of a principal lake, Watts Lake, to Lake Wailes. It is easy to understand how Wailes would have given way to Wales by 1915, when the post office was established. This is the site of the Singing Tower, a memorial to Edward W. Bok, who came to the United States from the Netherlands and became the famous publisher of *The Ladies' Homes Journal.* He died at his home in Lake Wales in 1930.

LAKE WORTH. *Palm Beach County.* A town called Hypoluxo by the Indians existed here as early as 1870. Later its named was changed to Lucerne, but, when it was incorporated in 1913, it was named after the nearby lake, which bears the name of Brig. Gen. William Jenkins Worth. His strategy brought the Second Seminole War to a conclusion, and he went on to win distinction in the Mexican War.

LAMONT. *Jefferson County.* McRory and Barrows (1935) trace the story of Lamont from the period when the stagecoach between St. Augustine and Tallahassee made a daily stop to change horses. Mail was left at Sam Beazley's store. Later, when trains replaced the stagecoaches, the mail went to McCain's store, and the settlement was known locally both as McCains Store and Lick Skillet. A candidate for the legislature suggested that neither name conveyed an image of the beauty of the tree-shaded village and urged adoption instead of Lamont, for Daniel Scott Lamont, secretary of war during the second administration of President Cleveland. Lamont recently had visited Florida and, being favorably remembered, his name was adopted.

LAND O'LAKES. *Pasco County.* Known for years as Ehren, the community changed its named in 1950 to capitalize on the promotional value of the numerous lakes in this area.

LANTANA. *Palm Beach County.* Named for the profusion of lantana blooming in the vicinity. N. B. Latham, a pioneer in the area, opened a store here early in this century. The town was incorporated in 1921.

LARGO. *Pinellas County.* Named for Lake Largo nearby. The lake itself was named by an associate of Hamilton Disston, the Philadelphia saw manufacturer whose acquisition of 4,000,000 acres from the state in 1881 included a tract in this vicinity. His associate, Mr. Livingstone, preferred *Largo,* Spanish for "long" or "big," to the more commonplace Big Lake by which the lake had been known. Old-timers say the community once nearly was called Luluville, in honor of the daughter of a pioneer settler, Gideon Blitch.

LAUDERDALE-BY-THE-SEA and **LAUDERDALE LAKES CITY.** *Broward County.* Two neighboring communities of Fort Lauderdale that wanted identification with the big city but independence of government. *See* Fort Lauderdale.

LAUDERHILL. *Broward County.* In 1959 envisioned as Fort Lauderdale's sister city. Officials of All-State Properties, Inc., the community's developers, and Mayor Harold Wolk held many meetings trying to select a name for the city-to-be. Mayor Wolk, a World War II artillery officer, found himself singing the caisson song, "over hill, over dale, we will hit the dusty trail . . . ." Eventually someone thought of Lauderhill to go with Lauderdale.

LAUREL HILL. *Okaloosa County.* During the Civil War, several boys who were not old enough to enlist in the Confederate Army but who formed a unit of the Home Guards met here where three laurel trees grew at the top of a hill for target shooting, drill, and other military practice. The town that grew up was named for the hill and its trees.

LAWTEY. *Bradford County.* Established in 1877 by a colony of twenty people from Chicago, Ill. The leader of the group was Col. V. J. Shipman, who had a son-in-law, William Lawtey, after whom the town was named.

LAZY LAKE. *Broward County.* Charles H. Lindfors acquired the land for a development in 1946 and named it Lazy Lake when a friend remarked that it looked "so lazy and peaceful." It was incorporated in 1953.

LEBANON. *Levy County.* Motorists on U.S. 19 and U.S. 98 along the west coast may be aware of Lebanon Station, but there also was a Lebanon settlement nearby. The first post office was opened at Lebanon in 1889. The name perhaps was suggested by a growth of cedar trees, which in turn suggests the cedars of Lebanon.

LECANTO. *Citrus County.* A post office has been here since 1883, but tradition says a man named Dr. Morton first settled here in 1862. Perhaps he selected the name, which combines the French *le*, "the," and the Italian *canto*, for "singing," in recognition of the numerous song birds of the area (Federal Writers Project, unpublished, 1939).

LEE County. The forty-first county established May 13, 1887. Named for Gen. Robert E. Lee. *See* Hendry.

LEE. *Madison County.* Named for Gen. Robert E. Lee, apparently by a settler, John Haven. This community was settled in the 1880s by Phillip Newland, who operated a store here.

LEESBURG. *Lake County.* Established in 1853 by Calvin and Evander Lee but unnamed until Calvin Lee went north several years later to order some goods. He realized that there was no town name to which the purchases could be consigned. He thought up Leesburg on the spur of the moment and it stuck.

LEIGH READ. *Almost a county.* A political duel and its chain of violent deaths from Tallahassee to Texas resulted in the flawed naming of a county. Leigh Read, a Tennessean, had been a member of the Florida Legislative Council and speaker of the House of Representatives. In the Indian campaigns, he was wounded, he was nicknamed "hero of the Withlacoochee Blockhouse" for his leadership of a relief column, and he was appointed brigadier general by President Jackson. Ironically, he was a signer of the 1839 constitution, which prohibited duels. Read's antagonist, Augustus Alston, challenged Read more than once. Finally Read, a Democrat, responded that if he must fight he would take on Alston, whom he described as the "bulldog" of the Whigs. Read killed Alston, but Alston's family refused to accept his death on December 12, 1839 as the chance duelers took. Alston's sister is said to have had a slug from his body molded into a bullet and sent as a symbol of revenge to Alston's brother, Willis. Read was once shot, then he was stabbed on another occasion before his luck finally ran out on April 27, 1841, when he was trapped in a shotgun ambush. Willis Alston, convicted of the murder, escaped from jail and fled to Texas, where a physician originally from Tallahassee denounced him as a fugitive. The physician was then murdered, and his friends, in turn, lynched Alston. The legislature in 1842 passed a bill changing the name of Mosquito County to Leigh Read County, but a clerk kept the act from reaching the governor for his consideration during the constitutional period. There is an 1842 map showing Leigh Read County, including the present counties of Orange, Volusia, and Lake, but the name never was to be.

LEISURE CITY. *Dade County.* Frank Vellenti, Sr., and Thomas E. Palmer headed the Florida Sun Deck Homes Company, which started this subdivision in 1952. They wanted to attract retired people and thus chose the name Leisure City.

LEMON CITY. *Dade County.* Known first as Motto in the 1880s, the separate community of Lemon City on Biscayne Bay was swallowed up by Miami in 1925. Lemon City gained its name from a grove of lemon trees planted by Samuel Filer.

LEON County. The seventh county, established December 29, 1824. Named for Juan Ponce de León, the Spanish explorer who gave Florida its name. *See also* Florida.

LEVY County. The twenty-sixth county, established March 10, 1845. Named for David Levy Yulee, whose career and background are as Nixon Smiley once said in the *Miami Herald,* "almost too improbable for fiction." Yulee's father, Moses, was born in a Moroccan harem. Moses' mother, Rachel Levy, was the beautiful daughter of a Jewish physician living in England. She was on an English ship bound for the West Indies when captured by Barbary pirates. As a young virgin, Rachel was a prize for the slave market in Fez, where she was bought for Jacoub ben Youli, grand vizier to the sultan of Morocco. A revolution enabled Rachel and her small son Moses to escape to Gibraltar. In time Moses took his mother and a sister to St. Thomas in the Virgin Islands. Moses married Hannah Abendanone; in 1811 she gave birth to a son named David. When David was nine he was sent to school in Virginia and his parents moved to Florida, settling near Micanopy. Nixon Smiley observes that David was as sharp and personable as his father, and he progressed rapidly. He became a member of Florida's first constitutional convention in 1838-39, and in 1841 he was elected territorial delegate to the U.S. Congress. After Florida was admitted to statehood in 1845, he became the first U.S. senator. He persuaded the legislature to change his name from David Levy to David Levy Yulee. A short time afterward, he married the daughter of Gov. Charles Wickliffe of Kentucky. Yulee developed a 5,000-acre plantation called Margarita, Spanish for "pearl," on the Homosassa River. His mansion there was burned by Union troops, but his sugar mill escaped. He headed a group that developed railroads, and he fought off, almost to the end of the Civil War, the efforts of the Confederate government to take up some of his rails to make connections more useful to the war effort. Yulee was imprisoned at Fort Pulaski, Ga., after the Civil War and was accused of aiding the flight of President Jefferson Davis and the Confederate cabinet. After release by order of President Grant, Yulee lived in Washington with a married daughter and died in New York in 1886. The name of the county was not changed when he changed his name, so Yulee has a county—Levy—and a community—Yulee, in Nassau County—which bear his name.

LIBERTY County. The thirty-second county, established December 15, 1855. Named for the great objective of the people who founded and built the United States. This is also the name of communities in Glades, Liberty, and Walton counties.

LIVE OAK. *Suwannee County.* The old wagon road from the military post at Suwannee Springs to the Gulf passed a clear, deep pond here under a huge live oak tree that offered shade and an attractive campground. As the population increased, the spot became a sort of parking center for horses, mules, and vehicles; when the railroad came through, the section hands working in the vicinity would say at noon, "Let's go to the big live oak and eat." The station was named Live Oak about 1885, and the town was incorporated in 1903. It is now the county seat of Suwannee County.

LLOYD. *Jefferson County.* Named for Walter Franklin Lloyd, who came here from Flatbush, N.Y., shortly after the Civil War, bringing his livelihood, a carpenter's tool chest. He first settled at Tallahassee, then moved to what was known variously as Bailey's Mill or Number Two, the second station from Tallahassee on the Jacksonville, Pensacola, and Mobile Railroad. Lloyd opened a mercantile business and married Sallie Dry Leonard, who brought an inheritance of farmland to the marriage.

LOCHLOOSA. *Alachua County.* Named from the Choctaw *luski,* "terrapin," and *lusa,* "black," hence black terrapin (Read, 1934). Lochloosa dates from the 1860s.

LONGBOAT KEY. *Sarasota County.* A name that probably has been around since the days of the explorers. It appears on eighteenth-century maps, but its origin has been lost. A longboat is the largest boat carried by a merchant sailing vessel.

LONGWOOD. *Seminole County.* Established prior to 1885 and named by E. W. Henck for a district of his native city, Boston, Mass. Henck was instrumental in promoting construction of the South Florida Railroad from Sanford to Orlando.

LOWELL. *Marion County.* The name dates from 1888 and is said to be taken from a Massachusetts textile milling city that, in part, used Florida cotton.

LOXAHATCHEE. *Palm Beach County.* The Indian name, meaning Turtle River (Simpson, 1964), of a river and a community in Palm Beach County and of a marsh that extends from Palm Beach County into Martin County. A map made by an Army topographer in 1856 did not name the Loxahatchee River (Will, 1964). "And, incidentally," wrote Will, "that name by rights was Locha-hatchee, which means Turtle Creek, but the soldiers, of course, couldn't pronounce that gutteral 'ch' so they spelled it to suit themselves, and came up with Loxahatchee, which in the Seminole lingo, would seem to mean a lying or false river, and maybe one where somebody once told a lie." Pronounced Lox-ah-HAT-che.

LULU. *Columbia County.* Who was Lulu? Tradition says she was the sweetheart of a pioneer. In any event, she is along in years if still living because the town was renamed in 1891 from Hagen.

LUTZ. *Hillsborough County.* Changed from Stemper in 1912 to honor a railroad official, C.E. Lutz.

LYNN. *Marion County.* Along with Lowell, also in Marion County, another of the transplanted names of Massachusetts textile mill cities, probably because these mills used Florida cotton. The postal register adds an e to the end of the name, but the map by the State Department of Agriculture spells it Lynn.

LYNN HAVEN. *Bay County.* Named for its promoter, W. H. Lynn, former New Yorker and publisher of *The National Tribune* of Washington, D.C., a magazine concerned with Union veterans of the Civil War. In the early 1900s Lynn conceived the idea of settling communities in Florida primarily for Union veterans of the Civil War. Out of Lynn's promotional energies two communities developed: St. Cloud in Osceola County and Lynn Haven. Haven was coupled with Lynn's name to suggest this place was to be for rest and security. Lynn Haven was incorporated June 10, 1913. Later, the veterans of the Civil War were joined by those who had served in the armed forces of the nation during the Spanish-American War. In the panhandle of Florida, where monuments to the Confederacy may be expected, in 1920, a typical memorial was erected in Lynn Haven—typical except that the soldier on top is in the uniform of the North.

MACCLENNY. *Baker County.* Originally called Darbyville, but renamed in 1885 for its founder, H. C. Macclenny, who owned large tracts of land in the vicinity. It is the county seat of Baker County.

MacDILL AIR FORCE BASE. *Hillsborough County.* Eight miles south of Tampa at the tip of Interbay Peninsula, the base was activated on April 15, 1941, and named in honor of Col. Leslie MacDill, who was

killed in an air crash near Washington, D.C., on November 8, 1938.
MacDill, a native of Monmouth, Ill., was 48 years old.

MADEIRA BEACH. *Pinellas County.* Named for Madeira, Portugal's
wine-producing Atlantic island off Africa. The word itself means
"wood"; when discovered the island was thickly forested. A. B.
"Bert" Archibald, an early Gulf Beach developer, is credited with
adopting the name.

MADISON County. The fourteenth county, established December 26,
1827. Named for President James Madison. This county drew many of
its settlers from Virginia. Carved from Jefferson County, Madison
originally included the present counties of Taylor, Lafayette, and
Dixie. San Pedro, on the Bellamy Road about 10 miles south of the
present city of Madison, was the first county seat. The first courthouse consisted of a one-room log building with a big open fireplace
in the south end. The county had perhaps 250 inhabitants, white and
black. Carlton Smith, the Madison county historian, wrote that if
Christopher Edwards, the first sheriff, found it necessary to travel to
Oldtown, in the southeastern part of the county, he would have to go
on horseback 15 miles to Charles' Ferry, then by riverboat to Fort
Fanning, then on horseback or foot for the remaining 6 or 8 miles to
Oldtown. Justice in those days relied upon the people of the community whenever immediate action was required.

MADISON. *Madison County.* Established May 2, 1838, as the county
seat of Madison County. First called Hickstown, after the Seminole
Indian chief John Hicks; later it was known as Newton. Mail kept
arriving addressed to Madison C. H., meaning the courthouse of Madison County—which had been named after James Madison, the fourth
president of the United States. After the Civil War the C. H. was
dropped and the Madison retained for the town. A little northwest of
Madison stood the Spanish mission of Santa Helena de Machaba. The
site is on the route of De Soto and on the upper route of the Old
Spanish Trail.

MAGNOLIA. *Wakulla County.* Imagination is required for one to stand
today on the west bank of the St. Marks River, eight miles above the
confluence of the St. Marks and Wakulla rivers, and realize a town
once existed here. Peering into the greenery on either side of the river,
we can far more easily imagine Indians concealed by the underbrush
than think of sailing ships taking Magnolia's cotton to New York and
New Orleans and of a town with four warehouses, a cotton press,
three stores, a bank, a newspaper, and dwellings. But such was the
scene in 1833. Now all that remains are graves, concealed from
strangers by trees and underbrush. Gravestones recall the founding
Hamlin family of Augusta, Maine. Magnolia failed, in part, because an

obstruction in the river limited the size of ships. This encouraged the building downstream of Port Leon, which was destroyed by the gale and tidal wave of September 13, 1843. Magnolia and Port Leon—two lost towns. The magnolia, tree and flower, long has served as a symbol of the Old South. Public fondness for the magnolia is evidenced by communities other than Magnolia on the St. Marks River that have borne the name. Magnolia in Clay County also was known as Magnolia Springs. Magnolia in Hernando County became Istachatta. Magnolia Mills in Clay County became Green Cove Springs. There was a Magnolia Point in Clay County and a Magnolia Point in Brevard County, which became City Point.

MAGNOLIA SPRINGS. *Clay County.* A popular resort even before the Civil War. In later years, a large riverfront hotel had President Grover Cleveland among its guests. A story goes that the president found the spring water so much to his liking that he had bottles sent to the White House.

MAITLAND. *Orange County.* The memory of Capt. William Seton Maitland, U.S. Army, a native of New York City and a member of the famous Maitland family of Lauderdale, Scotland, is preserved in Florida in the name of a fort, a lake, and a town, not one of which he ever saw (Hanna, 1936). Captain Maitland came to Florida in 1835 as an artilleryman in the Seminole War. He never recovered from a wound suffered in the Battle of Wahoo Swamp, and drowned in the Ashley River, S.C., on August 19, 1837, after jumping from a steamer in a moment of derangement. Fort Maitland was established in November 1838. The name of Lake Fumechelgia, which in Seminole dialect meant "place of the muskmelons," was changed about the same time to Lake Maitland. Later, Lake Maitland became the name of a settlement here. The Lake was deleted from the community name in 1905.

MALABAR. *Brevard County.* One of the older places on the east coast, the settlement dates from 1875 and its post office from 1883. C. W. and E. A. Arnold of New York and George U. Damon of New Hampshire are regarded as the founding fathers. The name probably was taken from the Malabar on the coast of India which, although it suggested the wealth of the Indies, meant "bad bar" in Spanish.

MALONE. *Jackson County.* Established in 1911 and named for its developer, John W. Malone.

MANALAPAN. *Palm Beach County.* An Indian word meaning "good bread" or "good country," and given to the community in the 1950s.

MANATEE County. The thirty-first county, established January 9, 1855. Named for Florida's manatees, or sea cows, an endangered species. Manatees were once found as far north as the Carolinas and all around the Gulf of Mexico. Now they survive only in isolated pockets of Florida, with man their only natural enemy. When Columbus thought he saw mermaids in 1493, he likely had sighted manatees. Science has preserved a vestige of the mermaid legend—a nineteenth-century taxonomist gave the order the scientific name of Sirenia, from the Spanish *sirenas* or "mermaids." The common name manatee came from the Spanish *manati*. Manatee eat submerged aquatic plants. They usually stay submerged about five minutes but will surface once a minute when swimming because of their need for oxygen. The typical manatee is 10 feet long and weighs 1,000 pounds. They are both friendly and harmless. The reproduction rate of one calf for each adult female every three years expresses the reason why the manatee has been unable to cope with man through loss of feeding areas, by hunting, and through injury resulting from the propellers of power-boats.

MANDARIN. *Duval County.* Known as San Antonia when Spain possessed Florida and St. Anthony under English dominion, but changed to Monroe in honor of President Monroe when the United States acquired Florida. In 1841 the town became Mandarin, presumably because Ebenezar Eveleth, an Oriental traveler, settled here. Mandarin is a variety of Chinese orange. The place became widely known after the Civil War as the winter home of Harriet Beecher Stowe, author of *Uncle Tom's Cabin.* Mrs. Stowe and her husband, a Presbyterian minister, spent their winters in Mandarin from 1868 until 1884. She wrote while here, continuing as the main support of her family. One of her works, *Palmetto Leaves,* possibly attracted tens of thousands of persons eager to see the semitropical land of which Mrs. Stowe wrote. As the home of America's best-known writer of the era, Mandarin was a favorite pause for the passenger steamboats on the St. Johns River. There is a legend that Mrs. Stowe received a fee from steamboat owners to sit on the porch of her cottage so the curious could see her (Smiley, 1972). In any event, the river served as a barrier against too much familiarity until 1878 when a pier was built amost next door to the Stowe cottage. After that, passengers could invade the Stowe property. Smiley reports they not only plucked oranges from the trees, but grabbed Mrs. Stowe's blouses from the clotheslines. The Stowe employees were unable to prevent invaders on the property, "even when armed with brooms and sticks," so the Stowes were forced to lock themselves against the rampages of the writer's admirers. Mrs. Stowe's brother, Rev. Charles Beecher, served as Florida's superintendent of public instruction from March 18, 1871, until January 23, 1873. A memorable picture in the State's Photographic Archives shows Mrs. Stowe standing with the governor and other officials and citizens on the steps of the Capitol at Tallahassee, which a few years earlier would have been an unlikely place indeed for the woman whom President Lincoln called "the little lady who hastened the Civil War."

MANGONIA PARK. *Palm Beach County.* This town, subdivided by a lawyer named A. R. Roebuck, resurrects a name that had died. The original Mangonia, on the northwest shores of Lake Worth, was settled by a family of Kansans and named because a parson interested in horticulture started cultivating mangoes there. It was absorbed by West Palm Beach.

MANNSFIELD. *Citrus County.* An example of the kind of happening that once caused a legislator to complain in the Florida House of Representatives "the trouble with politics is politics!" However, in this instance, justice appears to have triumphed. Senator Austin Shuey Mann was a prime mover in the creation of Citrus County in 1887, but those who had prepared for Inverness becoming the county seat were startled to discover the legislature had situated the seat at Mannsfield. This was a settlement mainly of homesteaders from Tennessee, Alabama, Georgia, and other Southern states while Inverness was the center of the so-called old-timers. It took a contested election to wrest the seat from Senator Mann and Mannsfield, and today Mannsfield is gone but Inverness remains.

MARATHON. *Monroe County.* Midway on the Overseas Extension of the Florida East Coast Railroad from the mainland to Key West, Key Vaca became the food supply depot for the 3,000 to 4,000 construction workers. Tradition says that someone remarked that by the time the railroad had reached Key Vaca the task had become a marathon, or endurance contest, and the name stuck to the place.

MARCO ISLAND. *Collier County.* The northernmost of the Ten Thousand Islands of the Florida west coast. The first post office here was known as Malco, since postal authorities thought there already was a Marco in Florida. In 1895 one of the richest collections of carved and painted Indian ceremonial and utilitarian objects found in Florida was unearthed here by accident. *See also* Collier City.

MARGATE. *Broward County.* So named by Jack Marqusee, one of the principal developers of this community, because Margate contained the first syllable of his name. He liked gate because the community is a gateway to the coastal area from the western part of the county. He liked the idea, too, that there were Margates in New Jersey, England, and South Africa.

MARIANNA. *Jackson County.* Established in 1823 and named by the original owners of the site, Robert Beveridge and his wife, for their two daughters, Mary and Anna. It is the county seat of Jackson County and was the scene of the Battle of Marianna in 1864, when

Union forces were resisted by old men and boys. Marianna is the county seat of Jackson County.

MARINELAND. *Flagler County.* Site of the famous Marine Studios, where sea creatures of many kinds, kept under natural conditions, may be viewed and photographed through portholes in the walls of large pools. The town has grown up around this unique enterprise on the coastal highway just south of St. Augustine.

MARION County. The twenty-fourth county, established March 14, 1844. Named for Gen. Francis Marion, the Swamp Fox of the revolutionary war. This county drew many of its early settlers from South Carolina, the hero's native state.

MARTIN County. The sixty-fourth county, established May 30, 1925. Named for John W. Martin, governor at the time. The belief is that the promoters insured themselves against a gubernatorial veto by giving the proposed new county the name of the chief executive. Martin was three times mayor of Jacksonville and governor in 1925-29.

MARTIN. *Marion County.* Named for John Marshall Martin of Ocala, who emerged from the Civil War as colonel of the Ninth Florida Regiment. He was wounded at Richmond, Ky. After return to duty, he was elected to the Confederate Congress from Florida but, after serving a year, he declined reelection and went back to the army.

MARY ESTHER. *Okaloosa County.* Professor Newton, a Presbyterian minister and teacher who came to Florida from Pennsylvania, passed through here in a boat on his way to settle in Walton County and found it so lovely and peaceful that he decided he would like eventually to have a home here. In Walton County he established Knox Hill School, where he taught for a number of years, but true to his promise to himself he came back to this spot. One version of the name says that the two names were those of his wife and daughter; another that they were the names of his two daughters. Both could be true if one daughter had been named after her mother.

MASARYKTOWN. *Hernando County.* Named for Thomas G. Masaryk (1850-1937), first president of Czechoslovakia. This agricultural colony was founded in 1924 by Joseph Joscak, editor of a Czech newspaper in New York.

MASCOTTE. *Lake County.* Established in 1885 by J. W. Payne of Boston and named after a ship that sailed a route from Boston to St. Petersburg. The word is the French spelling of mascot, meaning a person, animal, or thing supposed to bring good luck.

MATECUMBE. *Monroe County.* The name is a corruption of the Spanish words *matar hombre,* "to kill a man." Here crews of shipwrecked sailing vessels were said to have been killed or enslaved by Indians. There are two keys by the name: Upper Matecumbe and Lower Matecumbe. In this area more than four hundred persons drowned in the great Labor Day hurricane of 1935.

MAYO. *Lafayette County.* Established in 1874 by John B. Whitfield and named after James Micajah Mayo, who had been a colonel in the Confederate Army. In charge of a survey crew working nearby, Colonel Mayo delivered a Fourth of July speech that so impressed settlers they named their community for him. Colonel Mayo was the father of Nathan Mayo, longtime Florida commissioner of agriculture, and grandfather of William T. Mayo, member of the public service commission. This is the county seat of Lafayette County.

MAYPORT. *Duval County.* The St. Johns River was called the River of May by the French in the 1560s, and their name for the river is recalled in this community. Mayport is a base for the pilots who guide ships in the river. The town is also a landing for the St. Johns River ferries, a big U.S. Navy base, and the center of a seafood industry.

McALPIN. *Suwannee County.* Named by railroad officials for Daniel M. McAlpin, who represented Suwannee County in the Florida House of Representatives during the 1870s.

McDAVID. *Escambia County.* First known as Regia, but renamed in 1883 to honor Joel McDavid, member of a family here.

McINTOSH. *Marion County.* Named for a squatter from Georgia, who made himself at home on the VanNess acreage. Meffert (1955) best relates the origin of this name. "According to the twice-told tale related by Mrs. Annette Gist Haden, the squatter set up a sugar mill on what is now known as the Belk Place. Palatka, sixty miles away, was the nearest source of provisions. On his last shopping trip, the squatter was waylaid by Indians and scalped. A companion (either a black slave or a friendly Indian) got away and warned the victim's wife, who fled with her children. Though many years gone from the scene by the time the township was formed, the squatter had managed to identify himself so indelibly with the area that it was henceforth known by his name—McIntosh."

MECCA. *Pinellas* and *Seminole counties.* Mecca, a place reached after a pilgrimage, seemed just the right name for these communities in Pinellas and Seminole counties—at least that was the thought of E. T. Woodruff, who persuaded a railroad in 1912 to establish a stop in Seminole County for his farm products.

MEDLEY. *Dade County.* Named for Sylvester Medley, who settled here in 1905 and farmed until his death in 1950. The citizens chose his name not only to honor the man who had brought his cow up the creek 45 years before, but also because it was a pretty name.

MELBOURNE. *Brevard County.* Two accounts give slightly different dates for the founding of this town and ascribe its naming to different persons, but they agree it was named after Melbourne, Australia. One account says that C. I. Hector sailed into the harbor here in 1872, and the settlement was named after his former Australian home. Although Hector himself preferred the name of Park Ridge after the Illinois home of a local girl he evidently admired, she sought to return the compliments, and in a drawing of straws, she won. Another account says the town was founded in 1878 by Thomas Mason, a London schoolteacher, and that the name was given later by John Hector Cornwaith, a former resident of the other Melbourne. A number of satellite communities have grown up in the vicinity of Melbourne, and some of these have incorporated Melbourne in their names.

MELROSE. *Putnam* and *Alachua counties.* Straddling the line separating Putnam and Alachua counties, about half-way between Palatka and Gainesville, stands a small and quiet village with the highly conventional name of Melrose. Not many of those who pass through it or see its name on a map would know that it once bustled and thrived as a resort center, or that it once proudly went by the name of Shakerag. The activity that brought this community to birth and gave it its first and most poetic name was pony racing. Pony owners from miles in every direction brought their racers here on Sunday afternoons, for a fine track had been built. But the owners did not want the starter to waste perfectly good bullets; they gave him a large white cloth to wave to get the ponies off. Hence Shakerag. In 1882 a Scottish resident, thinking Shakerag was a bit crude and yearning for the poetry of his homeland, renamed the community Melrose. Seven years later two Canadian ladies came to Melrose, decided it had a future, and invested their money in the building of a 125-room wooden hotel. Three years later both of the original investors had died and the structure had become the property of C. P. Huffman. How profitably Huffman operated the hotel for the next decade and a half is not recorded, but in 1908 a man named George C. Looney rented the building for use as a military college. He was from Georgia and had had a similar school there. This one he named Phi Sigma College. He enrolled 180 students and put them into glamorous uniforms, but 18 months later the building burned to the ground and the light of learning went out. Shakerag certainly got off to a good start when they shook that rag.

MERRITT ISLAND. *Brevard County.* Once called Stony Point, but in documents as early as 1808 it is referred to as Merritt's Island, or Marratt's Island. The name may have come from Capt. Pedro Marratt, a surveyor for the Spanish government in East Florida. There was also a Mr. Merritt who had planted crops there before 1823.

MEXICO BEACH. *Bay County.* Named by two developers, Gordon U. Parker of Blountstown and W. T. McGowin, Sr., of Panama City, in 1948 for its proximity to the Gulf of Mexico.

MIAMI. *Dade County.* Deriviation of the name Miami is a mystery that has engaged the attention of many authorities in this field. The commonly accepted story is that it is an Indian word meaning "sweet water." That was the meaning understood by founding fathers, however wrong they may have been linguistically. Some wanted to name the new city Flagler in honor of Henry M. Flagler. Miami is not a Seminole word, phonetically, and no words have been found in the Seminole language meaning sweet water that sound like it. Another version translates it as "big water," which is said to refer to Lake Okeechobee, of which the present Miami River was once an arm. The Chippewas, a group of Algonquin Indians, have a word *Miami* in their language that means "people who live on a point," and these Indians lived on a peninsula. Their word is the origin of the name of Miami, Ohio, and the *Miami Herald*'s John Pennekamp says research indicates Indian trade routes could have brought the Chippewa word into Florida. Numerous speculations involve various Indian dialects as well as the Spanish language: In Choctaw the word means "it is so wide," referring to Lake Okeechobee; in Spanish it means "place of complete contentment." Still another version quotes an Indian chieftain as having said to an Indian maid, "You are beautiful," to which she replied, "My, am I?" None is authoritative, but all afford some pleasurable conjecture. Fort Dallas, established by the Army in January 1838, occupied a strategic place near the merging of the Miami River and Biscayne Bay. The fort was abandoned in June 1858. Remnants of the fort have been moved to a park upstream but still near the river. Today's Miami was chartered in 1896 with the coming of the Florida East Coast Railway. A number of satellite cities use Miami in their names. Miami is the county seat of Dade County.

MIAMI BEACH. *Dade County.* Much of the first part of Miami Beach to be reclaimed from mangrove swamp and Biscayne Bay was known as Alton Beach. Carl G. Fisher, the developer, took that name from a passing railway freight car marked Chicago & Alton Railroad (Redford, 1970). Fortunately that same whimsy did not prevail when the three developing companies put their territories together in a new city they called Miami Beach. It was agreed that Fisher's friend, James Whitcomb Riley, a Hoosier poet, would plant a tree symbolic of how the developers hoped their town should grow and flourish. The tree, now lost to history, was planted on what was to become Lincoln Road, and Riley recited:

> *We plant this tree*
> *Beside the sea*
> *In trust, that it yet may wave*
> *Through shower and shade*
> *In sunny hours*
> *For other eyes as glad as ours.*

The developers were ambivalent in their feeling toward the older city across Biscayne Bay. Although tied to Miami in many ways, the boosters of Miami Beach desired separate identification. When Julius Fleischmann, of the yeast family, dropped dead during a polo game, Steve Hannegan, the city's first publicist, telegraphed the news services in New York of Fleischmann's passing, then added, "Don't forget the Miami *Beach* dateline!"

MICANOPY. *Alachua County.* Named for Mikanope, chief of the Seminole Indians at the beginning of the Seminole War of 1835. The name itself signifies chief of chiefs. He was the leader of the Indians who perpetrated the Dade Massacre, December 28, 1835. Earlier that year, Dr. Payne, a Virginian, established a settlement here, and in 1837 the government established a military post here. Near this site once stood the Spanish Mission of Santa Ana. White colonists reached the area in 1817 to settle on a land grant of 290,000 acres owned by Don Fernando de la Maza Arredondo of Cuba. According to folklore, the name, pronounced Mik-an-O-pay, remembers a slow-paying Irish merchant—Micky-no-pay. Still another twist on the name is that a trader told an Indian creditor, "Me can no pay." Micanopy once was the seat of one of the two institutions of higher learning in Florida in the 1850s; they were 30 miles apart and had similar names: East Florida Seminary at Micanopy, a Methodist Episcopal school, and East Florida State Seminary at Ocala.

MICCO. *Brevard County.* Settled in 1884. Believed named after a Seminole known simply as Chief since the Seminole-Creek word for leader was *miko.*

MICCOSUKEE. *Leon County.* A community in Leon County, one of the oldest in mid-Florida, whose post office was established in 1831. This is also the name of a large lake in neighboring Jefferson County and of a famous road in Tallahassee, once the country lane that led to the community but now a bustling city thoroughfare. Simpson (1956) concludes the name derives from *nikasuki,* "hog eaters," from an Indian tribe whose principal village was in the vicinity of today's Tallahassee.

MIDDLEBURG. *Clay County.* Formerly spelled Middleburgh and first known as Carey's Ford. This community was a hub in the early nineteenth century, with ships traveling Black Creek to and from the St. Johns River and with overland routes from here both to Tallahassee and to the peninsula. Thus, it was in the middle of trade, but whether that had anything to do with the name is not known. Because of the deep-water port on the river and of the land routes, this location was important during the Seminole War, 1835-42. Fort Heilmann was constructed here.

MIDWAY. *Gadsden County.* Half-way between Tallahassee and Quincy and so named because travelers would say "we're midway" here on a journey between the two communities. A post office was opened in 1859.

MILES CITY. *Collier County.* Named in the 1920s for Miles Collier, youngest of the three sons of Barron Gift Collier. Miles Collier died in 1957 at West Palm Beach of bulbar polio. *See* Collier.

MILTON. *Santa Rosa County.* Formerly known by the eloquent names of Scratch Ankle and Hard Scrabble. Established as a trading post about 1825. As pioneer hardships gave way to modern culture, the poetic names gave way to more respectable ones. Just which Milton was honored by the final name is in dispute. Some say it is a contraction of an earlier Milltown; others that it was Milton Amos, a pioneer and ancestor of the present Amos family; still others say that it was John Milton—not the English poet but the Civil War governor of Florida. Milton is the county seat of Santa Rosa County. *See also* Scratch Ankle.

MIMS. *Brevard County.* An old community, its post office dating back to 1886, probably bearing a family name.

MINNEOLA. *Lake County.* An unnamed settlement was established here in 1870 by William A. Smith. In 1882 George W. Hull, a Canadian by birth, came here from Duluth, Minn.; he surveyed and mapped the town and, at the instigation of his wife, named it Minneola, a name found in several states and a Dakota Indian word meaning "many waters." The name was also applied by the Hulls to the lake here. Minneola was originally in Sumter County, until the county boundary was moved.

MIRAMAR. *Broward County.* The first mayor, James Gordon, borrowed the name at incorporation in 1955 from the community in Cuba named Miramar, "see the sea."

MONROE County. The sixth county, established July 3, 1823. Named for James Monroe, fifth president of the United States. His administration has become known as the Era of Good Feeling. Among other achievements of his eight years as president was obtaining the Floridas from Spain.

MONTE VISTA. *Lake County.* Spanish for "forest view," the name was bestowed in 1905 by Capt. R. D. Milholland when he erected a log house on Lake Crescent. The house became the site of the post office that had formerly been on Lake Nellie. The name was suggested by the Thlauhatka Hills, which can be seen from here.

MONTICELLO. *Jefferson County.* Named for the historic Virginia home of Thomas Jefferson. The post office here received the name in 1827. Near here stood the Spanish mission of La Concepcion de Ayabuli. This is the county seat of Jefferson County.

MONTVERDE. *Lake County.* Established in 1885 and incorporated in

1924. The name, assumed to be from Spanish for "green hill," referred originally to the hills of citrus groves near the site, although this area is now a grape-growing region.

MOORE HAVEN. *Glades County.* Named in 1916 for its founder, James A. Moore. It is the county seat of Glades County.

MOSQUITO. *Once a county.* Many places in Florida are named for the promotional value of a pleasant name. Mosquito County, however, was stuck with just the reverse. There were some 700 settlers, excluding Indians, in the huge territory embraced by Mosquito County at the time of its creation by the Territorial Council on December 29, 1824, and apparently those people had not been consulted about the name. The county, taken from St. Johns, embraced virtually all peninsular Florida, being 190 miles long and 60 miles broad. New Smyrna was designated the county seat in 1835, so the county probably was without a seat for about 10 years. Even then, the county records remained at St. Augustine until 1843. The county was given the name by which the Spanish had known the coast. Mosquito Inlet was named by the Spanish prior to 1573, and the land thereabouts was called Los Mosquitos. Although the name meant "gnat," certainly what the Spanish had in mind by mosquito was the insect that plagued the saltwater marshes of the coasts until comparatively recently. Now the marshes are drained and sprayed to control this pest. Even with the abundant mosquitoes, settlers cultivated the coastal area in the period prior to the Seminole wars. Many settlements were destroyed or abandoned in the hit and run guerrilla warfare that finally forced the Indians into the Everglades. An effort to change the name of Mosquito to Leigh Read *(which see)* in 1842 was aborted, but finally on January 30, 1845, Mosquito disappeared from the map when the Territorial Council approved the substitution of Orange. Meanwhile, another county, St. Lucie, had been carved from Mosquito; so, the old county had fewer people, approximately 175, than when it was created.

MOULTRIE. *St. Johns County.* Named for John Moultrie, lieutenant governor of Florida during the English occupation, 1763-83, who lived nearby in a stone mansion on his plantation, Belle Vista. He joined other English settlers in going to the Bahamas when Florida was returned to Spain.

MOUNT CARRIE. *Columbia County.* A post office was here from 1878 until 1885, and now a rest stop on U.S. 90 between Lake City and Jacksonville, but the name is a double mystery—why Mount in this flatland and why Carrie?

MOUNT DORA. *Lake County.* First known as Royellou, from the names of the three children—Roy, Ella, and Louis—of Mr. and Mrs. R. L. Remain, who were among the pioneer residents establishing the community in the 1880s. The post office and others had difficulty with the manufactured name. The post office spelled the name Royallen, Royallien, and Royalieu. The State Department of Agriculture spelled it Royalview. Perhaps it was a relief to nearly all but the offspring of Tremains when the name was changed on February 12, 1883, to Mount Dora. During a sectional survey in 1848, the U.S. surveyors ran their lines through this region, and Mrs. James A. (Dorra Ann) Drawdy offered them camping hospitality. In appreciation they named the lake here Lake Dora, and the town was later renamed after the lake. The town plat later was surveyed by a party that included John W. Weeks, afterward secretary of war in the cabinet of President Calvin Coolidge. Long afterward Weeks recalled Mount Dora as "a beautiful town, I laid it out." The two stories occasionally are merged, but apparently there were two survey teams, one that gave the name Dora to the lake and another, of which Secretary Weeks was a member, that platted the town of the same name. Mount refers to the elevation; the community is on a plateau 266 feet above sea level.

MOUNT PLEASANT. *Gadsden County.* Occupying a high ridge in this hilly region of Florida, the view here is pleasant indeed, as some early settler doubtlessly felt. Mount Pleasant is a pre-Civil War community.

MULBERRY. *Polk County.* There are four large phosphate plants in the immediate vicinity of this town, and at a point convenient to all four there stood a large mulberry tree. Freight for one of the plants was frequently marked "put off at the big mulberry tree," and, when a regular railroad agency was set up about 1889, it was named Mulberry.

MUNSON. *Santa Rosa County.* Named in 1913 for a lumber company manager, Capt. Charles Munson.

MYAKKA CITY. *Manatee County.* Variously spelled Myakka, Mayaca, Mayaco, Miakka, and Miaco and applied to communities, a lake, and a river in Manatee, Sarasota, and Martin counties, of obscure Indian meaning. Myakka City adopted the changed spelling to distinguish the new community from old Miakka (McDuffee, 1961).

NALCREST. *Polk County.* A retirement community for postmen sponsored by the National Association of Letter Carriers (NACL + rest). A bronze statue in the town square stood for a quarter-century in front of the William Penn Post Office Annex in Philadelphia. Nixon Smiley related the statue's travels in the *Miami Herald*. The statue is of Richard F. Quinn, a "thick-set, broad-shouldered and sawed-off Irishman with a Grover Cleveland mustache," letter pouch hanging from one shoulder and a raft of letters in his left hand. Quinn was immortalized in bronze because he was one of the organizers of the NALC and its first president, from 1881 until 1895. When the Philadelphia post office was rebuilt, Quinn's statue disappeared. In 1942 William C. Doherty, then president of the letter carriers, went searching and eventually found Quinn, crated and on his back in an attic of the new post office. Doherty had Quinn placed in the NACL's building in Philadelphia until 1963 when he was crated again and shipped to Nalcrest with the establishment of the retirement community.

NAPLES. *Collier County.* A beautiful resort town on the Gulf coast named for another beautiful city, Naples in Italy.

NARANJA. *Dade County.* Established in 1905 by M. L. Albury. When the post office department rejected the suggested name of Silver Palm because of another Silver Palm, the residents agreed on Naranja, Spanish for "orange," because of the many groves nearby.

NARCOOSEE. *Osceola County.* Derived from the Creek *nokose,* "bear." Among the first settlers in the mid-1880s were three groups from England: retired professional and military men, who came to Florida because of the climate and their limited incomes; a younger category of people, including sons of well-to-do families who had been sent abroad for various reasons and were supported by remittances; and workers, some employed as servants by the other groups. All expected to find comfortable living and cash for their cultivation of oranges.

NASSAU County. The tenth county, established December 29, 1824. Named for the Nassau River and Nassau Sound which, in part, separate Nassau and Duval counties. The river and the sound here and elsewhere in the United States and the capital of the Bahamas were named for the Duchy of Nassau, a former state in the western part of Germany whose seat was Wiesbaden. The line of William the Silent and his descendants, the princes of Orange-Nassau, became extinct when King William III of England died in 1702. The name was brought to Florida during the English occupation of 1763-83.

NATURAL BRIDGE. *Leon County.* Florida has a number of natural bridges where streams either go underground or emerge. Arch Creek in Miami is one. But the place best known is Natural Bridge, five miles east of Woodville in Leon County. Here on March 6, 1865, cadets from the West Florida Seminary (now Florida State University) joined Confederate regulars and home guards to halt the advance of Union forces seeking primarily to cut off St. Marks and Newport and maybe Tallahassee. In the battle at the Natural Bridge, Union losses were 8 dead, 105 wounded, and 35 missing. The Confederates had 3 men killed and at least 30 wounded. The people in the Tallahassee area were jubilant over their victory; "They had saved the capital, and indeed, at the end of the war it was the only Confederate capital east of the Mississippi River that had not been captured" (Dodd, 1959).

NAVARRE. *Santa Rosa County.* Named by the French wife of an army colonel who came here in the 1900s. The ancient kingdom of Navarre was a buffer state between France and Spain. Now Navarre is a province of Spain. Pamplona, its capital, is famous for the yearly running of the bulls. At Florida's Navarre a 2,640-foot bridge across Santa Rosa Sound links Santa Rosa Island and the mainland.

NEPTUNE BEACH. *Duval County.* One of a group of seaside communities about 18 miles southeast of Jacksonville which takes its name from that of the King of the Sea. *See* Atlantic Beach.

NEW BERLIN. *Duval County.* This name has survived the anti-German feeling of two World Wars. New Berlin's post office opened in December, 1875, but a Dr. von Balson, otherwise unidentified, is said to have bestowed the name on the community in the 1860s.

NEWBERRY. *Alachua County.* Named for Newberry, S.C. The town sprang up after phosphate deposits were discovered here about 1890.

NEWPORT. *Wakulla County.* Founded in October 1843, the fifth and last town started on the St. Marks River while Florida was a territory. Newport was just that, a new port reestablishing storm-ravaged Port Leon on another site (Cash, 1944). The port was intended to draw shipments of cotton, tobacco, lumber, naval stores, and furs from the Tallahassee Railroad. Newport became the seat of Wakulla County on February 1, 1844; by the end of 1843, it probably had a newspaper, a drugstore, and 1,500 inhabitants. The town began to decline by 1860 because St. Marks nearby kept the railroad and was five miles nearer to the sea. Among Newport's residents was the Reverend Charles Beecher, brother of Harriet Beecher Stowe and state superintendent of public instruction from March 18, 1871, to January 23, 1873.

NEW PORT RICHEY. *Pasco County.* Named for Old Port Richey, which had been located about a mile north of here and settled by A. M. Richey, merchant and postmaster.

NEW RIVER. *Bradford County.* Perpetuates the original name of the county. *See* New River County.

NEW RIVER. *Once a county.* The thirty-sixth county, established December 21, 1858, being created with Suwannee County in a division of Columbia County. Named from the river of the same name. The name of the county was changed December 6, 1861, to Bradford, in honor of Capt. Richard Bradford, the first Florida officer killed in the Civil War.

NEW SMYRNA BEACH. *Volusia County*. In 1767 Dr. Andrew Turnbull, under the English Occupation Act, obtained several thousand acres of land from the British crown and established a colony of Greeks and Minorcans on this site. He named the place for Smyrna, his wife's former home in Asia Minor. The location is said to have been occupied for a period of nine months by Menendez in 1565, after which his group abandoned it for St. Augustine. Near here stood the Spanish mission of Atocuimi. Seven miles south is Turtle Mound, said to be the only large Indian shell heap to survive to the present day with relatively little damage.

NICEVILLE. *Okaloosa County*. Formerly called Boggy Bayou. A group of citizens, including B. P. Edge, the postmaster, B. H. Sutton, George Parrish, S. S. Spence, John Allen, and G. B. Anchors, met and submitted a list of names to the Post Office Department. Portsmouth, the name preferred by the group, was rejected by the postal authorities because of its similarity to Portland, which was only 21 miles east. The name Niceville, suggested by Mr. Edge, the postmaster, was assigned.

NOCATEE. *De Soto County*. Euphony may have dictated the choice; the Seminole Indian word *nakiti* means "what is it?"

NOKOMIS. *Sarasota County*. A name doubtless inspired by Longfellow's poem, *Hiawatha*. This Ojibway Indian word means "grandmother."

NOMA. *Holmes County*. Named for the Noma Mill Company. Noma could be pronounced No Ma, but the town had two "pa's" in Drew Morris and Ira Hutchinson, who together operated a sawmill here at the turn of the twentieth century. Who or what was Noma remains unanswered.

NORTH PORT. *Sarasota County*. Unlike many Florida communities who have added Lake or Beach to their original name, North Port Charlotte's voters in 1974 lopped off Charlotte. Their reason was a closer identification with Sarasota County than with Charlotte County and its Port Charlotte. They were not deterred by the fact that a few canals are the city's only claim to being a port.

NORUM. *Washington County*. It has been said, perhaps in jest, that this name designated a dry community, where alcohol was not sold, but there must be some other explanation, yet unfound. The community had a post office from 1908 to 1921.

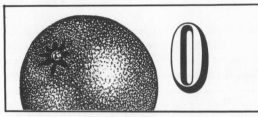

OAK HILL. *Volusia County.* Established about 1866 and named for an oak tree that grew on a shell mound near the home of J. D. Mitchell, the first settler.

OAKLAND. *Orange County.* Established in 1884 by settlers from South Carolina. Its name refers to the live-oak trees in the vicinity. It became a busy and thriving site of sawmills, sugar mills and cotton gins. In 1889 it became a junction for the Orange Belt Railway and Florida Midland Railroad: hotels, stores, and blocks of workmen's shanties sprang up with the establishment of large railroad shops. When the Florida Midland Railroad went bankrupt, the shops were removed, and later a disastrous fire swept the business district. Today Oakland's livelihood comes from the raising of citrus fruit and winter vegetables.

OAKLAND PARK. *Broward County.* So named in 1923 by men in the Oakland Development Company because of the large oak trees on the banks of the river. The name was later changed to Floranada and then in 1929 back to Oakland Park.

O'BRIEN. *Suwannee County.* Named in 1884 to honor an official of the Savannah, Florida and Western Railroad. Once known as Dod's Hole from a sink on the homestead of John F. White.

OCALA. *Marion County.* The literal meaning of this Indian word is heavily clouded, perhaps beyond discovery. Ocali was the name of an ancient Timucuan province through which De Soto almost certainly passed in 1539. The word later was used by the Indians to refer to the whole area of middle Florida, and there was at least one Timucuan chief who bore the name. During the Seminole War, Fort King, the principal fort in the state, stood on the present site of this town. The name was changed to Ocala in 1846, presumably by someone familiar with the history of the Indians and the Spanish in Florida. Some of the literal meanings that have been suggested for the name are "water margin," "lay on the fire," "kingdom," "fertile soil," "abundant," "green," "fair land," and "big hammock"—as wide a choice as any hobbyist of name origins could ask for. Read (1934) flatly states: "Ocala cannot be translated." Ocala is the county seat of Marion County.

OCEAN POND. *Baker County.* For a state with a boundary of several hundred miles on the Atlantic, ocean appears in relatively few place names—Ocean Breeze in Martin County, Ocean City in Okaloosa, Ocean Ridge in Palm Beach, and Oceanway in Duval—but the best known of all the Oceans is far from the Atlantic. It is Ocean Pond, a 1,700-acre lake in Baker County near the place where the major engagement of the Civil War in Florida was fought. Better known as the Battle of Olustee, the clash on February 20, 1864 resulted in Confederate casualties of 93 killed, 847 wounded, and 6 missing. Union losses were so great—203 killed, 1,152 wounded, and 506 missing—that in Union camps the battle was spoken of as the second Dade Massacre. For the remainder of the Civil War, Union forces in Florida were confined to Jacksonville, St. Augustine, and Fernandina.

OCEAN RIDGE. *Palm Beach County.* Originally the land east and west of the inland waterway here was named Boynton. In 1931 the property owners east of the inland waterway separated from Boynton, setting up their own government and taking the name Boynton Beach. About 1937 some of the residents desired to give up the name Boynton altogether. Several names were discussed, and the one chosen was Ocean Ridge. It was derived from the high coastal ridge at Boynton upon which a hotel stood until 1925. Several homes were built on the ridge by people who had earlier stayed at the hotel.

OCEANWAY. *Duval County.* The developer of this community, S. E. Gillespie, said in 1928, "We will call it Oceanway because it is on the way to the ocean."

OCHOPEE. *Collier County.* In 1974 the Associated Press was intrigued by Ochopee's 7-foot-by-8-foot post office, distributing nationally a feature article describing this as about the smallest in the United States. "When loads of mail arrive at the Ochopee post office in the middle of the Everglades, carrier Gerri Bates has to stay outside and sort it in the sunshine. That is because inside there is barely enough room for Postmistress Evelyn Shealy to turn around." Ochopee gained separate postal status in 1932. In Miccosukee-Seminole this word means "field" or "farm." Originally pronounced O-CHO-pee, now as O-CHOP-ee.

OCOEE. *Orange County.* Platted and named in 1885 by R. B. F. Roper for a small town in Polk County, Tenn., from which Roper's wife had come. It is a Cherokee Indian word that has been anglicized. Originally spelled *uwagahi*, it means "apricot vine place." Here Capt. B. M. Sims pioneered in the budding of wild orange trees. He started the first commercial citrus nursery in the United States, supplied many of the old groves in Florida with their first trees, and shipped many young trees to California. For several years Ocoee was known as Starke Lake for Dr. J. D. Starke who had a camp on the lake here.

OJUS. *Dade County.* Named in 1897 by Albert Fitch (Simpson, 1956). Fitch told an Indian that he hoped to raise many pineapples and asked what he should name the place. The Indian suggested *ojus,* "much, abundant, or plenty."

OKAHUMPKA. *Lake County.* Name of a lake in Sumter County and of a community in Lake County freely translated as Hitchita *oki,* "water," and Creek *hamken,* "one," or single lake. An Indian town was once where the modern community now stands. The present community was founded in 1880 by Rev. Edmund Snyder of Germantown, Penn. "Okahumpka is the English for the Indian word *Okeehumpkee,* meaning Deep Waters because of a spring of unknown depths that lies near the town of Old Okahumpka. This spring, whose depths have never been sounded, was named Bugg Spring because a man of that name was drowned there. Old Okahumpka was on Lake Dunham and was the last landing place of the steamboats coming up the Ocklawaha" (Kennedy, 1929).

OKALOOSA County. The fifty-second county, established June 13, 1915. The word is Choctaw *oka,* "water," and *lusa,* "black" (Read, 1934). Thus, the name probably referred to the Blackwater River in the same county. The county was taken from Santa Rosa and Walton counties.

OKEECHOBEE County. The fifty-fourth county, established May 8, 1917. The name means "big water," and is derived from two Hitchiti Indian words, *oki,* "water" and *chobi,* "big." The word Miami is thought to have the same meaning in another Indian dialect and to apply to the same body of water. *See also* Miami.

OKEECHOBEE. *Okeechobee County.* First called Tantie, after Tantie Huckabee, a red-headed schoolteacher from Carolina who had come to spread learning in this area. Early in the second decade of the twentieth century the Florida East Coast Railroad took over the settlement and laid out a model town that was then named for Lake Okeechobee. The town is the county seat.

OKEECHOBEE, LAKE. The second largest freshwater lake, of 700 square miles, entirely within one state. Alaska has the largest, of 1,033 square miles. Lake Okeechobee is the fourth largest natural lake entirely within the United States, Lake Michigan, which touches Wisconsin, Illinois, Indiana, and Michigan, being the largest, with 22,400 square miles. Lake Okeechobee is a remnant of a shallow sea, known as the Pamlico Sea, which once occupied what is now the Everglades-Lake Okeechobee basin. This basin formed when the Florida plateau emerged from the Atlantic Ocean as a result of movement of the earth's crust. Although large in area, Lake Okeechobee is shallow and probably contains less than 2 cubic miles of water. According to

Simpson (1956), the lake appeared as Mayaimi on the Solis de Meras map of 1565-67, Macaco on the Searcy map of 1828, and Wethlacco on the Poinsett map of 1838. "The spelling on the Poinsett map, *We Thlacco* is from the Creek *We,* 'water,' and *Thalka,* 'big,' and its present name is from Hitchitai *Oki,* 'water,' *Chubi,* 'big.' The entire synonymy apparently resolves itself into an expression of its size."

OKEELANTA. *Palm Beach County.* Situated on the North New River Canal, about six miles from Lake Okeechobee. The name was coined from the names of the lake and of the Atlantic Ocean. Newhouse (1932) relates how land development companies, as an inducement to settlement, gave a town lot to each purchaser of farmland in the Everglades. One of those purchasers was Laura V. McCullough of Washington, D.C., and she proposed that this townsite be known as Okeelanta (Clarke, 1949). The first Okeelanta was settled in 1913, but another, platted in 1915 by Dr. Thomas E. Will, a developer, emerged as New Okeelanta about a mile south of the first and ultimately this second town dropped the New.

OKLAWAHA. *Marion County.* A corruption of the Creek *ak-lowahe,* "muddy." This is the name of a tributary of the St. Johns River, of a town in Marion County, of the lake (but spelled Ocklawaha) formed by the Rodman Reservoir of the Cross-State Barge Canal, and of a creek in Gadsden County. For a river only 79 miles long, the Oklawaha has achieved much notice as a result of the efforts of naturalists to preserve the river from the digging of the cross-state canal. The Rodman Reservoir was named for a small community that was on the site. A congressional resolution gave the name Lake Ocklawaha to the body of water formed by the reservoir.

OLDSMAR. *Pinellas County.* Established in 1907 by the Reolds Farm Company, headed by R. E. Olds, Michigan automobile manufacturer. In 1925, to gain identification value during the land boom, the name was changed to Tampa Shores, but the old name was restored in 1937.

OLD TOWN. *Dixie County.* Inhabited by the Upper Creeks, Old Town, often called Suwannee Old Town, was one of the largest Indian villages in northern Florida. Old Town was captured by Gen. Andrew Jackson on a punitive expedition in April 1818. Among those trapped was Robert Chrystie Armbrister, a former British officer suspected by Jackson of fomenting Indians to warfare in Spanish territory. Jackson had Armbrister shot. Another Britisher, Alexander Arbuthnot, captured at St. Marks, was hanged by Jackson for the same reason. When the Indians were pushed out during the Seminole wars, the Americans took over Old Town. There has been a post office there since 1857.

O'LENO. *Columbia County.* Now a state park, but the name is a contraction of Old Leno. Once there was a town here known as Keno for the gambling game of the same name. To improve the reputation of the place, the name was changed to Leno. Bypassed by the railroad, Leno gradually went downhill until, by 1890, Old Leno was a ghost town.

OLGA. *Lee County.* A Norwegian sea captain with a long red beard, Peter Nelson came up the Caloosahatchee River in the early 1880s. There were stories that he was an offshoot of the Norwegian royal family—that he was, in fact, a prince. He fell in love with the Caloosahatchee and in 1883 founded two waterside towns, Olga and Alva. Miss Margaret Verdier Jones, niece of the first schoolteacher upriver, is quoted as saying Olga was named by Captain Nelson for a Russian princess then in the news (Fritz, 1963). Olga was an overnight stop for cattlemen in the nineteenth century as they drove herds from the ranges of the interior to ports on the coast, mainly for shipment to Cuba.

OLIVE BRANCH. *Osceola County.* A community beginning in 1894, but with its period of greatest activity between 1904 and 1910. The town was established by the religious group known as Shakers, the United Society of Believers in Christ's Second Appearing. Olive Branch was 1 of some 20 Shaker communities in the United States. The Florida communal establishment hewed to the Shaker maxim "Hands to work and hearts to God." There was farming, cattle raising, commercial fishing, and timbering. The quality of their pineapples earned a gold medal at the Jamestown Exposition in 1907 (Anderson, 1959).

OLUSTEE. *Baker County.* Corrupted from the Seminole-Creek *oklasti,* "blackfish" (Read, 1934). Here Union and Confederate troops fought the major engagement in Florida of the Civil War. *See also* Ocean Pond.

ONA. *Hardee County.* Named for a daughter of the Whiddon family, among the original settlers in 1897.

ONECO. *Manatee County.* An Indian name, but did it come from Oneka, oldest son of Uncas, a Mohican sachem? Or, did it come from Onaka, the fortune-teller and Seminole chief? Sources differ. The community dates from 1889.

OPA-LOCKA. *Dade County.* A Seminole Indian name referring to a hammock nearby. The word is made up of *opilwa,* "swamp" and *lako,* "big." That may have been a short form of *Opatishawaukalocka,* which roughly means "hammock in the big swamp." The community was born in the 1920s land boom by the combined efforts of Glenn H. Curtiss, pioneer of the aviation industry, and James H. Bright. These two men also originated Hialeah and Miami Springs on the doorstep of Miami. Curtiss is credited with having selected the name

Opa-locka, because the original buildings with their minarets and domes were reminiscent of a city from the *Arabian Nights.*

ORANGE County. The eleventh county, established December 29, 1824, under the name Mosquito. Renamed on January 30, 1845, for the many orange groves in the vicinity. *See* Mosquito.

ORANGE CITY. *Volusia County.* Established in 1876 by Dr. Seth French and a number of others from Wisconsin. By 1880 there were 175 citrus groves blooming on about 1,000 acres of land, and, when the town was incorporated in 1882, a name was chosen to reflect that fruitfulness. Prior to that change the community had been known simply as Wisconsin Settlement.

ORANGE PARK. *Clay County.* Founded in 1876 and during the 1880s the center of considerable wealth. Named for the orange groves that flourished here during that period. Previously the community had been known as Laurel Grove, the name of the old Kingsley plantation.

ORLANDO. *Orange County.* Several legends elbow one another in an effort to explain the origin of the name of this lovely central Florida city. One says that Judge James G. Speer, who came here from South Carolina in 1854 and became a state senator, took the name from that of a character in Shakespeare's *As You Like It,* and this version is supported by the fact that the city has a Rosalind Street. Another account says that a certain Mr. Orlando was leading an ox caravan to Tampa when he was seized by colic (now appendicitis) at this spot, died, and was buried where he fell; later passersby were said to have remarked, "There lies Orlando." What has become the official version concerns Orlando Reeves, who was on sentinel duty for a camping party while his companions slept. An Indian stealthily approached in the guise of a rolling log; Orlando saw him for what he was and fired his gun, waking the other campers and saving their lives, but not before the Indian had launched an arrow that killed Orlando. In 1939 students of Cherokee Junior High School at their own expense erected a tablet in Eola Park which says:

> *Orlando Reeves*
> *In whose honor our city*
> *Orlando was named*
> *Killed in this vicinity by*
> *Indians September, 1835*
> *"How sleep the brave who sink to rest*
> *"By all their country's wishes blest!"*
> —William Collins

Wherever and by whomever the name was chosen, the community was earlier known as Jernigan, after Aaron Jernigan, who came from Georgia and settled here in 1842. The first post office was opened in 1850, and the name was changed to Orlando in 1857. The city is the county seat of Orange County and has 30 lakes within its limits.

ORLOVISTA. *Orange County.* A combination of Orlando with the Spanish *vista,* "view" or "scene."

ORMOND BEACH. *Volusia County.* A group came here in 1873 from New Britain, Conn., where its members had been associated with the Corbin Lock Co. They included Daniel Wilson, George Millard, and Lucius Summers. At first they called the Florida community after their old hometown. Later settlers wanted a name more closely associated with local history, and Ormond was chosen on April 22, 1880. Strickland (1963) tells a story about the change of name that is reminiscent of the "Dr. Livingston, I presume?" meeting of Stanley and Livingston in Africa. A New Britain settler, John Anderson, was recovering from fever in 1880 when he heard a knock on the door of his log cabin. A distinguished-appearing stranger extended his hand and said, "My name is Ormond." He was James Ormond III, third in a line of Ormonds identified with this area. Captain James Ormond I settled Damietta, a 2,000-acre plantation on a Spanish land grant. He was killed about 1815. James Ormond II died in 1829 on the plantation, and his grave, which still may be seen near Ormond Beach, bears the legend, "An Honest Man." Anderson joined in proposing Ormond as a substitute for New Britain.

ORTONA. *Glades County.* An Italian established a subdivision here in the 1920s and gave it a name, understood to mean "garden spot," which he believed would appeal to fellow countrymen. Little remains.

OSCEOLA County. The fortieth county, established May 12, 1887. Named for the famous chief of the Seminoles, Osceola, who was imprisoned by Gen. Thomas S. Jesup after having been captured under a flag of truce. Osceola was first locked up at Fort Marion (Castillo de San Marcos) in St. Augustine; but, when some Indians escaped from there, he and other prisoners were transferred to Fort Moultrie at Charleston, S.C. Osceola died there on January 30, 1838. Weakened by chronic malaria and quinsy, he lost the will to live in captivity. "Had he not been captured under a flag of truce and sent away to die in prison, he might have died as ignominiously as many of his brethren. As it is his place as the most romantic if not the most heroic figure in the annals of the war seems secure" (Tebeau, 1971). Twenty years after the incident the criticism still was so great that Jesup found himself trying to explain his actions. Osceola was born on the Tallapoosa River, in Creek country, about 1803. Osceola is derived from the Creek *asi-yahola,* "black drink cry." The Creeks and later the Seminoles prepared a ceremonial black drink from the leaves of the yaupon. Research indicates Osceola was a half-breed: part Creek Indian, part Scotch. A Seminole leader of present days was quoted as saying that for the Seminoles, Osceola is a George Washington or an Abraham Lincoln, because of his unquenchable determination to keep the Seminoles free and to retain possession of the Indian lands (Hartley, 1974). Credit for naming the county belongs to State Senator J. Milton Bryan, who represented Orange County when Osceola was split away (Moore-Willson, 1935). The senator lived near Kissimmee, seat of Osceola. His daughter, Mrs. C. A. Carson, said: "When my father came home from Tallahassee there was a great celebration; every one in town [Kissimmee] turned out to meet him at the train and they carried him on their shoulders in celebration of the new county."

OSCEOLA PARK. *Broward County.* Named after the Seminole Indian chief. *See also* Osceola County.

OSLO. *Indian River County.* Supposedly transplanted from Oslo, the capital of Norway, a belief supported by the fact that Oslo's neighboring community on the Florida coast is Viking.

OSPREY. *Sarasota County.* An old community, said to date from John Webb's settlement in 1867, with the name of the hawklike bird found here.

OSTEEN. *Volusia County.* Known first as Saulsville for George Sauls, whose home was there in the 1850s, the name was changed in the 1880s to honor a pioneer cattleman, H. E. Osteen.

OTTER CREEK. There are Otter Creeks in Bay, Levy, Lafayette, and Wakulla counties, and an Otter Island in Sarasota Bay off Manatee County, all named for the abundance of otters at some time. There also is a community known as Otter Creek in Levy County, taking its name from the stream.

OVIEDO. *Seminole County.* A settlement was begun in about 1869, and in 1879 a post office was established. A name was sought that would not duplicate any other in the United States, and Andrew Aulin, one of the early settlers, selected the name of the capital of the Spanish province of Asturias, largely because of its euphonious sound. The Spanish pronunciation of Ove-yay-do, however, has long since been altered by Floridians to O-vee-do.

OXFORD. *Sumter County.* First named Sandspur, but in 1879 a group of town officials met to decide on a new name. W. J. Borden, later a state senator, submitted the name of Oxford. He thought it appropriate since there were several Oxfords in the United States. There is another story that the town got its name because during rainy seasons there was a pond on the road south of town where ox teams pulling heavy log carts would get stuck. Thus, Ox-ford.

OZONA. *Pinellas County.* First known as Yellow Bluff, after being settled by Walton Whitehurt in 1870 under the Homestead Act. The name was changed in 1878 to Bay St. Joseph and then in 1889 to Ozona. The story goes that Yellow Bluff was discarded because of the unpopularity then of any name suggestive of yellow fever. Two physicians, Whitford and Richardson, are said to have suggested Ozona because of the invigorating gulf breezes.

PACE. *Santa Rosa County.* Named in 1909 for a prominent lumberman, James G. Pace, Sr.

PAHOKEE. *Palm Beach County.* Incorporated in 1922 and named from a Hitchiti Indian word meaning "grass water," a term applied by the Indians to the Everglades. On Taylor's map of 1839 the name of the Everglades is given as Pay-ha-o-kee.

PALATKA. *Putnam County.* Established in 1821 as a trading post on the St. Johns River and said to have been known variously in its earliest years as Buena Vista, Gray's Place, Bush Post, and Fort Shannon. Its current name derives from a Seminole Indian word, *pilotaikita*, meaning "ferry," "ford," or "crossing." The Indians had long regarded it as an important place on the river; they held canoe races at this point. The first contraction of the Indian word used as the town's name was spelled Pilatka, but postal authorities complained that this spelling was too easily confused with Picolata, farther down the river, so the i was changed to an a. The settlement was burned in 1836 during the Seminole War. In 1838 the Army established Fort Shannon to serve as a garrison, supply depot, and hospital for the forts in the peninsula. Among the officers stationed here were Winfield Scott, Zachary Taylor, and William T. Sherman. During the Civil War, the community was occupied by Union troops. In the post-Civil War period, Palatka, because of its location on the St. Johns River, became one of the state's leading tourist centers. Palatka is the county seat of Putnam County.

PALM BEACH County. The forty-seventh county, established April 30, 1909. Named, quite logically, for the profusion of coconut palm trees on the Atlantic Ocean beach.

PALM BEACH. *Palm Beach County.* Named for the numerous palm trees bordering the beach. This fashionable resort, on an island between Lake Worth and the Atlantic Ocean, first gained its reputation for luxury and pleasure-seeking about 1890.

PALMETTO. *Manatee County.* Named for the abundant growth of small palms here by Samuel Sparks Lamb of Clarke County, Miss., who bought land here in 1868 and moved his wife and their six children to a new home (Abel, 1969). Palmetto was incorporated June 15, 1893.

PANACEA. *Wakulla County.* Named for the ancient Greek goddess of healing because of the springs here which were thought a possible remedy for ills.

PANAMA CITY. *Bay County.* George W. West, the original developer of this town, gave it this name because the town is on a direct line between Chicago and Panama City, Canal Zone. Panama City, Florida, is on St. Andrews Bay, and is the county seat of Bay County. Panama City Beach is a satellite community in Bay County.

PARADISE. *Alachua County.* This earthly paradise was settled soon after the Civil War. The name expressed the hopes of those first inhabitants. There are other Paradises in Florida: Paradise Park in St. Lucie County, Paradise Point in Citrus County, and Paradise Key in the Everglades National Park.

PARKER. *Bay County.* Named for W. H. Parker, who settled here many years ago. Other communities named Parker are in Escambia and Hillsborough counties, and probably derived their names from residents.

PARKLAND. *Broward County.* Founded by Bruce B. Blount, this agricultural community of less than 400 acres prides itself upon its resemblance to a park, hence the name.

PASCO County. The forty-fifth county, established June 2, 1887. Named for Samuel Pasco of Monticello, speaker of the Florida House of Representatives at the time the county was created. Pasco was elected by the legislature on May 19, 1887, as U.S. senator and served until December 4, 1899.

PASS-A-GRILLE BEACH. *Pinellas County.* This resort on Long Key, an island in the Gulf of Mexico, was incorporated in 1911, but maps dated as early as 1841 show the original form of the name as Passe-aux-Grilleurs. This name referred to the practice of fishermen, who, using this point to cross over the island, would stop here to cook or grill their meals. In time, and through usage by Americans unfamiliar with the French language, the name became shortened to its present form.

PAXTON. *Walton County.* A longtime resident, Mrs. G. W. Pittman, reports a sawmill was erected here around 1910 and one of the investors in the area was John Paxton of Chicago.

PEACE RIVER. A river of two names: Peace and Peas. Old maps and accounts called the river R de la paz, Sur el rio de la Paz, and F. Pacis. The oldest name that we know, therefore, was Peace. But the Seminoles called the stream Peas, from cowpeas or black-eyed peas, which grew in wild profusion along the river. On the Taylor military map of 1839 the stream was shown as Talakchopko or Pease Cr. The Summerlin family, whose cattle in this area numbered in the thousands in the years between the Civil War and the Spanish-American War, knew the river as Peas. Modern usage, however, has been Peace.

PEMBROKE. *Polk County.* Named in 1910 from an adjacent Pembroke mine of a phosphate company.

PEMBROKE PINES. *Broward County.* Named by Walter Seth Kipnis, who suggested at an incorporation committee meeting in 1960 that the development take the name Pembroke Pines. Pembroke came from the main access road, Pembroke Road, and Pines from the large number of those trees in the area. Pembroke Pines has spawned adjacent Pembroke Park.

PENIEL. *Putnam County.* Genesis 32:30, "And Jacob called the name of the place Peniel: for I have seen God face to face, and my life is preserved."

PENNEY FARMS. *Clay County.* This unusual community, eight miles west of Green Cove Springs, was founded by J. C. Penney, chain store magnate, for retired ministers, gospel workers, and their wives, in memory of his father, a minister, and his mother.

PENNSUCO. *Dade County.* Established about 1919 by the Pennsylvania Sugar Company, for sugarcane plantations. The name is formed from the first letters of the three words of the company name.

PENSACOLA. *Escambia County.* The Smithsonian Institution indicates that the most likely derivation of this name is from that of a tribe called Pansfalaya, "long-haired people." Other authorities suggest derivation from the same meaning but by a different route: Choctaw, *pansi,* "hair," and *okla,* "people." Note that the o and the k in the latter word have been transposed. Still another meaning from the Choctaw is "bread people." In the Pansfalaya or Pensacola tribe, the men as well as the women wore their hair long. Whatever the source of its name, the city was established by the Spaniard D'Ariola in 1698. Here was arranged the transfer of the Floridas to the United States by Spain, and here was located the first capital of the Territory of West Florida. Pensacola Bay has been given a variety of names: it was called Achuse by Ranjel, Achusi by Garcilaso, and Ochus by Elvas in 1540; in 1559 it was called Polonza by De Luna; and in 1693 Admiral Pez named it the *Bay of Santa Maria de Galve* (Simpson, 1956). Across Pensacola Bay from today's city, Tristan de Luna established a colony in 1559. This settlement, abandoned two years later after a storm wrecked de Luna's fleet, antedated by six years the founding of St. Augustine. The colony also antedated by five years the French at Fort Caroline. It is likely that the first Catholic white child born in the United States was born in de Luna's colony. Pensacola is the county seat of Escambia County.

PERRINE. *Dade County.* Named for Dr. Henry Perrine, a physician and botanist to whom the government granted a township of land here in 1838 for him to use in conducting experiments with tropical plants. This township ran from today's Coconut Grove, in suburban Miami, through the present community of Perrine to the Cutler Ridge area. He was killed by Indians on Indian Key, where he was living with his family. Dr. Perrine, a native of New York City, had decided while serving in 1827-38 as U.S. consul at Campeachy (now Campeche), Mexico, to devote the remainder of his life to introducing useful tropical plants into semitropical Florida. Offspring of some of the plants he brought to the vicinity of Biscayne Bay are to be found there now, in particular a species of vanilla (Walker, 1926). The site now called Perrine was chosen by the Model Land Company when the railroad opened. The Perrine heirs retained some of the grant, but as Perrine Palmer, Jr., former Miami mayor and great-great-great-grandson of Dr. Perrine, ruefully recalled in 1973, "all of the land was taken for taxes during the depression."

PERRY. *Taylor County.* Research by Mrs. Ed Brannon has established that Perry was in existence in 1859 and the name therefore probably commemorates Governor Madison Starke Perry (1857-61) rather than Governor Edward A. Perry (1885-89), as previously assumed. The town is the county seat of Taylor County.

PETERS. *Dade County.* A community in the farmlands of south Dade County named for Tom Peters, who was known as the "Tomato King" in the early 1900s.

PICNIC. *Hillsborough County.* A community on Hurrah Creek where S.R. 39 and S.R. 674 intersect. Nixon Smiley (1971) talked with Mrs. Bernice West, who was born "right here at Picnic" too long ago to remember. She did recall that when she was a child the settlement was known as Hurrah. People used to meet for a picnic or a fish fry at a "pretty prairie" where Hurrah Creek runs into the Alafia River. In time, the name of the settlement was changed from Hurrah to Picnic. "Hurrah isn't for what you think it is," Mrs. West told Smiley. "It's an Indian word, and it means something different from the word hurrah that most people think of." Mrs. West lived in a little cottage on a narrow, rutted road that was shaded by moss-laden live oaks. "That's the original road—the main road through Picnic when I was a girl," she said. "It's Picnic Road." When she was a girl, her father, traveling by wagon out along the Picnic Road, took two days to go to Tampa and two days to return.

PICOLATA. *St. Johns County.* Spanish for "broad bluff," which suggests the strategic importance of the place. Here, where the St. Johns River narrows, a natural crossing was used by Indians and later by the Spanish, who built forts on both sides of the river to protect the trail to the west in the Apalachee country around present-day Tallahassee. The English under Gen. James Oglethorpe captured this place in 1740. William Bartram, the naturalist, had an indigo plantation here in 1766. Actors in the cast of *Honeymoon* were waylaid in 1840 while en route to St. Augustine from Picolata by stagecoach. One actor was killed, and Indians wore the captured costumes for a while, an incongruous sight in the Florida wilderness.

PIERSON. *Volusia County.* Established in 1876 by Peter Pierson and his family, who gave it their own name.

PINECASTLE. *Orange County.* Will Wallace Harney, Kissimmee editor and poet of the 1880s, built a house here, some say in a large pine tree, where he ruminated and slept. He said this was his castle. The name then was applied to the community.

PINELLAS County. The forty-eighth county, established May 23, 1911, being separated from Hillsborough County across Old Tampa Bay. The peninsula that forms the larger part of the county was known to the Spaniards as Punta Punal, said to mean "point of pines," and the present name was fashioned from that. A number of its communities—Pinellas Park and Pinellas Point—have taken their name from the county.

PLACIDA. *Charlotte County.* Appears to be an Americanized form of the Spanish *placido*, "placid," for the pleasantly calm, tranquil waters of this noted fishing area. First named in 1907.

PLANTATION. *Broward County.* Most of this city is on lands that used to be known as the Frederick C. Peters plantation. Development of the city began with platting and sales of one-acre suburban sites usable for truck gardening called plantation homes. So, Plantation was selected as the name of the city when it was incorporated. Peters, whose family operated a shoe manufacturing company in St. Louis, came to Miami in 1934 and began land development. He died in 1964.

PLANT CITY. *Hillsborough County.* Settlers began moving into this area in 1842. First post office was established in 1849 at Itchepackesassa, once a Creek village whose name meant "tobacco field." An Irishman who had become postmaster coped in 1860 with the problems of spelling and pronouncing Itchepackesassa by rechristening it Cork, for his home city. In 1883 Henry Bradley Plant, of the Atlantic Coast

Line Railroad, purchased a charter to complete a cross-state railroad from Sanford to Tampa. Building southward was the Florida Railroad and Navigation Company. The intersection here of the two railroads not only determined the location but the prosperity of Plant City. Most if not all of the original east-west streets were named for men in some way connected with the Plant railroad, and Plant himself was honored when the town incorporated January 10, 1885.

PLYMOUTH. *Orange County.* Settled in the 1880s by English immigrants and first known as Penryn and then as Plymouth, both old-country names.

POINT WASHINGTON. *Walton County.* From here a view down a long stretch of Choctahatchee Bay makes this setting appropriate for a modern Eden, a mansion built in 1895 which has become a state-owned showplace. Washington derives from the county that once included the point.

POLK County. The thirty-ninth county, established February 8, 1861. Named for James Knox Polk, eleventh president of the United States (1845-49). Polk had the political distinction of twice being rejected for reelection as governor of Tennessee, the last time in 1843, a year before his election as president as the first dark horse nominee of the Democratic party. He was chosen over Henry Clay and Martin Van Buren because he demanded control of the Oregon Territory from Great Britain (the historic "54-40 or fight!") and favored annexation of Texas.

POLK CITY. *Polk County.* Established in 1922 by Isaac Van Horn and named after its county.

POMONA PARK. *Putnam County.* Named for Pomona, the Roman goddess of fruit trees, usually depicted holding fruits and a pruning knife.

POMPANO BEACH. *Broward County.* An interesting story regarding this name is that a survey party from the Florida East Coast Railroad was treated by local folks to a pompano dinner. To let future survey teams know about the delicious fish, the visitors jotted the word pompano on their charts. The persons who followed thought it was the name of the settlement. The name stuck. Another version credits Franklin Sheehan, a surveying engineer with the Model Land Company, with naming the town after the delicious fish. At any rate, Beach was added after 1940.

PONCE DE LEON. *Holmes County.* Established in 1875 and named for the Spanish explorer.

PONTE VEDRA. *St. Johns County.* Once known as Mineral City, for the ilmenite, rutile, and other heavy minerals associated with beach and dune sands. The National Lead Company wanted a Spanish-sounding name in the 1930s when the area was changed to a seaside development and accepted a New York architect's suggestion of Ponte Vedra for the city in Spain.

PORT CHARLOTTE. *Charlotte County.* Named in 1955 for the county where it is located. *See* Charlotte.

PORTLAND. *Walton County.* On Alaqua Creek near the Choctawatchee Bay, this community, its post office dating from 1884, seemed by its name to advertise its land-water location.

PORT MAYACA. *Martin County.* A variant of *mayaimi,* "big water," with Port prefixed.

PORT ORANGE. *Volusia County.* Came into being in 1867 through the energies of Dr. John Milton Hawks and two associates, James A. Fowler and George W. Dewhurst, three former Union army officers, who organized the Florida Land and Lumber Company and planned to settle a colony of blacks on public lands at Ponce de León Inlet (Strickland, 1965). Dr. Hawks, a native of New Hampshire, and his wife, also a physician, were interested in the plight of the Southern black. They were active in the Freedman's Aid Society of New York. Dr. Hawks helped organize a black regiment during the Civil War and was its surgeon. Hawks said he chose the name Port Orange because there was no other community by that name in the United States. "If a person forgot to add the state on the envelope, it would come to Florida alright (sic)," he explained. "Several times the Department at Washington addressed me at 'Orangeport' but I corrected them until finally letters came correctly addressed."

PORT RICHEY. *Pasco County.* Aaron McLaughlin Richey arrived in the early 1880s at a point of land on the Gulf of Mexico at the mouth of the Pithlachascotee River. He came to Florida after having served as a wagon master for settlers moving west from St. Joseph, Mo., across the Rocky Mountains to Sacramento, Calif. Richey concluded there was a need for public transportation in Florida, too, only this time by water. So he had a schooner built at Cedar Key. It was necessary to list a home port. Since there was no specific name for the place where it would be moored, he called it Port Richey (Bellwood, 1962). The newer and larger city of New Port Richey was established some 25 years later up the Pithlachascotee.

PORT ST. JOE. *Gulf County.* The first town established hereabouts. It was known as St. Joseph and was the scene of the convention that wrote Florida's first constitution in 1838. It was destroyed by a yellow fever epidemic and a tidal wave in 1841. The site is on St. Joseph Bay, which was named by the Spaniards for the husband of Mary, the mother of Jesus. Port St. Joe is the county seat of Gulf County.

PORT ST. LUCIE. *Martin* and *St. Lucie counties.* On the boundary between Martin and St. Lucie counties, taking its name in 1960 from the latter. This community is designed largely to attract retirees.

PORT SALERNO. *Martin County.* Named in 1959 from an older, nearby community of Salerno.

PORT SEWELL. *Martin County.* Named for a pioneer resident, Capt. Henry E. Sewell. The town has been a center for sports fishermen since the turn of the century.

PORT TAMPA. *Hillsborough County.* The port city for Tampa, located on Tampa Bay; founded in 1885 by Charles W. Prescott and Capt. James W. Fitzgerald. The community boomed when the Plant System extended its South Florida Railroad there in 1887, making Port Tampa its terminal. Port Tampa once was the headquarters of the Honduras national lottery.

PRINCETON. *Dade County.* The Model Land Company established a town here in 1904 and named it Modello. In 1905 Gaston Drake, with a group of Princeton University alumni, came to the community and named it for their alma mater.

PROVIDENCE. *Gadsden, Polk,* and *Union counties.* Florida has three communities named Providence, although the name is rare in other states. The rarity elsewhere probably resulted from "having been thought overly pious or even pretentiously so" (Stewart, 1970). A few habitation names were taken from country churches. The settlement Providence in Gadsden County preceded the creation of the county in 1823, and Providence in Union County dates from 1830.

PUNTA GORDA. *Charlotte County.* "Trabue, alias Punta Gorda" is Vernon E. Peeples's (1967) delightful account of a squabble over the community's name. Early in 1883, Isaac H. Trabue, a middle-aged attorney from Louisville, Ky., purchased a 30-acre tract on the south side of Charlotte Harbor. "Now as for naming the place . . . " Trabue (Peeples, 1967) wrote, "if we want to bring the place into notice—we must give it a name that will give it notority [sic]. I know of no name that will advertise it better than ours—will therefore name it Trabue." A squabble developed that resulted in the town being incorporated under the name Punta Gorda, explained by an anti-Trabue leader as having been "chosen almost unanimously because it was the original historical and geographical Spanish name." Trabue claimed that the teller who counted the votes and announced the Punta Gorda result was the leader of the opposition group. Trabue thereafter referred to the town he had birthed as "Trabue, alias Punta Gorda." After the election in 1888 of Benjamin Harrison, Trabue, as one of the few Republicans in this area, was asked to recommend someone to be appointed postmaster. Trabue suggested a black who had played an important political role in Florida during Reconstruction, and he was appointed. The Spanish had applied the name Punta Gorda, "wide point" or "fat point," to an arm of land jutting into

Charlotte Bay near the present city, which is the county seat of Charlotte County.

PUNTA RASSA. *Lee County.* Translated variously from the Spanish as "flat point" or "raveling point." The coastline of Sanibel Island, opposite Punta Rassa, to some observers appears ragged or raveled. Fort Delaney was established here in 1837, abandoned, then reoccupied in 1841. It was occupied again during the Civil War. Cable communications between the United States and Cuba were established at Punta Rassa in 1866, and it was here that the first news was received of the sinking of the battleship *Maine* in Havana harbor. This was a shipping point for cattle to Cuba at the turn of the century.

PUTNAM County. The twenty-eighth county, established January 13, 1849. Named for Benjamin Alexander Putnam (1801-69), lawyer, soldier, member of the Florida legislature, judge, and first president of the Florida Historical Society. Born on the Putnam plantation near Savannah, Ga., he attended Harvard, studied law privately at St. Augustine, and practiced there. In the Seminole Indian War, 1835-42, he served as major, colonel, and adjutant general. He served in both houses of the Florida legislature and as speaker of the House in 1848. By appointment of President Zachary Taylor, he was surveyor-general of Florida from May 1848 to 1854. He died at his home in Palatka on January 25, 1869.

PUTNAM HALL. *Putnam County.* Settled in 1850 by Elijah Wall and probably named for the same person as the county.

QUINCY. *Gadsden County.* Founded in 1825 when John Quincy Adams was secretary of state of the United States. Later, on February 15, 1828, Adams, as sixth president, signed a deed for the townsite of Quincy, further establishing his relationship with the community named in his honor. An act of the Legislative Council to incorporate the Town of Quincy was approved by Gov. William P. DuVal on November 19, 1828. Quincy is the county seat of Gadsden County.

RAIFORD. *Union County.* Named for a pioneer settler, Raiford has become synonymous for Florida's "big house," the state's main penitentiary and prison farm nearby.

RATTLESNAKE. *Hillsborough County.* For a number of years in the
1930s the throng of motorists crossing the Gandy Bridge between
Tampa and St. Petersburg passed a store, snake pit, and post office
called Rattlesnake, Fla. This story is told in the *Tampa Tribune,* November 30, 1958. The site at the east end of the approach to the
Gandy Bridge had been purchased by George End, a Connecticut
Yankee who came to Arcadia with his family during the boom of the
1920s. When the boom exploded, End was among the thousands of
Floridians who looked for something to make money. In time he met
Guy (Rattlesnake) Johnson of Nocatee, who confided that he had
orders for live rattlesnakes for medicinal purposes and that the area
they were living in had unlimited raw material. End decided to join in
the snake catching. His boys brought in a dead six-footer. "Well,
boys," he is quoted as having said, "we will skin him and maybe we
can sell the hide." The meat revealed by the skinning looked sufficiently inviting, so the family cooked and ate some. Ultimately, this
meal led to a business of canning rattlesnake meat and, because of
publicity that End engineered as a former newsman, to the purchase
of the Gandy site for public display of snakes and sale of canned
meat. End died from the bite of a snake that for several years "had
been very docile and gentle." James A. Clendinen, editor of the
Tampa Tribune, who turned up the story, added that when the territory containing Rattlesnake was annexed to Tampa in the 1950s "the
name of the Rattlesnake community disappeared—without any
mourning from the residents." The name, however, still appears on the
state's sectional map.

REDDICK. *Marion County.* Established in 1882 and named for its first
postmaster.

REDINGTON BEACH. *Pinellas County.* Named about 1960 for Charles
E. Redington, a developer of this area.

RED LEVEL. *Citrus County.* So named in the 1880s because the land was
level and because settlers saw a reddish tinge in the soil after plowing.

RICHMOND HEIGHTS. *Dade County.* Named for Dr. Richmond who
lived hereabouts before the turn of the century.

RIVERVIEW. *Hillsborough County.* On a stream leading into Hillsboro
Bay, and settled in the 1880s.

RIVIERA BEACH. *Palm Beach County.* Judge A. E. Heuser, an early
resident, named this town Oak Lawn, but a visitor's casual remark,
"This is the Riviera of America," brought about a change of name.

ROCKLEDGE. *Brevard County.* Established about 1875. Its name is
derived from the formation of coquina rock that crops out in ledges
along the shore. Coquina rock, from 1 to 30 feet deep, is a substratum
of the soil.

ROLLESTOWN or **ROLLSTON**. *Putnam County.* On the St. Johns River about a mile from today's San Mateo, the town was established in 1765 by Denys Rolle, English philanthropist and member of Parliament. He named it Charlotia, after Charlotte, Queen of George III. Rolle "brought a motley crew of men and women from the slums and streets of London, intending to rehabilitate these unfortunates, create a Utopia, and make Charlotia its capital. Disease, dissatisfaction, and desertion soon decreased the ranks of the colonists. Undaunted, Rolle purchased additional land until he controlled 80,000 acres; he worked his plantations with slave labor, and struggled along for several years, shipping rice, corn, beef, lumber, and naval stores. In one season he exported 1,000 gallons of orange wine. When Florida was returned to Spain in 1783, Rolle abandoned his plantation and removed with his slaves to the Bahamas" (Federal Writers Project, 1939).

ROMEO, JULIETTE. *Marion County.* Over the northwest corner of Marion County, just below where U.S. 41 enters the county on its way down from Williston to Dunnellon, you will find a little place called Romeo. You need not ask where Juliet is—she is 7.3 miles away. However, her name has inadvertently been misspelled Juliette. The story is that there were actually two Florida lovers whose families did not get along. The boy lived in what is now Romeo, the girl in what is now Juliette, and their story ended as tragically as the Veronese, though details are not to be had.

ROUND LAKE. *Jackson County.* Settled in the 1890s and named for a circular lake here.

ROYAL PALM BEACH. *Palm Beach County.* Located a few miles west of West Palm Beach and named to utilize the words Palm Beach. Similar examples are Palm Beach Shores, Palm Beach Lakes, Palm Beach Gardens, Palm Beach Isles, North Palm Beach, and, indeed, West Palm Beach. Palm Beach has magic in its name!

RUSKIN. *Hillsborough County.* Dr. George McA. Miller, a Chicago attorney and follower of John Ruskin, the English architect and critic, educator, economist, and social reformer, founded Ruskin in 1908 as a socialist community based on the teachings of Ruskin. Dr. Miller searched other states before finding on the shore of Tampa Bay the 12,000 acres he regarded as the most perfect site for his Utopia. With three Dickman brothers from Missouri, they platted in 1908 part of the land and spread the word that the town of Ruskin was ready for populating. Each new landowner became a member of the Ruskin Commongood Society; and, because Ruskin had advocated education for the working man, Dr. Miller opened Ruskin College, with emphasis on shops for weaving cloth, tanning leather, and printing books. Dr. Miller died in 1919, and with the loss of the driving force, the accidental burning of the college in 1919, and the refusal of so many of the young men to stay after their service in World War I, the socialist community withered. Now the town is better known for its "Ruskin Tomatoes," a trademark recognized nationally.

SAFETY HARBOR. *Pinellas County.* First settled by Dr. Odet Phillippi in 1823. It was first known as Espiritu Santo—"holy spirit." Later it was called Green Springs, and finally it was incorporated as Safety Harbor in 1917. The name indicates that it is a shelter for seamen and vessels.

ST. AUGUSTINE. *St. Johns County.* The oldest continuously settled city in the United States, having been founded in 1565 by Pedro Menéndez de Avilés, and named by him for St. Augustine, Bishop of Hippo, upon whose feast day, August 28, he sighted the coast. The city is situated between two saltwater rivers, the San Sebastian and the Matanzas. Its history is not only longer but perhaps richer and more colorful than that of any other in our nation. In or near St. Augustine were the missions of Nombre de Dios, San Sebastian, Nuestra Señora de la Leche, and San Diego de Salamototo. Saint Augustine is the county seat of St. Johns County.

ST. CATHERINE. *Sumter County.* Variously named: first known as Hiawatha in 1884; then the next year as Massacre, doubtlessly because the scene of the Dade Massacre was but a few miles away; and finally in 1902 as St. Catherine. The reason for the change to St. Catherine is not known, but a number of groups of German-Americans, of the Roman Catholic faith, settled in this area at the turn of the century. Nor is it known for which of the eight saints named Catherine the city was named.

ST. CLOUD. *Osceola County.* Originally the site of a sugar plantation established by the Hamilton Disston Company in 1882. In 1909 Raymond Moore of New York City succeeded in making this settlement a semiofficial residence for veterans of the Union Army. It was named for the suburb of Paris which was the location of the great palace occupied by Marie Antoinette, Napoleon, and other French sovereigns.

ST. JAMES CITY. *Lee County.* Founded on Pine Island in 1885 by a group of New Englanders who constructed buildings of spruce and white pine shipped from Maine. For a time before Flagler developed Palm Beach, St. James City was one of the most popular resorts in south Florida. Origin of name not known.

ST. JOHNS County. Paired with Escambia as one of Florida's first two counties, established July 21, 1821. Named for the St. Johns River. Five names have been applied to the river in its entirety and several others to portions of the river (Snodgrass, 1967). From Miss Snodgrass we learn that the Indians gave the river its first name, Welaka or Ylacco, two spellings with much the same pronunciation. A Spanish explorer called it Río de Corrientes, "River of Currents," in recognition of the spectacular way the currents at the river's mouth clashed with the surf. Jean Ribaut, a French explorer, entered the St. Johns on the first day of May, hence the name Riviere de Mai, "River of May." A Spaniard, Pedro Menéndez, captured France's Fort Caroline and renamed both fort and river San Mateo. About 1590 the Spanish mission San Juan del Puerto, "St. John of the Harbor," was established and ultimately gave its name, in shortened form, to the river. For a time in the mid-1700s both San Mateo and San Juan were shown on some Florida maps as two names for the one river. During the 20-year period of British ownership of Florida, 1763 to 1783, San Juan finally became St. John's and since has remained except for the dropping of the apostrophe.

ST. JOSEPH. *Gulf (then Franklin) County.* The most notable of Florida's lost towns. Named for Joseph, the husband of Mary, who was the mother of Jesus. Here Florida's first constitution was written during 1838 to 1839 in anticipation of the statehood that was to come in 1845. This seaport city was known as the richest and wickedest city in the Southeast. The Spanish and the French had built forts on this landlocked bay, but in 1822 the Americans came in throngs after the U.S. Supreme Court invalidated land titles in Apalachicola, 30 miles away. Saint Joseph was built fast and big. Wharves and warehouses, brick store and office buildings, and mansions regarded then as palatial—all were supported by a forest of spars and masts as vessels crowded the port. Then "in 1841 a ship from South America brought in yellow fever, and within a few weeks three-fourths of the town had succumbed. Panic-stricken survivors abandoned their homes and fled; ships avoided the port; hotels and business houses closed. For three years the town remained deserted. Fear of the plague was so great that only a few venturesome fishermen dared to approach the spot. In 1844 a hurricane and tidal wave swept in from the Gulf, leveling empty buildings and floating many out to sea. Devastating storms followed at intervals, and bit by bit all remains of the town were effaced" (Federal Writers Project, 1939). By 1854 the place was gone. Today the tangible reminders of St. Joseph are a cemetery and a state park with a constitution memorial and museum, both situated about a mile and a half from the landward limit of St. Joseph.

ST. LEO. *Pasco County.* Four Benedictine monks from Germany were sent in 1886 from the Belmont Abbey in North Carolina to minister to the spiritual needs of Seminole Indians and of German-Americans in the area. The monastery and subsequent college community were named for St. Leo, Leo the Great, who was Pope Leo I from 440 to 461 A.D.

ST. LUCIE County. First established as the twenty-fifth county on March 14, 1844, and recreated as the forty-sixth county on May 24, 1905. Named for St. Lucie of Syracuse. According to legend, she was born in Sicily of noble parents, made a vow of virginity, and was executed in 304 A.D. for being a Christian after having been reported to the Roman authorities by a rejected suitor. More commonly spelled Lucy, the name derives from "lux" or "light"; the saint has become associated with festivals of light and with prayers against blindness (Coulson, 1958). The original St. Lucie County was named Brevard County on January 6, 1855. The name of St. Lucie was first given in the area to a fort built by the Spanish near Cape Canaveral in 1565.

ST. LUCIE. *St. Lucie County.* First settled in 1868 and named for its county.

ST. MARKS. *Wakulla County.* First established in March 1718 by Don José Primo de Rivera, probably on the feast day of St. Mark. A wooden stockade had been erected by the Spanish in 1680. A Spanish masonry fort, San Marco de Apalache, was built here in 1759 and captured in 1799 by William Augustus Bowles and his band of Indians. The Spaniards recaptured the fort and imprisoned Bowles. The fort was taken by Gen. Andrew Jackson in 1819. Nearby was the Spanish mission of Santa Maria de Apalache. Before the Civil War the town of St. Marks was an important shipping port.

ST. PETERSBURG. *Pinellas County.* The "Sunshine City," but its name comes from that of one of the coldest great cities in the world— Russia's St. Petersburg, now Leningrad. When the Orange Belt Railway was being extended down to this part of the coast in 1887, its president was Peter Demens, a Russian by birth who had changed his own name from Dementief. Tales differ as to just why he was privileged to choose a name for this town—whether by drawing straws, flipping coins, or courtesy—but anyway he chose the name of his native city. Some of his associates objected, but they consoled themselves with the thought that the town would never amount to anything anyway. Its green benches and balmy breezes, which make it—among other things—a most pleasant haven, have caused it to be almost as famous as the arctic city of Peter the Great.

ST. TERESA. *Franklin County.* Settled in 1873, the area has been a way of life for some Tallahassee families for generations. When these families speak of "the coast," they mean the summer homes along a two-mile stretch of Apalachee Bay. The resort was named for Teresa Hopkins. Nobody remembers why or when the St. was added. In 1973, Mrs. R. B. "Miss Annie" Sensabaugh of Tallahassee reminisced about going to St. Teresa, first by horse and carriage, later by train and boat. It was a day's journey then, an hour now.

SALEM. *Taylor County.* Named for Jerusalem, which was called the "city of Salem" or the "city of Peace." Settlers hereabouts became numerous enough to justify a post office in 1878.

SALUBRITY. *Gadsden County.* Choosing place names that conjured up pleasant images is as old as American Florida, and not the product of the great land boom of the 1920s. There was, for example, Salubrity, "favorable to or promoting health." Salubrity was to be found in 1828 at the Ochlockonee River on the post road between Tallahassee and Quincy. Salubrity, or Salubria as it sometimes was spelled, passed out of postal existence in 1845.

SAM JONES OLD TOWN. *Hendry County.* The legend "Ruins of Sam Jones Old Town" appears on current highway and sectional maps. Smiley (1967) reported: "The map maker who put this site on the Florida road map was a practical joker." There is not a road within three miles, continued Smiley, "and nobody's lived here since 1861. That was the year when Sam Jones, a tough old Miccosukee veteran of the Seminole Wars, died." Smiley came here the easiest way, afoot, following then 80-year old Josie Billie across prairies and through the cypress. "But there's nothing to indicate that the place was ever a town," Smiley wrote. "The site is on an island which is covered by tall pines and a solid mass of head-high saw palmettos. If you could get through the palmettos you might kick up a pottery shred or two, but nothing more." Josie took Smiley to the spot where Sam Jones died and also to his grave, a mile beyond. A small monument, erected in 1951 by George Espenlaub of Clewiston, marks the site beneath the branches of an old live oak. The marker states: "In memory of Tuscanatofee, called Sam Jones, Valiant Seminole Leader." Smiley reports Jones also was known as Arpeika, but the palefaces knew him as "Sam Jones-be-damned." He was with Wildcat and Alligator when they and 150 other Seminoles stood off 1,000 men under Col. Zachary Taylor in the Battle of Okeechobee on Christmas Day, 1837.

SAMOSET. *Manatee County.* Established some time before 1931 and probably named for the Algonquin chief, Osamoset, whose name is said to mean he who walks over much.

SAN ANTONIO. *Pasco County.* Founded in the early 1880s by Judge Edmund F. Dunne, a former chief justice of Arizona. Family tradition says that when Dunne once lost his way in the Arizona desert while prospecting for silver, he prayed to his patron saint for rescue, vowing that he would give the name of San Antonio to a settlement he contemplated founding in Florida. The place in Florida that he finally selected had been called Clear Lake; in fulfillment of his promise he founded a settlement there and renamed it San Antonio. He later donated a 40-acre tract, on which in 1890 was built the Holy Name Academy, a Catholic girls' school.

SANDERSON. *Baker County.* Believed named for John P. Sanderson, prominent citizen of Jacksonville who represented Florida in the provisional Congress of the Confederate States. The site was used by both Union and Confederate soliders as a camp during the campaign of 1864.

SANFORD. *Seminole County.* This town grew from Fort Mellon, named for a U.S. Army officer killed in the Seminole War. The fort, established in 1837, stood about a mile east of the present city. In 1871 some 12,000 acres were purchased by Henry Sanford, a former U.S. minister to Belgium who bore an honorary generalship from the State of Minnesota, acquired during the Civil War. Sanford named the new town after himself. Sanford is the county seat of Seminole County.

SANIBEL. *Lee County.* An island and its community whose shared name is thought to combine health and beauty.

SAN MATEO. *Putnam County.* See Rollestown.

SANTA ROSA County. The twenty-first county, established February 18, 1842. Named for Santa Rosa Island, which in turn was named for St. Rosa de Viterbo, a Catholic saint. During Frederick II's campaign against Pope Gregory IX, Rose, then 12 years old, preached against submission to the emperor, resulting in the banishment of her family (Coulson, 1958).

SARASOTA County. The sixtieth county, established May 14, 1921. The origin of the name is shrouded in dispute and legend. The Spaniards are said by one version to have so named it to designate "a place for dancing," referring to the celebrations held by the Indians on or near the shore of the bay here, but no words in modern Spanish give this meaning to the name. A legend, more colorful but more obviously fabricated, ascribes the name to a beautiful daughter of De Soto, the great Spanish explorer—Sara Sota. An Indian prince is said to have allowed himself to be taken prisoner by the Spaniards so that he could be near her; when he fell sick she nursed him back to health, only to fall sick herself and die. The Indian prince and a hundred of his braves buried her beneath the waters of the bay, then chopped their canoes with their tomahawks, and sank to death themselves. Eighteenth-century maps show the name variously as Sarasote, Sarazota, and Sara Zota.

SARASOTA. *Sarasota County.* Founded on July 27, 1886, by Scotch and American settlers and named from the county. On December 23, 1885, a number of Scottish families came ashore here to settle land they had purchased for their homes in a new country. They met wilderness and hardship instead of the established town promised them. Many returned in disappointment to Scotland. The remaining colonists joined with American settlers to develop a town. Four satellite communities have developed around the modern city, all taking its name as part of their own. Sarasota is the county seat of Sarasota County.

SATELLITE BEACH. *Brevard County.* One of the communities that sprang up near the missile-launching center of Cape Canaveral and deriving its name from this activity.

SATSUMA. *Putnam County.* Named in 1886 for the satsuma oranges growing here. It also has been known as Satsuma Heights.

SCOTTSMOOR. *Brevard County.* Two Vermonters named Scott and Moore coined a Scottish-sounding name for a development in 1925 that outlasted the great land boom.

SCRATCHANKLE. *Palm Beach County.* John Tyner, Fred Reynolds, and Claude Santee settled on Lake Okeechobee around 1912. "Their location was called Tynersville, though it was better known as Scratchankle" (Will, 1964).

SCRATCH ANKLE. *Santa Rosa County.* So named because the smuggling going on here to avoid the official import-export center at Spanish Pensacola in the early 1800s, was "a lively and healthy trade . . . through Milton, often in those days spoken of as 'Scratch Ankle' since many of the surreptitious landings made here were at points where the briars came down to the water's edge." *See also* Milton.

SEA RANCH LAKES. *Broward County.* Named in the 1950s for a hotel, the Sea Ranch Hotel, a landmark across the highway from the townsite. There are two artificial lakes in the village.

SEBASTIAN. *Indian River County.* Named for St. Sebastian, a captain in the Praetorian Guard of the emperor Diocletian's palace. When Sebastian's Christian faith was discovered, Diocletian ordered him shot to death with arrows. Nursed back to health, Sebastian returned to the palace and reproached Diocletian for his persecution of Christians. Enraged, the Emperor had Sebastian cudgelled to death (Coulson,

1958). The community, established in 1882, took its name from the St. Sebastian River, named by Spanish explorers.

SEBRING. *Highlands County.* In 1912 founded and named for George Eugene Sebring, a pottery manufacturer of Sebring, Ohio. Family members scoff at the legend that he intentionally patterned the city plan after that of Heliopolis, the ancient Syrian city with its Temple of the Sun at the center and the streets radiating. It is the county seat of Highlands County.

SEFFNER. *Hillsborough County.* Because the first name, Lenna City, could become confused with Lemon City in Dade County, a change was required before a post office could be established. Named Seffner in 1884 after the first postmaster, F. P. Seffner.

SEMINOLE County. The fiftieth county, established April 25, 1913. Named for the Indian tribe. There is a tendency among non-Indians to think of Florida's Indians as Seminoles. Actually, there are two groups, the Seminoles and the Miccosukee. They are separated by language. The Miccosukees speak a dialect of the Hitchiti, once the most powerful Indian group in south Georgia. The Seminoles speak a dialect of the Creek, originating in Alabama. Simpson (1956) in tracing the development of the most recent aboriginal inhabitants of Florida says the name Seminole was applied by the Creeks to the emigrant Muskogean Indians who settled in Florida during the eighteenth and early nineteenth centuries. The Indians began to realize the completeness of the human vacuum in Florida subsequent to the extermination of the original aboriginal population in the early part of the eighteenth century. Simpson continues that as a consequence of the deserted condition of Florida, the names given to its natural features by the Timucuans, the Apalachians, and the Calusas were forgotten, unless preserved in the literature of European languages, and became supplanted by names derived from the languages of the immigrant Indians, from Creek and from Hitchiti. The derivation of the word Seminole is uncertain. Probably most authorities assume that the name is a corruption of the Creek *ishti semoli,* "wild men," an epithet applied by the Creeks to these separatists.

SENECA. *Lake County.* Large enough in the 1880s to support "a brass band of 14 pieces," but has since disappeared from the map. Seneca "was a very prosperous town before the Big Freeze, so wealthy in fact that it didn't 'consider a dollar bill anything, fives and tens were all that talked.' A settler who came after the Big Freeze was told that it was the 'wrath of Divine Providence that had wiped out the town' because of its wealth" (Kennedy, 1929). Seneca was given its name by an early settler from Seneca, N.Y.

SEVILLE. *Volusia County.* Established in 1879 and named for the ancient Spanish city, which in turn had been named Sephala, "marshy plain," by its founders the Phoenicians, a name that has been changed in time to Seville. The fertile hammocks of this region produce the small, wild, Seville orange, said to have been imported and planted by the Spaniards, but we do not know whether the town was named for the fruit or vice versa.

SEWALLS POINT. *Martin County.* Known first in the 1880s as Waveland. The name was changed in 1891 to Sewalls Point, probably for a family residing here.

SHADY GROVE. *Taylor County.* Settled in the 1860s and called Shady Grove for the old oaks. The name was changed to Luther in 1894 and then back to Shady Grove in 1909.

SHALIMAR. *Okaloosa County.* Said to have been named by one of the daughters of James E. Plew, probably after the river in Kashmir described in the popular song, "Pale Hands I Pressed." Plew, who was from Chicago, bought up the holdings of John Perrine; the land included most of Valparaiso and Niceville and all of Shalimar. Plew started a winery here just after repeal of prohibition; the grapes came from the old Bunte farm near Crestview, and the product was called Shalimar wine.

SHAMROCK. *Dixie County.* Named in the 1920s for a big lumber company whose mill was here and long a favorite pause for motorists on the Gulf coast highway.

SHARPES. *Brevard County.* From the name of settlers here in the 1890s.

SILVER SPRINGS. *Marion County.* Named from the celebrated spring, Florida's largest, whose crystal clearness inspired its name. A town has been here since 1852.

SLAUGHTER. *Pasco County.* This name could be regarded as a reminder of the Dade Massacre, which occurred 10 miles away, but actually Slaughter was the name of one of the families that settled here about 1880, primarily for turpentine farming. The area, better known now as Clay Sink, presently has some twenty families living on about 560 acres, mostly in Pasco County but some in Hernando County, and surrounded by the Withlacoochee State Forest, according to Joe Parsons, a forester. From April 13 to December 19, 1898, there was a post office for a Slaughter in Madison County. Again, this was a family name.

SNEADS. *Jackson County.* A community since the 1880s. Named for a pioneer dentist.

SOAK RUM. *Hillsborough County.* Robinson (1928) remarks upon the transition in the spelling of the names of places. "Perhaps as interesting as any is the gradual change of the name of a settlement in the southeastern part of the present Hillsborough County," writes Robinson. "It first appears about 1850 by the name Soak Rum, then Soccrum and now Socrum."

SOLANA. *Charlotte County.* Named in 1902 to honor the sun, Old Sol.

SOPCHOPPY. *Wakulla County.* From the Creek Indian *sokhe,* "twisted," and *chapke,* "long." Established in 1853, the town is on the Sopchoppy River, which is, indeed, long and twisted. A different version says Sopchoppy is Seminole-Creek for *lokchapi,* "(red) oak," a combination of *lokcha,* "acorn," and *api,* "stem" (Read, 1934). Sopchoppy has acquired the nickname "Worm Capital of Florida" because a score of families here follow an occupation that has thrived for generations in the Panhandle—grunting worms for fishermen. The worms are driven out of the ground by the weird grunting vibrations of roop iron on a stob. A roop iron is an old cut leaf spring, usually from a junked truck. "It is two feet long, three inches wide, two inches thick, the measurements selected to achieve the best vibrations. It is curled at the end for a handle. The stob is a wooden stake, 18 inches long, made of persimmon or oak for durability" (Cowan, 1973).

SORRENTO. *Lake County.* When the first settlers came about 1875, they could not agree on a name. "The settlers were enjoying the Italian novel, *Agnes of Sorrento,* at that time, and since Sorrento is a city in Italy that is noted for its oranges, that name was among those offered. It was finally decided to place them all in a hat and have a blindfolded person draw the chosen name. Sorrento was the one that was drawn" (Kennedy, 1929).

SOUTH BAY. *Palm Beach County.* Named in the 1900s for the southern arm of Lake Okeechobee, at a corner of which the town is situated.

SOUTH FLOMATON. *Escambia County.* An offshoot of Flomaton, Escambia County, Ala. The communities are separated by the Florida-Alabama boundary. Al Burt (1973) reports Flomaton was created about 1850 and first named Reuterville, after the man who built the railroad to Pensacola. Later Flomaton was called Whiting, for an early settler; then Pensacola Junction. The resultant mail confusion was settled for the moment by taking a fourth name—Floma—from the first three letters of Florida and the last two of Alabama. But the post office rejected Floma, finding it sounded too much like Florala, another border town to the east. So the townspeople decided on Flomaton.

SOUTH MIAMI. *Dade County.* Until the land boom of the 1920s, this area was called Larkin after a pioneer family whose descendants and friends still take a dim view of the change.

SOUTHPORT. *Bay County.* Established in 1893 as Anderson. The name was changed in 1907 to Southport to advertise the town as a shipping point.

SPARR. *Marion County.* The postmaster, M. S. Sparr, gave his name to the place in 1882.

SPRINGFIELD. *Bay County.* So named by the founding fathers in the 1950s because the name, popular in other states, had not been used in Florida.

STARKE. *Bradford County.* Two versions ascribe the name to two different persons. The *Bradford County Telegraph,* in a 75th anniversary edition on November 12, 1954, said: "Since the earliest residents of the little village included more people from South Carolina than any other state it is not surprising that the town was called Starke in honor of Madison Starke Perry, Governor of Florida from 1857 to 1861. Governor Perry was born in South Carolina in 1814 and his mother was a member of the prominent Starke family of that state." The other version says the town was named for Thomas Starke, also of South Carolina, who in 1854, with 50 black women slaves, purchased the land around DeLeon Springs in Volusia County. Established prior to 1867, the city is the county seat of Bradford County.

STEELE CITY. *Jackson County.* Named for A. B. Steele, builder in 1895 of the Atlanta & St. Andrews Bay Railway.

STEINHATCHEE. *Taylor County.* First a community was so named in Lafayette County in 1876 and then, when the post office for Lafayette County's Steinhatchee was discontinued in 1937, a Taylor County community took over the old name. The present Steinhatchee is on the river of the same name, which forms the boundary between Taylor and Dixie counties. From the Creek *ak,* "down," *isti,* "man," and *hatchee,* "creek," together meaning "dead man's creek." Dead Mans Bay is at the mouth of the river.

STUART. *Martin County.* Named for Samuel C. Stuart, first telegraph operator and station agent, when the Florida East Coast Railroad was built across the St. Lucie River in 1893. Originally, the townsite was known as Potsdam. Stuart is the county seat of Martin County.

SUMATRA. *Liberty County.* Established in 1908 and named from the variety of wrapper tobacco cultivated hereabouts, a variety known as Sumatra because it is similar to the tobacco grown in Sumatra, the second-largest island of the Malay Peninsula.

SUMMERFIELD. *Marion County.* An area of rich muck soil, once the bed of ancient lakes, named in 1885 to emphasize the long agricultural season.

SUMTER County. The twenty-ninth county, established January 8, 1853. Named for Gen. Thomas Sumter (1736-1832), a native of

South Carolina who was prominent in the southern campaigns of the revolutionary war. Many South Carolinians were early settlers in this area.

SUN CITY. *Hillsborough County.* Originally named Ross, but during the boom of the 1920s the name was changed to Sun City and a motion picture studio was built in the hope of enticing some of the film industry. Sun City was a relic of the boom for many years, but revival signs appeared in the 1960s.

SUNRISE. *Broward County.* This community reversed the usual order of a day, going from Sunset to Sunrise. According to Mayor John Lomelo, Jr., in 1974, the community originally was planned as a retirement area and called Sunset. The developers quickly found retirees did not like to be reminded they might be in the sunset of life; hence, the switch in 1961 to Sunrise Golf Village, the Golf emphasizing the two golf courses bordering the community. In 1971 the village was incorporated as the City of Sunrise.

SUNSHINE BEACH. *Pinellas County.* This community on Treasure Island, northwest of St. Petersburg, was formerly called Sunset Beach; but, when it was incorporated in 1937, the present name was adopted. Another portion of Treasure Island was first called Coney Island when it was platted in 1920. Because protests arose over the amusement-park associations of this name, the community adopted the name of Sunset Beach, the name abandoned by the other town.

SURFSIDE. *Dade County.* A community along the Atlantic Ocean to the north of Miami Beach, originally named as a subdivision.

SUWANNEE County. The thirty-fifth county, established December 21, 1858. One of the few counties in the United States whose name has been immortalized in song: Stephen Collins Foster wrote in "Old Folks at Home" about "Way down upon the Swanee River." The river that Foster spelled Swanee has become a world symbol of love for family and home. Etymologists disagree on the origin of Suwannee. Utley (1908) says the name comes from a Cherokee Indian word *sawani,* "echo river." Gannett (1947) agrees. Brinton (1859) suggests it may have been a corruption of the Spanish *San Juan.* He mentions a Shawnee tradition that their tribe originated on this river and claims that the name may be a corruption of Shawanese. Simpson (1956) says Suwannee seems to be identical with the name of a village in Gwinnett County, Ga., that stands on the site of a former Cherokee town called Suwani. According to Read (1834), the Cherokees claim their village is from Creek origin. If this is true, the derivation of the name is probably from the Creek *suwani,* "echo." Simpson mentions that good echoes are a feature of this stream. He continues, saying that the stream is probably the one called River of the Deer by De

Soto. During the seventeenth century, a Franciscan mission called San Juan de Guacara was located somewhere along the left bank. This name for the river persisted despite the destruction of the mission and the change of flags; an English surveyor named Romans in 1774 called the river the River St. Juan de Guacara vulge Little Sequana. Sequana appears to be an Indian attempt to pronounce San Juan.

SWEETWATER. *Dade County.* One of the popularly accepted English translations of Miami. Hence, this community to the west of Miami adopted a version of its big neighbor's name. The name also stirs desirable images in the mind.

SYCAMORE. *Gadsden County.* Randall Johnson came here in 1822, the first immigrant to settle in what today is known as the Sycamore community. Stanley (1948) tells how after Johnson built a stockade around his log home he stuck his sycamore riding switch into the damp earth inside the stockade. The switch took root and grew into a Gadsden County landmark from which a community, a church, and a post office derived the name of Sycamore.

TAFT. *Orange County.* Originally called Smithville for M. M. Smith who operated a turpentine camp here. Then Prosper Colony was started in 1909. Six thousand acres were platted for a town site—the town to be surrounded by small farms. After a long advertising campaign, a contest was conducted to name the town. The winner honored William H. Taft, twenty-seventh president of the United States.

TAINTSVILLE. *Seminole County.* The *Florida Times-Union* for December 16, 1971, reported the Seminole County Commission had sanctioned the name Taintsville for a formerly nameless community between Oviedo and Chuluota. The delegation spokesman, Theodore Peterson, was quoted as having told the commission: "We are tired of telling people that we live behind the fire tower on the road that doesn't have a name." He also said the community "tain't in Oviedo and tain't in Chuluota."

TALLAHASSEE. *Leon County.* Virtually every authority agrees that the name of the capital city of Florida is derived from a Creek Indian word meaning "old town." And an old town it is indeed, if you count the residence of the Indians and the Spaniards. The first date we know definitely is 1539, when De Soto met here with the Apalachee tribes, who controlled the fields and streams in this area. We have no way of knowing how long before that the Indians had been using this spot as a center of activity. About 1633 the Spanish mission of San Luis was established; it stood a few miles northwest of the present city of Tallahassee. The spot was chosen for the capital of Florida on March 4, 1824, while Florida was still a territory. Legend says the name and spelling were finally chosen by Octavia Walton, daughter of a territorial governor of Florida and granddaughter of a signer of the Declaration of Independence. In addition to being the capital of Florida, Tallahassee is the county seat of Leon County.

TAMARAC. *Broward County.* In 1963 named by Kenneth E. Behring, the original developer, for the tamarack, a tree of the larch family not ordinarily found in Florida. As the story goes, a tamarack tree discovered here was taken as an omen that transplanted people also would flourish. A metal sculpture of a tamarack branch has been placed in the community's country club and the representation of a branch is also shown in the city seal.

TAMIAMI TRAIL. "The Trail" opened a highway between Tampa and Miami and took its name from the first three letters of Tampa and the last four of Miami. The idea of this cross-state highway through the Everglades was ramrodded by a number of people along the route, William Stuart Hill of the *Miami Herald* being among the first in 1914. Tebeau (1957) reports "it was E. P. Dickey who formally suggested the name of 'Tamiami Trail' at this first meeting of the State Road Department. The name was such a natural that it was almost immediately accepted. The *American Eagle* (at Estero) at first objected that it sounded 'like a bunch of tin cans tied to a dog's tail and clattering over cobblestones,' and queried, 'Why not call the Jacksonville to Miami Dixie Highway "Jackiami Joypath" and the road through Arcadia to the east coast "Pair-o-Dice Loop"?' " The Tamiami Trail was officially opened on April 25, 1928, nearly 13 years after the first dirt was turned for its construction.

TAMPA. *Hillsborough County.* As with so many names of Indian origin, tracers of the name of this important Florida west coast city have a choice among three unrelated suggestions as to meaning. One is "near it" or "close to it," another is "split wood for quick fires," and the third is a source in a fifteenth-century Spanish city. The "near" presumably referred to the closeness of an Indian village to what is now Tampa Bay. The "split wood" is said to have been used because of the quantities of driftwood found along the shore. The bay was first known as Espiritu Santo or "Holy Spirit, and was entered in 1528 by Narvaez, who found the Indian village. Karl H. Grismer (1950), Tampa historian, says Hernando de Escalante Fontaneda, a Spanish lad of 13 when shipwrecked off the Florida coast in 1545, was responsible for preserving Tampa's ancient name. Friendly Indians gave Fontaneda hospitality and the opportunity to travel in the Florida peninsula for 17 years before he returned to Spain. He learned the languages of four tribes and compiled a list of 22 towns within the Caloosa territory of south Florida, "and the name 'Tanpa' led all the rest. He spelled the word with an 'n' instead of an 'm'. Contemporary writers and map makers who saw Fontaneda's *Memoir* apparently liked 'Tampa' better than 'Tanpa' and when they picked up the word and used it they gave it more euphonic spelling" (Grismer, 1950). Fontaneda did not give a meaning for the name. Dr. John R. Swanton of the Smithsonian Institution, an authority on the languages of the primitive Indians of the Southeastern United States, says there is little hope an authentic interpretation ever can be ascertained unless a Caloosa vocabulary is discovered. Present-day Tampa grew from Fort Brooke, named in the spring of 1824 for its commanding officer, Col. George Mercer Brooke. "The farm and fishing village which grew up outside the military reservation also was called Fort Brooke but eventually was known by the Indian name of Tampa" (Dunn, 1972). Settlers objected to the military name and adopted the name Tampa Bay for their first post office in 1831. It was soon decided that the Bay could be dropped. The city is the county seat of Hillsborough County.

TANGERINE. *Orange County.* Named in 1881 for the citrus fruit.

TARPON SPRINGS. *Pinellas County.* Established around 1880 by A. P. K. Safford, a former governor of Arizona. The name is said to have originated with a remark of Mrs. Ormond Boyer, who had come here with her father from South Carolina, and who, while standing on the shore of the bayou and seeing many fish leaping in the water, exclaimed, "See the tarpon spring!" For the most part, however, the fish seen splashing in the water here are mullet, not tarpon.

TASMANIA. *Glades County.* The name selected in 1916 when a new generation wanted to shed the old name, Fisheating Creek. Tasmania remains on the map although Nixon Smiley reported in 1973 that not a single relic remains. Writing in the *Miami Herald,* Smiley reported other replacement names for the community were rejected by the Post Office Department because these already were in use. "Call it Tasmania," said a retired sea captain, "I'll bet there ain't no name like that in the postal guide." So they did.

TAVARES. *Lake County.* Established around 1880 by Maj. Alexander

St. Clair Abrams and named by him for a Spanish ancestor of his. It is the county seat of Lake County.

TAVERNIER. *Monroe County.* A protected anchorage here has attracted mariners since small boats began sailing in the vicinity some two centuries ago. How the key got its name is a matter of conjecture. Earl Adams, a former newsman who in later years served as clerk of the Circuit Court at Key West, is quoted as having said an enterprising saloonkeeper had a place near the site of the modern settlement of Tavernier. To attract trade, he stuck a sign in the mangroves. It misspelled the message "tavern near," and the misspelling has been preserved. Less fanciful is the belief the name may be a corruption of the Spanish Cayo Tabona, or "Horsefly Key," given to a small island on the seaward side of Tavernier harbor (Stevenson, 1970). Commencing in the 1760s, Bahamian turtle catchers and woodcutters added wrecking to their occupations. With the original savages now gone from the Keys, the Bahamians, known also as "Conchs," would anchor in summer off Tabona to wait for sailing ships to provide a good living for the "Conchs," who rescued the shipwrecked crews and passengers and salvaged the cargoes (Brookfield and Griswold, 1949).

TAYLOR County. The thirty-fourth county, established December 23, 1856. Named for Zachary Taylor, twelfth president of the United States and commander of the U.S. Army forces in Florida during a part of the Second Seminole War.

TELOGIA. *Liberty County.* Another version of the Seminole word, *taluga,* "cow peas." Telogia dates from 1908 or perhaps earlier.

TEMPLE TERRACE. *Hillsborough County.* Named for the temple orange, whose trees bear glossy, dark-green leaves and brilliant golden fruit. These 1,500 acres of land were bought from Mrs. Potter Palmer of Chicago in 1921 by a group of Tampa financiers and laid out in groves of temple oranges.

TERRA CEIA. *Manatee County.* Spanish for "heavenly land." Hernando De Soto landed somewhere in Tampa Bay in May 1539. An U.S. commission, headed by Dr. John R. Swanton of the Smithsonian Institution, concluded De Soto landed at Shaw Point and made Terra Ceia Island his headquarters during the six weeks he remained in the vicinity. Bickel (1942) writes, "We know the Mangrove Coast Indians were sun worshipers. The fine, high temple mound at Terra Ceia Island shows the long ramp coming up from the west to the top of the pryamid where the temple, facing eastward, once stood. De Soto's soldiers destroyed it in 1539."

TEQUESTA. *Palm Beach County.* The obsolete aboriginal name for Biscayne Bay. Tekesta Indians formerly lived on its shores. The Spaniards called the entire coastal region south of Cape Canaveral the Province of Tequesta. Today's community of Tequesta was established in the mid-1960s.

THONOTASASSA. *Hillsborough County.* A lake and town named from Seminole-Creek *thlonoto,* "flint," and *sasse,* "is there," likely from the quarries in the vicinity where flint was extracted for making arrowheads and spear heads. Pronounced Tho-note-oh-SAS-sa.

TICE. *Lee County.* Early in the 1900s, Chauncey O. Tice and an uncle, former Chief Justice W. W. Tice of Kentucky, who at that time lived in Fort Myers, decided to start an orange grove. They bought acreage between the Atlantic Coast Line Railroad and the Caloosahatchee River about three miles east of Fort Myers. Later C. W. Tice bought out his uncle's interest. He built his own packinghouse, on which he one day found a sign saying "TICE." It had been put there by the railroad people, who wanted to use his packinghouse for a station. Later a new station was built nearby, and the same name continued to be used.

TITUSVILLE. *Brevard County.* Established just after the Civil War by Col. Henry T. Titus, who had been a fierce antagonist of John Brown in the struggle over Kansas which preceded the war. The locality had been known as Sand Point, but Titus, who was postmaster and something of an autocrat, changed the name to perpetuate his own. Titusville is the county seat of Brevard County.

TREASURE ISLAND. *Pinellas County.* To promote lot sales in 1913, Noel A. Mitchell floated a rumor that buried treasure was on this island. The scheme failed, but the name stuck. The community took its name from the island.

TRENTON. *Gilchrist County.* Named after Trenton, Tenn., by Ben Boyd, who, at the age of 18, ran away from home following a fistfight at a racetrack. He first settled in Lafayette County, Fla. He married a girl from near Mayo named Sarah Sapp; shortly thereafter, they moved to what is now Trenton, but then was known as Joppa. Boyd served in the Confederate Army, and sometime between 1875 and 1885, having established a sawmill at Joppa, he renamed the town after his Tennessee home. Trenton is the county seat of Gilchrist County.

TRILBY. *Pasco County.* Commenced as McLeod in 1885, changed to Macon six weeks later, then renamed Trilby in 1901. At the turn of the century many people were reading George du Maurier's novel *Trilby.* Not only was the town's name changed to Trilby, but streets were given names after the characters in the book. There was a Svengali Square and Little Billee Street.

TURKEY SCRATCH. *Jefferson County.* In the 1880s, before inhabitants became self-conscious about the names of their communities, a settlement in Jefferson County was known as Turkey Scratch. A resident of Turkey Scratch suggested to the people of Lick Skillet that another name would be more suitable for their settlement. Lick Skillet was changed to Lamont, and Turkey Scratch was renamed Panola.

TWO EGG. *Jackson County.* A sign on U.S. 90 in Jackson County delights tourists. It points the way to a place called Two Egg. The story goes that two brothers started a country store there but had not decided on a name until their first customer asked for two eggs. Another story says that a child came in, placed two eggs on the counter, and said, "Mammy says send her one egg's worth of bladder snuff and one egg's worth of ball potash."

TYNDALL AIR FORCE BASE. *Panama City.* Named on June 13, 1941, for Lt. Frank B. Tyndall, a World War I ace who was killed in line of duty near Mooresville, N.C., on July 28, 1930. Lieutenant Tyndall was born at Sewalls Point near Fort Pierce, Fla., on September 28, 1894. He entered combat with the Air Corps of the American Expeditionary Forces in 1918 and took part in the St. Mihiel and Meuse-Argonne offensives. He was credited officially with four victories over German pilots and was flight commander of his squadron.

UMATILLA. *Lake County.* An Indian word apparently imported from Oregon thought to mean "water rippling over sand." The town was established in 1862, and its first postmaster was N. J. Trowell. The name was suggested by William A. Whitcome, formerly of Cincinnati, who had been in correspondence with some people in Umatilla, Oreg., where Umatilla is also the name of a county. In Washington State it is the name of a waterfall.

UNION County. The sixty-first county, established May 20, 1921. Originally, the name of the county was to have been New River, thereby reestablishing a county name that had existed from December 21, 1858, until December 6, 1861, when New River was changed to Bradford to honor a fallen soldier (*see also* Bradford). The sponsor of the bill to change the name in 1921 amended the bill to replace New River with Union. Union County was separating from Bradford, and a reason for the name the new county chose may be found in the sponsor's statement, quoted in the *Florida Times-Union* for May 6, 1921, that the counties "were united this time in asking for the divorce though the two parts of the [Bradford] county have never before been able to get together on this proposition." This explanation for the use of "Union" seems more logical than the lofty reasons used through the years, one of which has been for the "Union of the United States."

UTOPIA. *Okeechobee County.* One of the first settlements on Lake Okeechobee was started by Clifford Clements in 1897, eight miles southeast of Taylor Creek on the north shore. "At first he hunted there," recalls Will (1964), "but others joined him later to trot lines and set pound nets in the lake. Clements called his place Utopia. The settlement grew to be a cluster of palmetto shacks with a two story store and a school, both presided over by Clements. Of course it had a post office too, but when catfishing expired, so also did Utopia." There was another Florida Utopia, in Holmes County, for a short time in the 1880s. Thus, alas, Utopia can no longer be found in Florida today.

VALKARIA. *Brevard County.* Ernest Svedalius, a Swede who settled here in 1886, gave the place a name reminiscent of his homeland, the Valkyries of Scandinavian mythology—with a Latin ending.

VALPARAISO. *Okaloosa County.* Name taken from that of the city in Indiana, which in turn had been named for the famous Chilean port. The word is Spanish for valley of paradise. It was chosen for this community by John Perrine, who came here from Valparaiso, Ind., about 1918.

VALRICO. *Hillsborough County.* When Valrico, meaning valley of gold, was founded in 1890, inhabitants prided themselves on having chosen a name not shared with any other place in the country. Settled before the Civil War, the area previously had been known as Long Pond.

VENICE. *Sarasota County.* Named in 1888 by Franklin Higel, an early settler who felt that the blue waters of the bays, rivers, and Gulf gave the place a resemblance to the famous Italian city. In years long ago the area was known as Horse and Chaise to boatmen who saw a likeness to a carriage in a distinctive clump of trees on the shore.

VENUS. *Highlands County.* A hamlet of turpentine and agricultural workers on S.R. 17. We do not know who gave this name signifying all loveliness to this obscure little settlement, but the wife of Vulcan, the mother of Cupid, the mistress of Adonis, by her name brightens the scene here as she does wherever she appears throughout the world. Nearby is Old Venus.

VERNON. *Washington County.* Since the county is named Washington, and this community, established in 1850, was once the county seat, we can presume that it was named for Mount Vernon. Some persons, however, say the name was derived from a place in France.

VERO BEACH. *Indian River County.* Name derived from Vero Gifford, the wife of John T. Gifford, a former sheriff of Royalton, Vt. (Smiley, 1972). Gifford moved his family to Florida in 1888, settling on the west side of the Indian River. Gifford received postal permission in 1891 to establish a post office and selected his wife's name for the place. The Beach was added later. Vero Beach is the county seat of Indian River County.

VICKSBURG. *Bay County.* So named not as a reminder of a great siege of a city on the Mississippi during the Civil War, but rather, through the collaboration of two turpentine distillers, Messrs. Vickers and McKenzie. Mr. Vickers suggested part of his name, and Mr. McKenzie added the "burg."

VOLUSIA County. The thirtieth county, established December 29, 1854. Named for a landing called Volusia on the St. Johns River near Lake George. How the landing was named is uncertain. Tradition says the name is of Indian origin, but Simpson (1956) does not include Volusia. Another story attributes the name to a Frenchman or Belgian named Veluché, pronounced Va-loo-SHAY, who owned a trading post at the landing during the English period. Veluché was then anglicized into Volusia. Gold (1927) says "there is no record either in the Spanish, Territorial or County titles of any land being owned at any time in that vicinity or in the county for that matter, under the name 'Veluche' or any name that resembles it. If such a man held title to land under the English regime, there would be no way of ascertaining the fact, as all English titles were denied."

WABASSO. *Indian River County.* Settlers from Ossabaw, Ga., in 1898 spelled the name of their hometown backward.

WACISSA. *Jefferson County.* A river and hamlet, the meaning of whose names is lost. Well remembered, however, is that Achille Murat, nephew of Napoleon Bonaparte and son of Joachim Murat, king of

Naples, settled on a plantation 15 miles from Tallahassee. He owned this land in partnership with Col. James Gadsden and named it Wacissa. During a picnic at San Luis, a ruined Spanish mission now within the city limits of Tallahassee, he met and fell in love with Catherine Daingerfield Willis Gray, a grandniece of George Washington. They were married July 12, 1826. In anticipation of their marriage, the prince had a tract on Wacissa cleared for a new plantation. The couple's own home he called Lipona.

WAHNETA. *Polk County.* Probably the phonetic spelling of Juanita. Wahneta Farms was developed by the Inland Realty Co., which was spearheaded by William G. Brorein of Tampa. The post office was organized in 1901.

WAKULLA County. The twenty-third county, established March 11, 1843; name also of the famous Wakulla Springs, of a river that unites with the St. Marks River and falls into Apalachee Bay, and of a community. Although the word is interpreted to mean mystery by some, Simpson (1956) says there is no factual basis for this meaning. "Since Wakulla was probably a Timucuan word, it is unlikely that its meaning will ever be known. It may contain the word *Kala* which signified a 'spring of water' in some Indian dialects." Read (1934) suggests Wakulla comes from the Creek *wahkola,* "loon," two species of which winter in Florida.

WALDO. *Alachua County.* Named about 1856 for Dr. Benjamin Waldo, a physician and member of the legislature who was born in South Carolina in 1816 and died in Marion County in 1871.

WALNUT HILL. *Escambia County.* A settlement here has been so named since 1823, although the post office was not established until 1888. Named for the walnut trees here.

WALTON County. The eighth county, established December 29, 1824. Named for Col. George Walton, secretary of the Territory of West Florida during the governorship of Andrew Jackson, 1821-22, and of the combined territory, 1822-26. The colonel was the son of George Walton, governor of Georgia and signer of the Declaration of Independence. Colonel Walton's daughter Octavia suggested the name Tallahassee for the new capital.

WARD RIDGE. *Gulf County.* Ward Ridge was created by the legislature in 1953 and named by Sen. George Tapper in honor of his friend, Dr. Albert Ward, a physician, who died that year.

WARRINGTON. *Escambia County.* Named for Cmdre. Lewis Warrington of the U.S. Navy. The community was established during the 1840s when the Pensacola Navy Yard was first being built. About 1929 the village was moved to make way for expansion of the government facilities, and the new settlement, on the banks of Bayou

Grande was called New Warrington. Officially, however, the name remains as it was at first.

WASHINGTON County. The twelfth county, established December 9, 1825. Named for George Washington. Chipley is the county seat.

WATERTOWN. *Columbia County.* Probably settled in 1895 and probably named for Watertown, N.Y.

WAUCHULA. *Hardee County.* Once spelled Wauchuta (Norton, 1894). Simpson (1956) says this spelling allows two logical interpretations: Wauchula could be derived from the Creek *wakka*, "cow," and *hute*, "house or tank," or it could be a contraction of the Creek *wewa*, "water," and *hute*. Still another guess is that it comes from *watula*, "sandhill crane." Wauchula is the seat of Hardee County.

WAUKEENAH. *Jefferson County.* In 1827 Col. John G. Gamble named his plantation in honor of a Spanish lady from Pensacola who was his guest. Her name was Joachina, the English pronunciation of which approximates Waukeenah. Colonel Gamble's land grant was known as Welaunee, near the Marion Crossroads where, according to McRory and Barrows (1935), the Tallahassee Road crossed a local north-south road. Among the other plantations in the area were William Nuttall's El Destino, Prince Achille Murat's Lipona, Kidder Meade Moore's Pinetucky, and Judge Randall's Belmont.

WAUSAU. *Washington County.* In 1972 Lloyd Grantham, mayor of Wausau, wrote that the town was named by John Glen, a Scot who first settled in Wausau, Wisc., and then, traveling south, found this area to so resemble Wisconsin that he transplanted both himself and the name of his first American home. The original name is from a Wisconsin Indian word meaning far or distant.

WAVERLY. *Polk County.* W. D. Campbell and his family from Waverly, N.Y., were the first settlers here in 1882. For a while the place was called Buffalo Ford, but the name was changed to Waverly. After the big freeze of 1894-95, the settlement fell on hard times, and its name reverted to Buffalo Ford. When the railroad came through, Waverly was revived.

WEBSTER. *Sumter County.* First named Orange Home in the 1850s. The postmaster, G. F. Hays, learned there was another Orange Home, so he chose Webster in honor of Daniel Webster.

WEEKI WACHEE SPRINGS. *Hernando County.* From the Creek words *wekiwa*, "spring," and *chee*, "little."

WELAKA. *Putnam County.* From a combination of Indian words meaning tide or intermittent springs. The town, dating at least since 1850s, is on the St. Johns River, which the Seminoles called Ylacco or Welaka. Another interpretation given the word is river of lakes, which is most applicable to the St. Johns.

WELLBORN. *Suwannee County.* L. W. Wellborn laid out this townsite in the 1860s.

WEST PALM BEACH. *Palm Beach County.* After Henry M. Flagler decided he would extend his railroad and hotel chain to Palm Beach, he purchased several hundred acres across Lake Worth in April 1893 and laid out the townsite of West Palm Beach to provide housing first for his workers and thereafter for commercial development. "The workmen rowed across Lake Worth each morning to their jobs at the Royal Poinciana and then back across the lake in the afternoon" (Martin, 1949). The streets of West Palm Beach were named for trees, fruits, and flowers common to the area: clematis, datura, narcissus, sapodilla, and tamarind. By 1909, Palm Beach County was carved out of Dade County and the newly created county seat of West Palm Beach had outgrown its sister city, as Martin points out, both in size and commercial importance.

WESTVILLE. *Holmes County.* Once the seat of Holmes County, having wrested this honor from Cerro Gordo about 1900. Another dandy squabble over the seat occurred in 1905 and Bonifay won. The story goes that people in Westville hid the county records in a swamp, but these were recovered. The resistance in Westville to giving up the county seat was said to have caused men from Bonifay to drive mules and wagons to Westville at night, take the courthouse apart, and haul the pieces to Bonifay.

WEWAHITCHKA. *Gulf County.* Established in 1875 by Dr. William C. Mitchell and others, who chose this complex Indian name believing that it meant water eyes. A perfect pair of eyes is formed by two oblong lakes along the edge of the town; these are separated by a pronounced ridge a few feet wide that corresponds to the bridge of the nose. An aviator can easily distinguish this formation from the air. Other interpretations of the name are water view or place where water is obtained.

WHITE CITY. *St. Lucie County.* Settled shortly after 1893 by Danish immigrants from Chicago, who became interested in citrus culture after reading a series of articles on growing oranges written by a Danish newsman covering the Chicago World's Fair. The settlers named the main street Midway for the thoroughfare of that name at the fair and the settlement White City after a Chicago amusement park.

WHITE SPRINGS. *Hamilton County.* Known as Rebel's Refuge during the Civil War because many plantation owners moved here with their families and slaves and lived in safety throughout the war, out of the path of Union invasion. The modern town was founded about 1900 by Dr. R. J. Camp. The name was selected because of the clear, white spring in whose water there are said to be more than fifty minerals of medicinal value.

WILBUR-BY-THE-SEA. *Volusia County.* J. W. Wilbur in 1915 founded this community which lies between the Atlantic Ocean and the Halifax River.

WILDWOOD. *Sumter County.* Named long before there was any town. A telegraph construction engineer ran out of wire at this point, and so notified his headquarters, heading his dispatch Wildwood. The town was established in 1877.

WILLISTON. *Levy County.* Established prior to 1885 by J. M. Willis, who named it after himself.

WILTON MANORS. *Broward County.* Developed during the 1920s by E. J. Willingham, and presumably he devised a name that in part perpetuates his own.

WIMAUMA. *Hillsborough County.* Formed for the first letters of the names of Wilma, Maud, and Mary, daughters of the first postmaster, Captain Davis, at the turn of the century.

WINDERMERE. *Orange County.* Platted in 1887 by engineers of the Florida Midland Railroad and named by John Dawe, in remembrance of the Lake Country of England, where he had grown up.

WINSTON. *Polk County.* Named for the Winn family, who settled here in the 1880s. The community first was known as Youmans.

WINTER BEACH. *Indian River County.* First known as Woodley, then Quay, and finally by its present name in 1925, when many communities took names during the great land boom that suggested their natural advantages for the northern homeseeker.

WINTER GARDEN. *Orange County.* Established by Henry Harrel of Alachua in 1857 and formerly called Beulah. In 1908 the name Winter Garden was chosen because of the perennial blossoms and greenery here and the mild temperature in winter.

WINTER HAVEN. *Polk County.* Platted in 1884-85 and so named by P. D. Eyclesheimer, the developer, because this area was considered a haven from the severities of winter. Also known as the City of a Hundred Lakes.

WINTER PARK. *Orange County.* First settled by David Mizell of Alachua County in 1836. There is said to have been a town here called Lakeview, founded in 1858 and rechristened Osceola in 1870. In 1882 Loring A. Chase and Oliver E. Chapman laid out a new 600-acre townsite very much along the lines of the New England towns from where they had come and gave the town its present name because it is a veritable park in winter.

WITHLACOOCHEE. Two rivers with the same name taken from the Creek *we,* "water," *thlako,* "big," and *chee,* "little," or little big water. One river is a tributary of the Suwannee and flows through southern Georgia, then 23 miles into Florida, and unites with the Suwannee near Ellaville in Madison County, Fla. The other river flows in south-central Florida to empty into Withlacoochee Bay and the Gulf of Mexico at Port Inglis. Its length is variously reported from 86 to 157 miles. Pronounced With-la-COO-chee.

WOODVILLE. *Leon County.* Down the St. Marks Highway from Tallahassee, this community has had a post office since 1888 and was settled perhaps a half-century earlier.

WORTHINGTON SPRINGS. *Union County.* Established in 1825 and named for William G. D. Worthington of Maryland, secretary and acting governor of the Territory of East Florida.

YALAHA. *Lake County.* After the first of the permanent settlers—there had been some living here as early as 1847—in 1869 or 1870 decided a name was needed, they selected Yalaha, which they understood to be Indian for yellow orange. Pronounced Ya-LA-ha.

YANKEETOWN. *Levy County.* Founded in 1923 by Judge A. F. Knotts of Gary, Ind., and his nephew, Eugene Knotts, who set up a small fishing camp and a few houses and hoped to start a community. They advertised the community under the name of Knotts. In derision of the northerners, however, the southerners who lived in this vicinity—especially Hugh Coleman, rural mail carrier—called the place Yankeetown. When the town was incorporated by an act of the 1925 legislature, Yankeetown was adopted. The word Yankee, according to *Random House Dictionary,* originated in the Dutch *Jan Kees,* John Cheese, a nickname applied by the Dutch of colonial New York to English settlers in Connecticut.

YEEHAW. *Indian River County.* A modern Indian name, a corruption of Creek *yaha,* "wolf." This is a station on the abandoned Okeechobee branch of the Florida East Coast Railroad.

YOUNGSTOWN. *Bay County.* Named for T. B. Young, who came here from Georgia as a pioneer and naval stores operator in the early 1900s. The place formerly was known as Lawrence.

YULEE. *Nassau County.* Once known as Hart's Road, but in 1893 named Yulee in honor of David Levy Yulee. *See* Levy County.

ZELLWOOD. *Orange County.* Named for Col. T. Elwood Zell of Philadelphia, Pa., publisher of *Zell's Cyclopedia,* who spent the winters of 1875 and 1876 here with his brother-in-law and business associate, John A. Williamson, and then built his own home. He called his home Zellwood, and the community adopted the name in his honor.

ZEPHYRHILLS. *Pasco County.* Originally called Abbott's Station, but renamed in 1915. The name calls attention to the cooling breezes that blow over the hills in this section of the state.

ZOLFO SPRINGS. *Hardee County.* Named for the large number of sulphur springs in this area. Zolfo is the Italian word for sulphur; the name was applied in 1885 by Italian laborers in the vicinity.

BIBLIOGRAPHY

Abel, Ruth E. *One Hundred Years in Palmetto*. Palmetto: Palmetto Centennial Association, 1969.

American State Papers. Military Affairs, 1832-59. Vol. I. Washington, D.C., p. 744.

Anderson, Russell H. "The Shaker Community in Florida." *Florida Historical Quarterly* 38(1), July 1959.

Audubon, John James. *The Birds of America*. 1827-1838. Reprint. New York: Macmillan, 1953.

Barbour, George M. *Florida For Tourists, Invalids and Settlers*. New York: Appleton, 1883.

Barbour, Ralph Henry. *Let's Go To Florida*. New York: Dodd, Mead & Company, 1926.

Bell, Harold W. *Glimpses of the Panhandle*. Chicago: Adams Press, 1961.

Bellamy, Jeanne. "The Everglades: Unlike Anything Else." In *The Florida Handbook 1973-1974*, compiled by Allen Morris. Tallahassee: Peninsular Publishing Company, 1973.

Bellwood, Ralph. *Tales of West Pasco*. Hudson, Fla.: Albert J. Makovec, 1962.

Bishop, E. W. *Florida Lakes*. Tallahassee: Florida Division of Water Resources, 1967.

Blackman, Ethan V. *Miami and Dade County, Florida*. Washington, D.C., Victor Rainbolt, 1921.

Blackman, William Fremont. *History of Orange County Florida*. DeLand: E. O. Painter Printing Company, 1927.

Boyd, Mark F. "Early Highways of Florida." In *Florida Highways*. Tallahassee: Florida State Road Department, 1951.

Boyd, Mark F. "Historic Sites in and Around the Jim Woodruff Reservoir Area, Florida-Georgia." *Bureau of American Ethnology Bulletin 169*. Washington, D.C.: U.S. Government Printing Office, 1958.

Bradbury, Alford G., and Hallock, E. Story. *A Chronology of Florida Post Offices*, Handbook No. 2. Vero Beach: The Florida Federation of Stamp Clubs, 1962.

Bradbury, Alford G., and Hallock, E. Story. *A Chronology of Florida Post Offices*, Handbook No. 2, Addenda No. 1. Vero Beach: The Florida Federation of Stamp Clubs, 1966.

Brigham, Florence S. "Key Vaca." Tequesta 17(1957).

Brinton, Daniel Garrison. *Notes On The Floridian Peninsula: Its Literary History, Indian Tribes and Antiquities*. Philadelphia: Joseph Sabin, 1859.

Brookfield, Charles M., and Griswold, Oliver. *They All Called It Tropical*. Miami: The Data Press, 1949.

Brooks, T. J. Foreword to *Seventh Census of Florida*. Tallahassee: State Department of Agriculture, 1945.

Browne, Jefferson B. *Key West, The Old and The New*. St. Augustine: The Record Company, 1912.

Buchholz, F. W. *History of Alachua County*. St. Augustine: The Record Company, 1929.

Burke, Emily P. *Reminiscences of Georgia*. 1850. (Quoted in *Dictionary of Ameri-*

can English, edited by William A. Craigie. Chicago: University of Chicago Press, 1940.)

Burt, Al. "Small Towns Deserve Visitor's Second Look." *The Miami Herald,* 14 October 1973.

Cantrell, Elizabeth A. *When Kissimmee Was Young.* Kissimmee: First Christian Church, 1948.

Cash, W. T. "Newport as a Business Center." *Apalachee.* Tallahassee: Tallahassee Historical Society, 1944.

Clarke, Mary Helm. *South Florida Treasure Trails.* Tallahassee: Kay Publishing Company, 1949.

Cohen, Isidor. *Historical Sketches and Sidelights of Miami, Florida.* Miami: Privately printed, 1925.

Compiled General Laws of Florida. Atlanta: The Harrison Company, 1929.

Cooke, C. Wythe. "Scenery of Florida Interpreted by a Geologist." *Geological Bulletin No. 17.* Tallahassee: State of Florida Department of Conservation, 1939.

Coulson, John, ed. *The Saints.* New York: Hawthorn Books, 1958.

Covington, James W. *The Story of Southwestern Florida.* New York: Lewis Historical Publishing Company, Inc., 1957.

Cowan, Allen. "Sopchoppy is on the Worm Standard." *St. Petersburg Times,* 22 July 1973.

Crow, C. L. "East Florida Seminary—Micanopy." *Florida Historical Quarterly* 14(3), January 1936.

Dau, Frederick W. *Florida Old and New.* New York: G. P. Putnam's Sons, 1934.

Davis, Jess G. *History of Alachua County.* Alachua County Historical Commission, 1970.

Davis, Mary Lamar. "Tallahassee Through Territorial Days." *Apalachee.* Tallahassee: Tallahassee Historical Society, 1944.

De Young, Karen. "Ruskin: The Years Wear Thin a Dream." *St. Petersburg Times,* 9 May 1974.

Dickison, Mary Elizabeth. *Dickison and His Men.* Louisville, 1890.

Dodd, Dorothy. "Florida in the War, 1861-1865." In *The Florida Handbook 1959-1960,* compiled by Allen Morris. Tallahassee: Peninsular Publishing Company, 1959.

Douglas, Marjory Stoneman. *The Everglades: River of Grass.* New York: Rinehart, 1947.

Douglas, Marjory Stoneman. *Florida, the Long Frontier.* New York: Harper & Row, 1967.

Dovell, J. E. *Florida: Historic, Dramatic, Contemporary.* New York: Lewis Historical Publishing, 1952.

DuBois, Bessie Wilson. "Jupiter Inlet." *Tequesta* 28(1968).

Dunn, Hampton. *Re-Discover Florida.* Miami: Hurricane House, 1969.

Dunn, Hampton. *Yesterday's Tampa.* Miami: E. A. Seemann Publishing, 1972.

Eidge, Frank. "Mr. Perky's Bat Tower Stands as Lone Monument." *Tallahassee Democrat,* 8 February 1973.

Fairbanks, George Rainsford. *Florida: Its History and Romance.* Jacksonville: Drew Company, 1904.

Federal Writers Project, Work Projects Administration. *Florida: A Guide to the Southernmost State.* New York: Oxford University Press, 1939.

Federal Writers Project, Work Projects Administration. *A Guide to Key West.* New York: Hastings House, 1949.

Federal Writers Project, Work Projects Administration. "Place Names in Florida." 1939. Unpublished manuscript, Florida State Library.

Florida Board of Conservation, Division of Water Resources. *Florida Lakes.* Part III. Gazetteer. Tallahassee, 1969.

Florida Board of Conservation, Division of Water Resources and Conservation. *Gazetteer of Florida Streams.* Tallahassee, 1966.

Florida Department of Agriculture Sectional Map of Florida. DePew, N.Y.: J. W. Clement Company, 1963.

Florida Department of State. Division of Archives, History, and Records Management. *Guide to Florida's Historic Markers.* Tallahassee, 1972.

Florida State Advertising Commission. Unpublished replies to 1953 questionnaire on place name origin sent to Chambers of Commerce and postmasters.

Florida State Gazetteer 1886-7. New York: The South Publishing Company, 1886.

Fontaneda, Hernando de Escalante. *Memoirs.* Translated from the Spanish, with notes by Buckingham Smith. Washington, D.C.: 1854.

Forbes, James Grant. *Sketches Historical and Topographical of the Floridas; More Particularly of East Florida.* 1821. Reprint. Gainesville: University of Florida Press, 1964.

Forshay, David A. *Lure of the Sun: A Story of Palm Beach County.* Lake Worth: First Federal Savings & Loan Association of Lake Worth, 1967.

Franklin County . . . Its Resources, Advantages, Possibilities. Apalachicola, 1901.

Fritz, Florence. *Unknown Florida.* Coral Gables, Fla.: University of Miami Press, 1963.

Fuller, Walter P. *This Was Florida's Boom.* St. Petersburg: Times Publishing Company, 1954.

Gannett, Henry. *American Names.* Washington, D.C.: Public Affairs Press, 1947.

Gold, Pleasant Daniel. *History of Duval County Florida.* St. Augustine: The Record Company, 1928.

Gold, Pleasant Daniel. *History of Volusia County Florida,* DeLand, Fla.: The E. O. Painter Printing Company, 1927.

Gore, Eldon H. *History of Orlando.* Orlando: Eldon H. Gore, 1949 and 1951.

Goulding, Francis R. *Marooner's Island.* 1869.

Grismer, Karl H. *The Story of Sarasota.* Sarasota: M. E. Russell, 1946.

Grismer, Karl H. *The Story of St. Petersburg.* St. Petersburg: P. K. Smith, 1948.

Grismer, Karl H. *Tampa.* St. Petersburg: St. Petersburg Printing Company, 1950.

Hanna, Alfred J. *Fort Maitland, Its Origin and History.* Maitland: The Fort Maitland Committee, 1936.

Hanna, Alfred J. *A Prince in Their Midst.* Norman: University of Oklahoma Press, 1946.

Hanna, Alfred J., and Hanna, Kathryn Abbey. *Florida's Golden Sands.* Indianapolis: Bobbs-Merrill Company, 1950.

Hanna, Alfred J., and Hanna, Kathryn Abbey. *Lake Okeechobee: Wellspring of the Everglades.* Indianapolis: Bobbs-Merrill Company, 1948.

[Hanna], Kathryn Abbey. "The Story of the Lafayette Lands in Florida." *Florida Historical Quarterly* 10(3), January 1932.

Hartley, William, and Hartley, Ellen. *Osceola, The Unconquered Indian.* New York: Hawthorn Books, 1974.

Hathway, James A. *Key Largo.* Coral Gables, Fla.: The Key Largo Foundation, 1967.

Heatherington, M. F. *History of Polk County Florida.* St. Augustine: The Record Company, 1928.

Heitman, Francis Bernard. *Historical Register and Dictionary of the United States Army from its Organization, September 29, 1789, to March 2, 1903.* Vol. 2. Washington, D.C.: U.S. Government Printing Office, 1903.

Hellier, Walter R. *Indian River: Florida's Treasure Coast.* Miami: Hurricane House, 1965.

Hines, Bea L. "Eatonville: Sleepy Old Town Starting to Come Alive." *The Miami Herald,* 27 February 1972.

Hollingsworth, Tracy. *History of Dade County.* Miami, 1936.

Jeffreys, Thos. *The Coast of West Florida and Louisiana.* London, 1775.

Johnson, Allen, ed. *Dictionary of American Biography.* New York: Scribner's, 1964.

Johnson, Malcolm. "Old Street Names are Index to History of Tallahassee." *Tallahassee Democrat,* 24 August 1973.

Jones, Eloise Knight. *Ocala Calvacade.* Ocala: S. F. McCready, 1946.

Judge, Joseph. "Florida's Booming—and Beleaguered—Heartland." *National Geographic,* November 1973.

Kennedy, William T., ed. *History of Lake County Florida.* St. Augustine: The Record Company, 1929.

King, M. Luther. *History of Santa Rosa County: A King's Country.* Milton: Mrs. M. L. King, 1972.

Kjerulff, Georgiana Greene. *Tales of Old Brevard.* Melbourne: Florida Institute of Technology Press, 1972.

Lambert, John. *Travels Through Lower Canada, and the United States of North America.* 1810.

Le Moyne de Morgues, Jacques. Florida ca. 1565. In T. DeBrys, *Historia Americae,* 1591.

Longstreet, R. J. *The Story of Mount Dora Florida.* Mount Dora: Mount Dora Historical Society, 1960.

Lowery, Woodbury. *Spanish Settlements Within the Present Limits of the United States.* New York: G. P. Putnam's Sons, 1905.

McDuffee, Lillie B. *The Lures of Manatee.* Atlanta: Foote and Davies, Inc., 1961.

McNeely, Ed, and McFayden, Al R. *Century in the Sun.* Orlando: Robinsons, 1961.

McRory, Mary Oakley, and Barrows, Edith Clarke. *History of Jefferson County Florida.* Monticello: Kiwanis Club, 1935.

Madison County Jaycees Official Program. Madison, 1963.

Martin, Sidney Walter. *Florida's Flagler.* Athens: The University of Georgia Press, 1949.

Mayo, Nathan. *Sixth Census of the State of Florida.* Winter Park: The Orange Press, 1936.

Meffert, Neil S. *Florida Times-Union,* 13 February 1955.

Moore-Willson, Minnie. *History of Osceola County: Florida Frontier Life.* Orlando: The Inland Press, 1935.

Moore-Willson, Minnie. *The Seminoles of Florida.* 7th ed. New York: Moffatt, 1920, pp. 255-81.

Morris, Allen, compiler. *The Florida Handbook.* Tallahassee: Peninsular Publishing Company, biennially since 1947.

Morris, Allen, and Waldron, Ann. *Your Florida Government: Five Hundred Questions and Answers.* Gainesville: University of Florida Press, 1965.

Motte, Jacob R. *Journey Into Wilderness.* Gainesville: University of Florida Press, 1953.

Muir, Helen. *Miami, U.S.A.* New York: Henry Holt and Company, 1953.

Newhouse, John (Jan Van Nijhuis). "History of Okeelanta." 1932. Unpublished manuscript in P. K. Yonge Library, University of Florida.

Norton, Charles Ledyard. *A Handbook of Florida.* 2nd ed. rev. New York: Longmans, Green & Company, 1894.

Ogleby, Joe. "A Coming of Age." *St. Petersburg Times,* 23 April 1972.

Peeples, Vernon E. "Trabue, Alias Punta Gorda." *Florida Historical Quarterly* 46(1967).

Perkerson, Medora Field. *White Columns of Georgia.* New York: Rinehart, 1952.

Pickett, Mrs. Harold Major; Rice, Kenneth L.; and Seplman, Henry M., III. *Florida Postal History and Postal Markings During the Stampless Period,* Handbook No. 1. Palm Beach: Palm Beach Stamp Club, 1957.

Pierce, Charles W. *Pioneer Life in Southeast Florida.* Coral Gables, Fla.: University of Miami Press, 1970.

Plowden, Jean. *History of Hardee County.* Wauchula: *The Florida Advocate,* 1929.

Proby, Kathryn Hall. *Audubon in Florida.* Coral Gables, Fla.: University of Miami Press, 1974.

Random House Dictionary of the English Language. New York:Random House, Inc., 1967.

Read, William A. *Florida Place Names of Indian Origin and Seminole Personal Names.* Baton Rouge: Louisiana State University Press, 1934.

Read, William A. *Indian Place Names in Alabama.* Baton Rouge: Louisiana State University Press, 1937.

Redford, Polly. *Billion-Dollar Sandbar: A Biography of Miami Beach.* New York: E. P. Dutton & Co., Inc., 1970.

Rerick, Rowland H. *Memoirs of Florida.* Edited by Francis Phillip Fleming. Atlanta: The Southern Historical Association, 1902.

Rhodes, Harrison Garfield, and Dumont, Mary Wolfe. *A Guide to Florida for Tourists, Sportsmen and Settlers.* New York: Dodd, Mead & Company, 1912.

Robinson, Ernest L. *History of Hillsborough County Florida.* St. Augustine: The Record Company, 1928.

Scruggs, Mrs. Oliver. History of Aucilla." 1966. Unpublished manuscript.

Simpson, J. Clarence. *Florida Place-Names of Indian Derivation.* Edited by Mark F. Boyd. Florida State Board of Conservation Special Publication No. 1. Tallahassee, 1956.

Simpson, J. Clarence. "Middle Florida Place Names." *Apalachee.* Tallahassee: Tallahassee Historical Society, 1946.

Smiley, Nixon. Columns in *The Miami Herald.* 13 August 1971, 1 and 4 September 1968, 11 December 1968, 12 December 1971, 7 May 1973, 24 June 1973.

Smiley, Nixon. *Florida, Land of Images.* Miami: E. A. Seemann Publishing, 1972.

Smith, Elizabeth F. *Wakulla County Pioneers 1827-1967.* Crawfordville, Fla.: The Magnolia Monthly Press, 1968.

Snodgrass, Dena. In *Papers.* Vol. 5. Jacksonville: Jacksonville Historical Society, 1969.

Snodgrass, Dena. "The St. Johns: River of Five Names." In *The Florida Handbook 1967-1968,* compiled by Allen Morris. Tallahassee: Peninsular Publishing Company, 1967.

Stanley, J. Randall. *History of Gadsden County.* Quincy: *Gadsden County Times,* 1948.

Stevenson, George B. *Keyguide to Key West and the Florida Keys.* Tavernier, Fla.: Stevenson, 1970.

Stewart, George R. *American Place-Names.* New York: Oxford University Press, 1970.

Stewart, George R. *Names on the Land.* Boston: Houghton Mifflin Company, 1958.

Straub, William L. *History of Pinellas County Florida.* St. Augustine: The Record Company, 1929.

Strickland, Alice. "Ponce de Leon Inlet." *Florida Historical Quarterly* 43(3), January 1965.

Strickland, Alice. *The Valiant Pioneers.* Coral Gables, Fla.: University of Miami Press, 1963.

Swanton, John R. *Early History of the Creek Indians and Their Neighbors.* Washington, D.C.: U.S. Government Printing Office, 1922.

Swanton, John R. *Final Report of the United States De Soto Expedition Commission.* Washington, D.C.: U.S. Government Printing Office, 1939.

Tebeau, Charlton W. *Florida's Last Frontier: The History of Collier County.* Coral Gables, Fla.: University of Miami Press, 1966.

Tebeau, Charlton W. *A History of Florida.* Coral Gables, Fla.: University of Miami Press, 1971.

Tebeau, Charlton W. *The Story of the Chokoloskee Bay County.* Coral Gables, Fla.: University of Miami Press, 1955.

Tebeau, Charlton W. *They Lived in the Park.* Coral Gables, Fla.: University of Miami Press, 1963.

Utley, George W. "Origin on the County Names of Florida." *Florida Historical Quarterly* 1(3), October 1908.

Walker, Hester Perrine. "Massacre at Indian Key, etc." *Florida Historical Quarterly* 5(1), July 1926. Excerpts from unpublished 1885 journal.

Webb, Wanton S. *Webb's Historical, Industrial, and Biographical Florida.* New York: Webb & Company, 1885.

Weidling, Philip J., and Burghard, August. *Checkered Sunshine, The Story of Fort Lauderdale.* Gainesville: University of Florida Press, 1966.

Whitfield, J. B. *Florida Statutes, 1941.* Vol. III. Tallahassee: State of Florida, 1946.

Will, Lawrence E. *Cracker History of Okeechobee.* St. Petersburg: Great Outdoors Publishing Company, 1964.

Will, Lawrence E. *A Dredgeman of Cape Sable.* St. Petersburg: Great Outdoors Publishing Company, 1967.

Will, Lawrence E. *Okeechobee Boats & Skippers.* St. Petersburg: Great Outdoors Publishing Company, 1965.

Williams, Edwin L., Jr. "Negro Slavery in Florida." *Florida Historical Quarterly* 28(2), October 1949; continued in no. 3, January 1950.

Williams, John Lee. *The Territory of Florida, etc.* New York, 1837.

MAPS CITED IN THE TEXT

Highway map of Florida, published by the Florida Department of Transportation, Tallahassee, 1971.

Map of the Seat of War in Florida, compiled by orders of Gen. Zachary Taylor and others. War Department, Corps of Engineers. Washington, D. C., 1839.

Military Map of the Peninsula of Florida, South of Tampa Bay. Compiled by order of the Honorable Jefferson Davis, Secretary of War. Washington, D. C., 1856.

Sectional map of Florida, issued by the Department of Agriculture, Tallahassee, June 1963.